FLORIDA STATE
UNIVERSITY LIBRARIES

AUG 9 1995

Tallahassee, Florida

Chinese Historical Microdemography

This volume and the conference from which it resulted
were sponsored by the Joint Committee on Chinese Studies
of the American Council of Learned Societies and the
Social Science Research Council with funds provided
by the Andrew W. Mellon Foundation.

Chinese Historical Microdemography

EDITED BY
Stevan Harrell

UNIVERSITY OF CALIFORNIA PRESS
Berkeley   Los Angeles   London

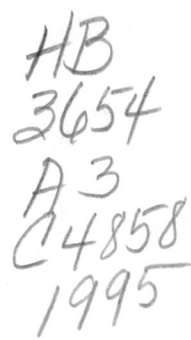

University of California Press
Berkeley and Los Angeles, California
University of California Press, Ltd.
London, England
© 1995 by
The Regents of the University of California

Library of Congress Cataloging-in-Publication Data
Chinese historical microdemography / edited by Stevan Harrell.
    p. cm. — (Studies on China ; 20)
    Papers from the conference sponsored by the Joint Committee on Chinese Studies.
    Includes bibliographical references and index.
    ISBN 0-520-08306-7 (alk. paper)
    1. China—Population. 2. Family—China—History. 3. Marriage—China. 4. China—Social conditions—1644–1912. I. Harrell, Stevan. II. Series.
HB3654.A3C4858 1995
304.6'095—dc20   94-6116

Printed in the United States of America
9   8   7   6   5   4   3   2   1

The paper used in this publication meets the minimum requirements of American National Standard for Information Sciences—Permanence of Paper for Printed Library Materials, ANSI Z39.48-1984.

STUDIES ON CHINA

A series of conference volumes sponsored by the Joint Committee on Chinese Studies of the American Council of Learned Societies and the Social Science Research Council.

1. The Origins of Chinese Civilization
   edited by David N. Keightley
   University of California Press, 1982

2. Popular Chinese Literature and Performing Arts in the People's Republic of China, 1949–1979
   edited by Bonnie S. McDougall
   University of California Press, 1984

3. Class and Social Stratification in Post-Revolution China
   edited by James L. Watson
   Cambridge University Press, 1984

4. Popular Culture in Late Imperial China
   edited by David Johnson, Andrew J. Nathan, and Evelyn S. Rawski
   University of California Press, 1985

5. Kinship Organization in Late Imperial China, 1000–1940
   edited by Patricia Buckley Ebrey and James L. Watson
   University of California Press, 1986

6. The Vitality of the Lyric Voice:
   Shih Poetry from the Late Han to the T'ang
   edited by Shuen-fu Lin and Stephen Owen
   Princeton University Press, 1986

7. Policy Implementation in Post-Mao China
   edited by David M. Lampton
   University of California Press, 1987

8. Death Ritual in Late Imperial and Modern China
   edited by James L. Watson and Evelyn S. Rawski
   University of California Press, 1988

9. Neo-Confucian Education: The Formative Stage
   edited by Wm. Theodore de Bary and John W. Chaffee
   University of California Press, 1989

10. Orthodoxy in Late Imperial China
    edited by Kwang-Ching Liu
    University of California Press, 1990

11. Chinese Local Elites and Patterns of Dominance
    edited by Joseph W. Esherick and Mary Backus Rankin
    University of California Press, 1990

12. Marriage and Inequality in Chinese Society
edited by Rubie S. Watson and Patricia Buckley Ebrey
University of California Press, 1991

13. Chinese History in Economic Perspective
edited by Thomas G. Rawski and Lillian M. Li
University of California Press, 1991

14. Bureaucracy, Politics, and Decision Making in Post-Mao China
edited by Kenneth G. Lieberthal and David M. Lampton
University of California Press, 1992

15. Pilgrims and Sacred Sites in China
edited by Susan Naquin and Chün-fang Yü
University of California Press, 1992

16. Ordering the World:
Approaches to State and Society in Sung Dynasty China
edited by Robert Hymes and Conrad Schirokauer
University of California Press, 1993

17. Chinese Families in the Post-Mao Era
edited by Deborah Davis and Stevan Harrell
University of California Press, 1993

18. Voices of the Song Lyric in China
edited by Pauline Yu
University of California Press, 1993

19. Education and Society in Late Imperial China, 1600–1900
edited by Benjamin A. Elman and Alexander Woodside
University of California Press, 1994

20. Chinese Historical Microdemography
edited by Stevan Harrell
University of California Press, 1995

CONTENTS

LIST OF TABLES / *ix*
ACKNOWLEDGMENTS / *xiii*

1. Introduction: Microdemography and the Modeling of Population Process in Late Imperial China
Stevan Harrell / *1*

2. Marriages among the Song Elite
Patricia Ebrey / *21*

3. Fertility and Population Growth in the Lineages of Tongcheng County, 1520–1661
Ted A. Telford / *48*

4. A Comparison of Lineage Populations in South China, ca. 1300–1900
Liu Ts'ui-jung / *94*

5. Demographic Constraint and Family Structure in Traditional Chinese Lineages, ca. 1200–1900
Liu Ts'ui-jung / *121*

6. Marriage, Mortality, and the Developmental Cycle in Three Xiaoshan Lineages
Stevan Harrell and Thomas W. Pullum / *141*

7. A Century of Mortality in Rural Liaoning, 1774–1873
James Lee, Cameron Campbell, and Lawrence Anthony / *163*

8. Migration in Two Minnan Lineages in the Ming and Qing Periods
Wang Lianmao / *183*

GLOSSARY OF CHINESE TERMS / *215*
GLOSSARY OF DEMOGRAPHIC TERMS / *217*
REFERENCES / *221*
CONTRIBUTORS / *231*
INDEX / *233*

TABLES

1.1. Survivorship Values (1_x) for Two Xiaoshan Lineages / *9*

1.2. Total Death Rates for Males, Ages 20–99, Shi and Wu Lineages / *9*

1.3. Death Rates of Adult Males, by Birth Cohort, Lin Lineage / *10*

1.4. Percentages of Heirless Males, by Cohort, Five Lineages / *11*

1.5. Number of Consorts per Man, Lin and Wu Lineages / *12*

1.6. Ages at First Son's Birth, Xiaoshan Wu Lineage / *12*

2.1. Distribution of Men's and Women's Ages at Marriage / *27*

2.2. Distribution of Age Differences / *30*

2.3. Distribution of Ages at Death of Men and Women Who Lived to Marry / *31*

2.4. Lineages Whose Genealogies Were Used for Birth Dates of Couples / *38*

2.5. Age Differences of Spouses in Genealogies / *39*

2.6. Distribution of Ages at Marriage from Ming Paired Epitaphs / *42*

3.1. Fertility Measures by Lineage Group / *51*

3.2. Family Characteristics by Husband's Social Status / *62*

3.3. Family Characteristics by Wife's Ten-Year Birth Cohort / *69*

3.4. Family Characteristics by Standard Market Area of Residence / *71*

3.5. Family Characteristics by Lineage Group / *76*

x   LIST OF TABLES

3.6. Summary of Expected Relationships, All Variables with Net Growth Rate / *83*

3.7. Multiple Regression of Social Demographic Variables on Net Growth Rate, Models I–III / *86*

3.8. Stepwise Regression of Model III on Net Growth Rates / *87*

    Appendix 3.A. Husband's Social Status Variable Coding / *92*

    Appendix 3.B. Zero-Order Correlation Matrix / *93*

    Appendix 3.C. Zero-Order Correlation Matrix / *93*

4.1. Male-Based Fertility Rates, Zhu Lineage / *97*

4.2. Fertility of Husbands and Consorts, by Lineage / *99*

4.3. Numbers of Sons, by Cohorts of Fathers / *102*

4.4. Parity Progression Ratios (a_x) / *107*

4.5. Distribution of Family Sizes / *108*

4.6. Mortality Patterns of Lineage Males, by Age / *110*

4.7. Graduated q_x of Lineage Males / *112*

4.8. Life Expectancies (e_x) of Lineage Adult Males / *114*

4.9. Distribution of Deaths of Shaoyang Li Males, by Cohort / *118*

4.10. Life Expectancies (e_x) of Shaoyang Li Adult Males, by Cohort / *119*

5.1. Summary of Family Possibilities in the Five Lineages / *123*

5.2. Summary of Conjugal Families, by Lineage / *129*

5.3. Summary of Conjugal Families, All Lineages / *131*

5.4. Three-Generation Families / *132*

5.5. Fathers' Ages at Birth of the First Son in Conjugal Families / *133*

5.6. Fathers' Ages at Birth of the First Son in Three-Generation Families / *134*

5.7. Ages at Death, All Men / *135*

5.8. Ages at Death, Grandfathers in Three-Generation Families / *136*

5.9. Four-Generation Families / *137*

6.1. Age- and Period-Specific Death Rates from the Genealogies / *147*

6.2. Estimated Life Expectancies at Birth, by Time Period, Lin, Wu, and Shi Lineages / *148*

6.3. Sonlessness and Median Death Age, by Time Period, Wu and Shi Lineages / *149*

6.4. Men Who Potentially Belonged to a Stem Family at Birth / *151*

6.5. Men Who Potentially Belonged to Stem Families in Middle Life / *152*

6.6. Men Who Potentially Belonged to Stem Families as Grandfathers / *153*

6.7. Probability of Being a Member of a Potential Stem Family / *154*

6.8. Men Who Potentially Belonged to a Joint Family in Childhood / *157*

6.9. Men Who Potentially Belonged to a Joint Family in Middle Life / *158*

6.10. Men Who Potentially Belonged to a Joint Family as Grandfathers / *159*

6.11. Probability of Being a Member of a Potential Joint Family / *160*

7.1. A Summary Profile of the Population Registers / *168*

7.2. Ages at First Appearance ("Birth"), 1774–1864 / *170*

7.3. Frequency and Mean Ages at First Registration / *171*

7.4. Common Discrepancies between Reported Age and Corrected Age / *172*

7.5. Discrepancies in Age Reporting by Age Group / *173*

7.6. Female Life Table, 1792–1867 / *174*

7.7. Male Life Table, 1792–1867 / *175*

7.8. Differences in Male and Female Life Expectancy (F–M) / *176*

7.9. Female Life Expectancies during Good Periods versus Bad Periods / *178*

7.10. Male Life Expectancies during Good Periods versus Bad Periods / *179*

8.1. Destinations of Yan Lineage Migrants / *191*

8.2. Destinations of Lin Lineage Migrants / *198*

8.3. Birth Orders of Migrants from Selected Minnan Lineages / *209*

8.4. Comparison of Longevity in the Yan and Lin Lineages / *211*

ACKNOWLEDGMENTS

The papers that became chapters in this book were originally presented at a conference at Asilomar, California, in January, 1987, sponsored by the Joint Committee on Chinese Studies of the American Council of Learned Societies and the Social Science Research Council. The monetary and moral support, not to mention the patience, of the Committee and of the ACLS, represented by Jason Parker, throughout the long process of bringing the results to publication, are gratefully acknowledged. I am also grateful to the other scholars who attended the conference, but whose work does not appear in this book: Guo Songyi, Keith Hazelton, Ju Deyuan, William R. Lavely, G. William Skinner, and Edward Wagner. Liou Hsiao-hsiun was an able and resourceful assistant for a multilingual, multicultural group of conferees. Richard Barrett read the manuscript through in two different versions, and made challenging but constructive criticisms that led to significant improvements in the quality of the final product. For editorial and research assistance with the manuscript, I thank Harlan R. Dorfman and Gabrielle O'Malley. Sheila Levine and Laura Driussi of the University of California Press have lent their considerable editorial skills to the difficult task of editing a manuscript full of tables, figures, and sometimes obscure vocabulary.

ONE

Introduction: Microdemography and the Modeling of Population Process in Late Imperial China

Stevan Harrell

The study of Chinese historical demography is still in its infancy.[1] Since the publication of Ho Ping-ti's impressive summary work, *Studies on the Population of China*, in 1959, however, a sort of "standard model" of what happened has been accepted in most Western scholarship. This model sees a gradual but bumpy rise in population, from about 50,000,000 in the Han dynasty to over 430,000,000 in the mid-Qing, and the numbers rise and fall with the fortunes of the dynasties (Ho 1959:277–78).

This model has recently been challenged explicitly from two directions. Bielenstein (1987) has asserted that the whole idea that mortality crises were serious enough to cause declining population for more than a few years is one that does not make sense either in terms of what we know about demographic rates or in terms of the figures we can derive from censuses and tax-registration records throughout various dynasties. He sees instead a curve that although bumpy is always rising, with changes in slope but never an actual turn downward. At the same time, Skinner (1987) has challenged the standard model from a different direction: he has shown through an internal statistical analysis that some of the records thought to be among the most accurate used by Ho and others to formulate the standard model are in fact based not on any kind of empirical population counts but on a simple algorithm applied annually to the previous year's records. Skinner's demonstration was for Sichuan in the mid-Qing only, but if those records are spurious, Skinner asks, how can we trust other records from remoter times based on even more obscure methodologies?

There is also a third, and more implicit, challenge to the standard model: a challenge that accuses the model less of inaccuracy than of incompleteness and oversimplification. The standard model has been accepted on the rather naive assumption that processes were similar everywhere in the country, that the effects of the dynastic cycle were similar within and across regions. But we now know from the grand conceptual model put forth by Skinner (1985) and from various locally based empirical studies that the economic conditions faced by different regions, or by core and peripheral areas within the same region, were in fact different in their nature and in their timing. We would expect regions to be affected differentially not only by factors that raise or lower fertility and mortality but also by migration, as indeed Ho pointed out in his original work (Ho 1959:136–68). But as in the case of other factors, migration has been studied from data that purport to portray its aggregate results rather than from descriptions of its actual process.

If the standard model stands challenged, then, it is more than anything because it is based on aggregate figures compiled by governments for taxation and land-registration purposes rather than on any kind of population records built upon life histories of individuals. The great advances made by European historians of population in the last two decades have been based on individual records, upon the detailed analyses of small populations taken as representative of a particular section of the larger whole. For certain European populations we now know not just aggregate counts but also the fertility, nuptiality, and mortality processes that have contributed to these counts. (See Stone 1981.) If we are going to understand population process in China, we are going to have to study the process at the individual and family level. A start has been made in this direction for the twentieth century. The articles published in Hanley and Wolf (1985) represent the beginning of historical microdemography in China. In their introduction to that volume, for example, Wolf and Hanley develop the idea that there was a "Chinese regime" of demographic process, with basic features of early and universal marriage, moderate to high marital fertility,[2] and joint (or grand) family organization.[3] They contrast this regime with the "Japanese regime" of later marriage, low fertility involving conscious fertility limitation, and stem family organization, as well as with the northwestern European regime described by Hajnal (1965), in which marriage is late and not universal, marital fertility high, and family organization primarily nuclear (Wolf and Hanley 1985:1–6).

There has been particular progress in recent decades in understanding one aspect of this demographic regime—the developmental cycle of the Chinese family. Beginning with the work of Maurice Freedman in the postwar period (1958, 1966) and proceeding to the empirical studies of Arthur Wolf (1985a), Wolf and Huang (1980), Myron Cohen (1968, 1970, 1976), Burton Pasternak (1983), and others, we have gained an understanding of the demographic and ecological/economic conditions under which the Chinese joint family system does or does not reach full fruition. We find in general that prosperity itself encourages the development of joint families, both by increasing fertility and by delaying family division, and that certain economic conditions, particularly those that encourage pooling of either labor or capital, also delay family division (Cohen 1976; Harrell 1982). We have come, in fact, to the point of challenging earlier assertions by anthropologists Francis L. K. Hsu (1943) and Fei Xiaotong (1939), who surmised that the joint family was an exclusive preserve of the elite. Wolf (1985a) in particular has shown that opportunities to form joint families extended to all but the poorest strata of the population in the nineteenth and twentieth centuries, and Lee's recent work (Lee and Eng 1984, Lee 1990) has demonstrated a developmental cycle for nineteenth-century Liaoning farmers in which families commonly grew to the joint stage of married brothers and their wives living together, and often even beyond that.

These initial steps toward understanding the actual processes behind China's population history are very useful, but they also lack something vital to the whole enterprise: historical depth. That their detailed analyses are based entirely on late-nineteenth- and twentieth-century records leaves open the possibility that something very different might have been going on in earlier periods. If we wish to understand the bumps in the long-term population curve, we need to extend to earlier periods the study of the same factors—fertility, nuptiality, mortality, family organization, migration—that have made at least provisional sense of the twentieth-century data.

The conference that gave rise to this volume was suggested by Professor G. William Skinner on the basis of his hope that the study of genealogies (and secondarily other available historic microsources) would be able to bring the detailed examination of particular cases to bear on the general problems of China's population history. All of the papers represented in this volume approach Chinese population history from this perspective: they consider detailed evidence for small populations in order to observe trends in the regional history of populations. To understand how they do this, we must first look at the nature of the sources.

GENEALOGIES AND HOUSEHOLD REGISTERS AS SOURCES FOR DEMOGRAPHIC RESEARCH

Genealogies (more properly, genealogical records) have been compiled by Chinese lineages since the Song period (Ebrey 1986). By the Ming and Qing, it is quite probable that most large lineages in China (and a great number of smaller ones) compiled genealogical records of some kind. These records range in size from hand-scribbled notes on odd scraps of paper, kept by a few families to keep track of their ancestors' birth and death dates, to multivolume, printed sets published by large and wealthy southern clan associations. However, neither of these extremes is particularly useful for demographic research: the scribbled scrap has too few cases and the encyclopedic reference probably included people in return for a subscription fee rather than according to any real genealogical principle.

What interests the demographic historian is the midsized genealogy containing a few hundred to a few thousand entries. These genealogies were compiled and usually printed (though sometimes handwritten) by literate members of large local lineages and typically included all members of the lineage on purely genealogical grounds. Such genealogies still survive in great numbers in the home towns and villages of the lineages themselves (Wang, chap. 8), in spite of the great amount of genealogy-burning that went on during the Great Proletarian Cultural Revolution. A not quite so large but still impressive number are found in libraries both inside and outside China, and many of these, in turn, have been collected by the Genealogical Society of Utah, a research arm of the Church of Jesus Christ of Latter-Day Saints.[4]

A good genealogy is much more than just a table of names and dates. It typically includes a series of prefaces by famous members or friends of members of the lineage, a history of the lineage, biographies of prominent members, detailed diagrams of how to find the graves of certain important ancestors, descriptions of ancestral halls, texts to be used in hall and grave worship, rules of conduct for lineage members, tables of land held by the lineage or by its constituent branches, and other documents relating to history, administration, and ritual. It is a wealthy lode of information about local society and history, one but minimally utilized by historical researchers so far.

For demographic purposes the most important part of the genealogy is the *shixi tu* (chart of the system of generations) and/or *shixi biao* (table of the system of generations), which contain detailed entries for each male member of the lineage who reached a certain age, as specified in the rules of compilation. A complete entry for a lineage member typically contains the following information: the man's personal name (*ming*), courtesy name (*zi*), and style (*hao*), if he had one; his generation and birth-order rank within that generation (*hang*); the name of his father and his birth order among the surviving sons of that father; if he was adopted, the name of the natural father; any official titles or imperial honors the man may have held; the year, month, day, and time of his birth; the year, month, day, and time of his death; and the place where he was buried. The entry also includes the name of his first wife, occasionally together with the name of her father and her birth order among her sisters; the year, month, day, and time of her birth and death; her place of burial; and the number of her sons, along with their names (a few genealogies list daughters and the men they married). Then the information is repeated for any subsequent wives the man might have had after his first wife's death and for any concubines who bore sons.[5]

On the surface, this kind of data appears to be a historical demographer's dream; there are thousands of cases, each gives detailed information, and birth and death dates are given directly and do not have to be deduced from self-reported ages. One must remember, however, that genealogies were compiled not for the convenience of historical demographers but in order to record the birth and death dates of ancestors to whom lineage members owed worship obligations. There are thus certain gaps. Although women marrying into the lineage, the wives and mothers who eventually become ancestors, are recorded, in many genealogies the information on these women is much less complete than that on their husbands and sons. However, the daughters of lineage members, who eventually move out and become someone else's ancestors, are rarely recorded and then not in much detail.[6] Since children who die young are typically not accorded full ancestral rites, most genealogies have a compiler's rule that excludes from full entries those boys who died before a certain age, usually eighteen or twenty *sui*.[7] The purpose and methods of compilation thus introduce gaps and biases into the available data.

That genealogies are compiled for ritual rather than demographic reasons also contributes to a further problem: the incompleteness of records. Not all entries in any genealogy contain the full range of data; studies (Harrell and Pullum, chap. 6; Telford, chap. 3; Harrell 1987) show that wives' entries usually contain less complete data than their husbands' and that the entries of men who had many descendants are usually more complete than those of men who had no sons or whose lines of descent died out after a few generations. To perform demographic analyses based on genealogies, then, one must infer what is not there; one must strike a delicate balance between making unwarranted conclusions based on incomplete data and making no conclusions at all because the data are incomplete. One must find ways to infer without imputing too much. The papers in this book that are based on genealogies (Harrell and Pullum; Telford; Liu; and Wang) continue a line of research that began with papers by Liu Ts'ui-jung (1985) and Harrell (1985), both of whom attempted to derive demographic information from genealogies, something that had not been done previously. Each of us made a different assumption: Liu took the data in the genealogies as complete and calculated actual vital rates, whereas I assumed that we could not know the nature of the biases and thus attempted only comparisons of one subpopulation with another and refused to estimate actual rates. It now seems clear that we both had much to learn. Liu's rates were probably off because she did not allow for infant mortality in her computations of such measures as life expectancy and total fertility. My analysis was overly cautious, not even looking for ways to estimate actual rates, and thus not allowing comparison of the Chinese population with other historic populations.

In this volume, however, having learned from those early works, all the authors working with genealogies have calculated demographic rates based on some more realistic assumptions about the relationship between what actually happened and what is recorded in the genealogies. Many of the assumptions used are no doubt still somewhat off the mark; but we are closer than we were, and we can begin to use genealogical data to ask questions about topics of general interest such as long-term fertility and mortality trends, the nature of the developmental cycle, and the demography of overseas migration.

As for genealogies, so for other kinds of historical demographic sources. At least two papers in this volume (Ebrey and Lee) rely partly or wholly on sources other than genealogies: Ebrey on epitaphs and Lee on the household registration records of the Qing imperial banner system. Like genealogies, these sources were not compiled for demographic purposes and thus can be assumed to have certain biases, as will be explained more fully by the authors in their papers. But as does the work based on genealogies, the work based on epitaphs and records attempts to understand and adjust for the biases introduced by the nature of the data and thus helps us come close enough to what must have been the historic reality that we can ask questions that should be of interest to historical demographers and demographic historians everywhere.

A PROPOSED DEMOGRAPHIC REGIME FOR LATE IMPERIAL CHINA

The first use to which the papers in this volume put demographic data derived from genealogies and similar sources is in making preliminary guesses about the nature of the demographic regime in the empire as a whole, or at least in its constituent geographic regions. This demographic regime has two salient characteristics. First, the regime is driven primarily by mortality factors rather than fertility factors: age-specific marital fertility in particular seems to remain remarkably constant, whereas mortality changes cause differences in years of exposure and cause net reproduction to rise or fall. Second, the factors that drive this regime rise and fall with the regional manifestations of the dynastic cycle. Using the specific data and calculations from the empirical studies of fertility and mortality found in the papers by Ebrey, Telford, Lee, Liu, and Harrell and Pullum, as well as other published and unpublished work, I want to formulate a preliminary model of this regime based on a curious and very significant fact: even though genealogies and household registers studied so far encompass a tiny fraction of the Chinese population (a few tens of thousands out of a few hundred million, or perhaps a one-in-ten-thousand sample), they all show more or less the same trends happening at the same time. This fact suggests that these sources, no one or few of which may have any significance in itself as far as empire-wide trends, when combined force us to sit up and take notice. Is it a coincidence that they all show the same patterns? At least we have data that are reasonably accurate (Harrell 1987; Telford 1990), though not representative, on which to base further research.

The model I wish to propose on the basis of these data is thus a simple one: population growth did indeed go up and down with the dynastic cycle,[8] and it did so as a consequence of a particular combination of vital rates. In periods of economic prosperity and political peace, mortality went down for both sexes at all ages, age at marriage for males went down, and the proportion of married males went up. Conversely, in periods of turmoil, age-specific mortality went up at all ages for both sexes, male age at marriage increased, and the proportion of married males declined. Throughout all this, female age at marriage remained fairly constant, as did age-specific rates of marital fertility. These factors in themselves, of course, would be sufficient to cause twists and turns in rates of population growth. Mortality increases at premarital ages would preclude people from being born, and mortality increases at marital ages would eliminate women from the reproductive pool if they or their husbands died, since widow remarriage was frowned upon (though hardly unknown) in the traditional family system. Increased male age at marriage would also increase the likelihood of early widowing, and would thus lower crude birth rates in the absence of changes in marital fertility. It would be nice to know more about the reasons for the lower proportion of males marrying. Was this caused by a higher rate of female infanticide or differential care that discriminated against girls, which would mean that fewer males could marry because there were fewer women to marry (assuming the impossibility of polyandry, which was rare enough to be nothing but a curiosity among the Chinese), or did it somehow derive purely from economic conditions that either skewed the marriage market, leaving unmarried females at the top and males at the bottom, or otherwise made it impractical for young people to arrange marriages? A skew in the marriage market would mean that a lowered proportion of males ever married happened along with a continued virtually 100% marriage rate for women; difficulties in arranging marriages would lead to a lower nuptiality rate for women also. Since genealogies typically don't give us very much information about daughters, we have no way of telling. So let us look at the figures we do have, for age-specific mortality rates, for nuptiality of males, and for age at marriage for both sexes.

Mortality

Several studies on mortality suggest a common pattern: mortality was moderate in the mid-Ming, rose with the interdynastic turmoil of the seventeenth century, went down again quite rapidly with the Qing pacification, and then rose slowly from the first half of the eighteenth century to the end of the Imperial period. Let us look at some of the case studies that support this generalization.

Telford (chap. 3) finds big net changes in reproduction rates during the crisis period of 1635–45 in Tongcheng, Anhui. Before this period, reproduction rates were fairly high, though they did show a steady decline in the sixteenth century, perhaps owing to gradually deteriorating social conditions in the middle and late Ming. Then, with the interdynastic crisis, reproduction rates dropped suddenly and were even negative for a single cohort whose prime reproductive years came during the transition. After social stability was restored at the beginning of the Qing, the rates went up again and remained high for the remainder of the period studied by Telford, which ends before the decline of the Qing would be expected to become visible. When Telford examines the causes of the decline in a multiple regression analysis, he finds the variable that explains the greatest portion of the variance is the average age of the wife at the birth of the last son, which, given the natural fertility that Telford has found in this population and the general ban on widow remarriage, should be a fairly accurate proxy for the age at which the first parent dies. The next most important factor in his stepwise analysis is the percent of men unmarried, which is of course a nuptiality factor. Last comes the wife's age at marriage (also see Table 3.3).

Similarly, Liu Ts'ui-jung (chap. 4) shows for a single lineage in Shaoyang, Hunan, that both mean age at death and life expectancies at particular ages follow the same kind of curve. High in the early Ming, they go down steadily and then bottom out in the cohorts that show the effects of the Ming-Qing transition. Then they rebound again at the beginning of the Qing before starting another decline that continues throughout the eighteenth and nineteenth centuries. (See Table 4.9.)

In a previously published paper, Liu (1985) used different measures to demonstrate similar findings for two lineages in Xiaoshan, Zhejiang. In Table 1.1, reproduced from her paper, survivorship values can be seen to go down between the mid-eighteenth century and the mid-nineteenth.

Harrell and Pullum (chap. 6) have found similar figures for death rates in three lineages in Xiaoshan County, Zhejiang. Unfortunately, their material does not extend back beyond 1600, but it shows the expected pattern of fairly high death rates 1600–50, much lower rates 1650–1700, and then a progressive climb afterwards. Because of some questions about the data in the Wu lineage genealogy, the figures for the Wus stop at 1800 (see Table 1.2).

Another analysis, by birth cohort, for another lineage in the same area shows a similar pattern, though perhaps not as clearly, given that the Ns are very small for the Lin lineage (see Table 1.3).

TABLE 1.1. Survivorship Values (1_x) for Two Xiaoshan Lineages

	Females				Males			
	Shen Lineage		Xu Lineage		Shen Lineage		Xu Lineage	
Ages	1695–1709	1785–1799	1695–1709	1785–1799	1695–1709	1785–1799	1695–1709	1785–1799
15–19	35643	32900	37773	27308	38795	32680	38970	33575
20–24	34488	31583	36710	25750	37863	31438	38050	32388
25–29	33200	30058	35488	24050	36738	29955	36940	30755
30–34	31745	28295	34155	22310	35508	28353	35725	28565
35–39	30083	26265	32723	20495	33878	26373	34183	25753
40–44	28170	23920	30883	18573	31495	23748	32048	22318
45–49	25958	21273	28228	16510	28228	20458	29208	18368
50–54	—	—	—	—	24063	16608	25603	14143
55–59	—	—	—	—	19193	12460	21278	10003

SOURCE: Liu Ts'ui-jung 1985:59, Table 2.17.

TABLE 1.2. Total Death Rates for Males, Ages 20–99, Shi and Wu Lineages (× 1000 Person-Years)

Years	Shi	Wu
1601–1650	34	23
1651–1700	13	17
1701–1750	24	23
1751–1800	24	29
1801–1850	29	—
1851–1875	53[a]	—

SOURCE: Harrell and Pullum, chapter 6, Table 6.1.
[a] Includes the mortality crisis years of 1862–65, when the Taipings occupied Xiaoshan.

Finally, we have the analysis by Lee, Campbell, and Anthony (chap. 7) of mortality in a Liaoning peasant population in the late eighteenth and early nineteenth centuries. Although the time span of the analysis is short, there is a definite trend downward in life expectancy from the first two decades of the nineteenth century to the second two. We eagerly await the extension of this analysis to the 1870s.

At the same time, however, there are now grounds for believing that the downturns in Chinese reproduction rates at times of dynastic or regional crises were probably not sufficient to cause the kind of massive population declines posited by the standard model for the Ming-Qing transition, for example, or for the Taiping rebellion of the mid-nineteenth century. Pop-

TABLE 1.3. Death Rates of Adult Males, by Birth Cohort, Lin Lineage

Birth Cohort	Death Rate
1600–1649	31.5
1650–1699	13.5
1700–1749	26.2
1750–1799	27.7
1800–1849	24.5
1850–1899	58.0

SOURCE: Harrell and Pullum, chapter 6, Table 6.1.

ulation growth rates declined during these crises, to be sure, but it is now doubtful whether they declined to below replacement level for more than a few years. Keith Hazelton's analysis in an unpublished paper (n.d.) provides the first hard evidence (at least for some of the genealogical populations), and it finds that these mortality crises were not as severe as had previously been thought. Even in the Ming-Qing transition, the actual population decline was short-lived, and the precrisis level was reached again within a decade. The genealogical populations examined here might well have weathered the crises better than the populace as a whole, but even with this caveat it still seems improbable that there were ever any large-scale or long-lasting population declines in late imperial Chinese history. We may have been misled previously by the data, which consisted of impressionistic descriptions, surely exaggerated, and population registers, surely rendered less complete by the conditions of disruption.

Nuptiality

Mortality is one component of the temporal variation in reproduction rates; nuptiality is another. We have already mentioned the figures cited by Telford, in which, after mortality, the most important factor in explaining differential rates of population growth from one period to another is the percentage of a cohort of males who married. Other scholars have found the same thing.

Liu Ts'ui-jung (chap. 4) provides a suggestive analysis for several lineages scattered throughout central and southern China. Although she does not give figures for percentages of men who died unmarried, she does record figures for percentages of heirless males for the five lineages (see Table 1.4).

A previous paper (Harrell 1985) shows the same trends through a different kind of procedure. In that paper, I demonstrate that differential growth rates of different lineages and lineage branches are correlated with a series of factors, including the number of consorts (wives or concubines)

TABLE 1.4. Percentages of Heirless Males, by Cohort, Five Lineages

Cohort	Zhu	Zhao	Xu	Li	Mai
1548–1597	7.8	25.8	0	4.7	13.5
1598–1647	21.9	6.7	0	13.7	21.2
1648–1697	16.1	11.6	13.5	9.6	16.2
1698–1747	15.9	13.5	18.5	18.2	21.0
1748–1797	16.9	19.4	22.8	20.9	20.1
1798–1847	21.0	21.9	26.2	24.2	31.0

SOURCE: Liu, chapter 4, Table 4.3.

brought in per man. Although this analysis shows lots of variation according to the differential economic successes of different branches at different times, the overall trends are quite clear, as can be seen from Tables 1.5 and 1.6.

That the trends at the beginning of the period studied are not as predicted is almost certainly because these lineages were getting started at that time, and men who found successful lineages or are the sons and grandsons of founders of successful lineages are by definition more successful reproductively than the average. What is more interesting is the steady decline in almost all branches after 1700; the decline becomes particularly noticeable in the nineteenth century.

Telford (chap. 3) provides similar evidence for the Tongcheng lineages in the late Ming and early Qing in a tabulation by birth cohort of percentages of sons unmarried (see Table 3.3). Notice the clear pattern in Table 3.3. The variable being measured is the percentage of the *sons* of the members of that particular birth cohort who remain unmarried; the changes over time thus reflect trends forty to sixty years after the date indicated in the left column. Thus percentages of unmarried men are very high during the turbulent final decades of the Ming, begin to fall around 1650, the date of the Qing consolidation of power, and continue to drop to a plateau that lasts until about 1700; it is not clear if the slight rise in the unmarriage rate of the sons of men born in the latter half of the century (men who would be marrying in the early and middle 1700s) is the beginning of a longer Qing downswing, but it is a hint in that direction.[9]

Age at Marriage

Age at marriage is our final factor. Because the birth dates of the wives and mothers of lineage members are usually listed in genealogies, this is one area where we can look at both male and female figures. And we find that the age at marriage also plays a large part in determining reproduction rates.

TABLE 1.5. Number of Consorts per Man,
Lin and Wu Lineages

Cohort	Lineage or Fang			
	Lin 1	Lin 2	Lin 3	Wu
1601–1650	.93	1.00	2.00	1.83
1651–1700	.87	.90	1.4	1.36
1701–1750	.97	.85	1.2	1.02
1751–1800	1.00	.73	1.2	.84
1801–1850	.77	.62	1.0	.74

SOURCE: Harrell 1985:105, Table 4.18.

TABLE 1.6. Ages at First Son's Birth, Xiaoshan
Wu Lineage

Cohort	Father's Age	Mother's Age
1601–1650	27.5	24.6
1651–1700	26.8	23.8
1701–1750	28.9	25.3
1751–1800	31.3	26.1
1801–1850	33.1	24.6

SOURCE: Harrell 1985:102, 104, Tables 4.14 and 4.16.

Age at marriage cannot be calculated directly from data given in the genealogies, since they only give birth and death dates. But a reasonable proxy can be found in the age of the parent at the birth of the first surviving son. Various methods have been proposed (Liu 1985; Harrell and Pullum, chap. 6; Ebrey, chap. 2) for reckoning back from this figure to age at marriage for fairly large populations, which damp out the effects of individual variation. For our analysis here, what is important is change over time, and for this we can use age at birth of first son. In fact, the direct effect on population is greater for this variable than for age at marriage; age at marriage is only indirectly related to reproduction rates, whereas age at birth of first son is actually a contributing factor to reproduction rates. Let us examine some of the changes over time in age at birth of first son. We can begin with my analysis of the He, Lin, and Wu lineages of Xiaoshan. I have shown in that paper that the father's age at birth of first son is an important contributing factor to differential growth rates among lineage branches, and mother's age at birth of first son makes a weaker or perhaps no contribution (Harrell 1985:101–3). For one lineage, the Wus, there is a definite change over time in the father's age at birth of first son, but there is a much less obvious change for the mother's age (see Table 1.6).

Telford (chap. 3) reports information that sheds doubt on this simple hypothesis; in his stepwise regression analysis he finds the mother's age at birth of first son to be more important than the corresponding father's age. Since his unit of analysis is the individual, however, this variable does not really say anything about changes over time in age at marriage; it just says that women who marry earlier will have more children, or more accurately, that women who have a son earlier will be more likely to end up with a larger number of sons. Telford, unfortunately, does not provide a measure of changes over time in age at birth of first son for either mothers or fathers.

We do have, however, one more set of data that bears on this hypothesis: Ebrey's (chap. 2) analysis of age at marriage in the Song and Ming dynasties, in which she comments that although male age at marriage varied widely, female age varied little. If the late Ming and Qing followed the same pattern, it was likely to be the male age that varied. Incidentally, male age at marriage ought to correlate with nuptial rates: the greater the age difference between spouses, the greater the percentage of males that remain unmarried, which is what we saw in some of the tables on nuptiality.

Possible Sources of Spurious Findings

Given the nature of genealogies as sources, we ought to look for sources of bias before we herald the findings herein as marking a new era in our understanding of China's population history. There are three that come to mind: inaccuracies in genealogies, a skewed sample of genealogies, and the possibility that genealogies are unrepresentative of the total population.

I have treated the issue of inaccuracies in genealogies in a separate paper (Harrell 1987), so I will not elaborate on the issue here. Suffice it to say that the biases inherent in genealogy compilation—underrecording of women and children—have been allowed for by the authors of the works from which the figures in this analysis are taken.

The second possible source of spurious findings is that ours is a skewed sample of genealogies; that is, the genealogies sampled here are not representative of the population recorded in genealogies—members of medium to large lineages with at least some prosperous and successful members. Since all the genealogies we have examined show the same trends in the same directions at the same times, it is unlikely (though not impossible) that an error in sampling genealogies is the source of the remarkable uniformity of our results. More likely, our results are only representative of the particular macroregions represented by the genealogies used by the authors of this volume. If we had a few from Lingnan, say, or the Southeast Coast, macroregions whose regional economic cycles were quite different from those of the Yangzi and North China regions represented here, then I think we would have made a strong argument for the whole empire. (Liu's analysis in chapter 4 does include the genealogy of the Mai of Xiangshan in Guangdong, in the core area of Lingnan, but that is the only Lingnan genealogy analyzed in this volume.) As it is, if we do find some sorts of regional variations, they can still be accommodated within the model of the three primary factors affecting rates of growth. Skinner has taught us not to be disappointed to find regional cycles superimposed on empire-wide ones.

If we are fairly certain that we have sampled genealogies fairly, we still need to consider whether or not we are studying an unrepresentative sample of the Chinese population by using genealogies at all. And the answer is yes, of course. Lineages tended to command various kinds of resources in their areas, resources that gave them mortality advantages in the face of bad years as well as fertility advantages in playing the marriage market for more and earlier brides. The question we need to ask is whether the *direction of change* in the rates we are examining is different in lineages than it is in the population at large.

For mortality, I think we are pretty safe in saying that the direction of change is the same. Telford (1990a) has recently demonstrated that there are considerable differences in mortality rates between elite and non-elite members within Tongcheng lineages, so we are studying a population that is growing faster than the general populace. It is also quite probable that the population decline in the brief periods of serious crisis was less severe in the genealogically recorded proportion of the population than in the population as a whole. But I cannot think of any reason why the *temporal trends* of mortality would be different for lineage populations than for the rest of the population; there is no reason why their mortality rates would go down in hard times (when everyone else's were going up), and it is even more unlikely that there would be a situation where their rates would increase as the mortality of their less fortunate neighbors went down.

For nuptiality rates and age at marriage, however, the representativeness of lineages for the population as a whole is questionable. If lineages were able to exercise effective dominance, they might have monopolized brides and driven down the age at marriage for their male members and driven up the age at marriage for people in nonlineage communities. Conversely, a decline in lineage dominance would mean an evening out of percentages of unmarried males and of male ages at marriage between lineages and their neighbors. So we need to determine the kinds of circumstances in which lineages were able to dominate a marriage market and to try to plot these against the historical cycles of rises and declines in the population growth rate. Only then will we know whether the nuptiality variations over time noted here were very important in explaining *overall* trends in population growth rates in China or whether they were confined to large lineages and other dominant groups within local populations. The distribution of nuptiality variations is an important subject for future research.

If Telford's analysis is any hint, however, nuptiality should make less difference in the overall growth rate of populations than mortality, which seems to be the prime determiner of total fertility and of reproduction rates in this population.

Implications for the Demographic History of China

We thus have a hypothetical model of population growth in Ming and Qing China, one which is in disagreement with the received wisdom in several ways.

First, there is a real question of whether the population actually dipped from the late Ming to the early Qing. The growth rate certainly went down, but if it ever became negative it probably remained negative for only a few years in any one place and probably never amounted to a large drop in population.

Second, there is a real question of whether the Chinese populations were characterized by low marital fertility or not. I think not. Telford agrees that Chinese were a natural-fertility population: he has come up with estimates of total fertility of somewhere between 8 and 9.5. Estimates to the contrary are of two kinds: (1) the Buck survey, as reassessed by Barclay et al. (1976), which was a retrospective survey in which total fertility is expected to be reported as low because previous infant deaths are not reported (Wolf 1985)[10] and (2) Liu Ts'ui-jung's observations (1985) that are based on genealogies that did not record infant mortality. We need more data on the latter to fit rates to model life tables and the like, but my guess is moderate or high and uniform age-specific fertility. Liu's estimates in chapter 5 of this volume of both female and male total marital fertility of around 4.5 to 6.0 seem to be at odds with Telford's figures, but Liu has not accounted for infant mortality in her calculations. If a 250 per 1,000 infant mortality rate is figured in, these figures jump to a range of 6.0 to 8.0, which while not high is still much closer to Telford's high range.

Third, as Telford points out (p. 56), population in late imperial China thus appears to be regulated more by mortality factors than by fertility factors. Insofar as reproduction rates change with the dynastic cycle, they reflect not a change in age-specific fertility but rather a change in years of exposure, itself a consequence primarily of mortality levels in the childbearing years and secondarily of age at marriage. Insofar as marriage rates also vary, as shown by Liu in chapter 4, they seem to vary with the degree of imbalance in the sex ratio; higher sex ratios in hard times perhaps reflect increased female infanticide, which itself is a mortality factor.

The only real factor in differential population growth, then, is the change in years of exposure per person. If a person dies early, has a spouse die early, marries late, or doesn't marry at all, total fertility will change; if mortality is higher for the children, then net reproduction rates will change even if total fertility remains constant. The three factors examined here all contribute to expansion and contraction of years of exposure, and in the preliminary state of our analysis, we can hypothesize that years of exposure vary with the dynastic cycle.

FAMILY ORGANIZATION AND THE DEVELOPMENTAL CYCLE

In light of the various advances made in understanding the developmental cycle of recent Chinese families, as mentioned above, the detailed study of genealogical materials ought now to be addressed to the question of whether the modern-day models apply to Chinese families in past eras. Now that anthropologists have shown convincingly that residence in stem and joint families was part of the life experience of most Chinese in the late nineteenth and twentieth centuries, we need to ask whether residence in extended families was the continuation of a centuries-long pattern or whether the prevalence of complex families in recent years has resulted from lowered mortality due to public-health improvements in places such as Taiwan, a Japanese colony, and Ding Xian (Gamble [1954] 1968), a model of rural reconstruction on the mainland.

Two of the contributions to this volume address this question explicitly: the papers on family and the developmental cycle by Liu Ts'ui-jung (chap. 5) and by Stevan Harrell and Thomas Pullum (chap. 6). Using somewhat different assumptions and methods of calculation, both come up with the same answer: a resounding affirmation of the proposal that the stem and joint family forms were part of the life cycle of most of the families in the lineages studied from late Ming through late Qing times and that the ideal was achievable for centuries before modern health and sanitation measures lowered mortality appreciably. Consider the following figures derived from those two papers. Liu shows that 47.7 to 74.5% of the men in her sample of five lineages experienced life in a three-generation family; in Harrell and Pullum's lineages the values varied from 66 to 80%. Although Liu does not actually compute the chances of living in a joint, or grand, family, she estimates that about 50% of the men had a chance to become grandfathers in such families, since that many men had sons who lived to adulthood. Mortality would of course reduce the number of men who actually attained such patriarchal status, but undoubtedly some men were members of grand families at earlier stages of life. Harrell and Pullum's paper (chap. 6) provides more explicit evidence for the possibility of forming joint families: in the three lineages they studied, a little over half the men probably experienced life in such complex households. Although the methods used to calculate these percentages and the detail with which the questions are pursued vary somewhat from author to author, it is important to note that all the methods used are quite conservative: they only count a man as having lived in a three-generation family if the man was alive at the same time as his father's father, as his father and his sons, or as his sons' sons. They miss all the stem and joint families headed by widowed matriarchs, which are, at least in most census studies, a plurality if not a majority of the total number of extended families; they also miss those joint families in which one of the brothers has only daughters for several years and the sons, later in the birth order, are born only after the grandparents die. And since these methods assume division at the time of the grandfather's death, they entirely miss joint families of the *frèreches* form, a form that appears to have been common during the Qing period in Liaoning, at least (Lee 1990).

The findings of Liu and of Harrell and Pullum are of potentially great significance for Chinese family history, since they seem consistent across two rather disparate study populations. At the same time, both sets of findings raise questions regarding the representativeness of lineage populations for studying the total population of China in the Ming and Qing periods. Lineages that had enough wealthy members to be able to fund the compilation and printing of genealogies represented a biased sample of the general Chinese population, as has been demonstrated by Rubie Watson (1985). Even poor families belonging to large and influential lineages had certain economic advantages over poor families who were not members of any lineage at all, and it is quite possible that these economic advantages translated into lower age at marriage or lower age-specific mortality, two of the demographic phenomena that, as we have seen above, contributed to comparative demographic success in traditional China. So although we do not know for sure that lineage members were more likely to form stem and joint families than were their nonlineage neighbors, we can postulate that it was so, and we must be cautious about the overall significance of these findings on complex families.

At the same time, however, Wolf's (1985a) statement of the revisionist position indicated that his attribution of common stem and grand (joint) family structure did not apply to the poorest people, those who had no stable connection with the land or with the community. If we take Wolf's caution into account, then our figures from genealogy-bearing lineages, which after all include both wealthy and poor families, may be reasonably representative of all but the poorest in Ming and Qing China generally, and our case studies certainly contribute to the project of "revitalizing the myth" of Chinese family size.

MIGRATION AND REGIONAL CYCLES

As have long-term fertility and mortality trends, population migration has been of interest to scholars for a long time (Ho 1959; Averill 1983). But most previous accounts have been regional in nature, describing the effects on a region of large-scale in- or out-migration but not detailing the family-level processes through which regional population changes were accomplished.

The study of genealogies and similar local sources can contribute to the filling of this gap in the same way that it contributes to our understanding of fertility and mortality. There are, of course, enormous local differences in rates of migration: one village may send most of its inhabitants away while a neighboring village sends nobody. Nevertheless, migration from a region is not randomly distributed; there are patterns across a region as a whole and within certain subregions and ecological niches in that region. And through the study of local-level migration, we can begin to discern these intraregional patterns and then relate them to family-level processes.

The paper by Wang Lianmao in chapter 8 is a first attempt to study the processes of migration from a traditional emigrant area and to relate these processes at the same time to family strategies and to the broader intraregional and regional patterns of variation; the paper is based on a comparison of two genealogies from the Zhangquan subregion of the Southeast Coast macroregion (Skinner 1985:277). On the basis of detailed study of two genealogies in two very different ecological situations within this subregion (the Yans of Anping were a coastal, periurban, commercial lineage, and the Lins of Pushan were an inland, agricultural lineage), we can discern local patterns of participation in the great demographic and economic swings that characterized the Southeast Coast region in the late Ming and early to mid-Qing.

Specifically, the great high tide of migration for the commercial Yans came in the late Ming, when the Southeast Coast macroregion as a whole and the Zhangquan subregion in particular were experiencing an upswing caused by increased coastal trade in southern China and Southeast Asia (Skinner 1985:278). Most of the migrants from this lineage, as Wang demonstrates, went to coastal cities in China or to overseas ports; from anecdotal evidence it is clear that they went to trade and that many of them made their fortunes at it. The Lins, however, mostly migrated later, during and after the economic disasters of the long and painful Ming-Qing transition, when the Southeast Coast was in serious economic decline (Skinner 1985:279). Although there was some migration to coastal cities, most was either overseas, where most of the Lin migrants seem to have gone as laborers rather than merchants, or, significantly, to the new frontier of Taiwan, where the purpose of migration was ordinarily not to get rich in trade but simply to make a living in the newly opened agricultural areas.

The nature of the family process also differed somewhat in the two lineages; most of the overseas and coastal migration, which was predominant among the Yans, was of single men who intended to return; it was rare for families to emigrate. In the wave of migration to Taiwan in the Qing in which the Lins participated, however, there were many more families migrating as units, indicating once again the influence of ecology on migration strategies at the family level.

The study of Chinese historical microdemography is, as stated above, still in its infancy; much remains to be done before the educated guesses made in this volume are either rejected or become the historical commonplaces of tomorrow. We hope, however, that we have made a start toward an understanding of the connection between local phenomena and broad national and regional trends in Chinese population history.

NOTES

1. For a recent summary of the state of the field of Chinese historical demography, see Lavely, Lee, and Wang (1990:816–823).
2. There is disagreement between Wolf's (1985b) and Coale's (1985a) analyses of the level of marital fertility: Coale, and also Liu (1985), see a much lower level than does Wolf. I tend to side with Wolf, on the grounds that those who talk of moderate fertility neither take infant mortality rates (which were unrecorded but probably very high) into account nor provide, as Wolf does, a cultural rationale for the fertility strategy they portray.
3. To say that a family system is nuclear, stem, or joint is to say that its developmental cycle can expand to nuclear, stem, or joint composition, respectively, as its maximal form. Thus in a joint family system, one will never find all the families in a sample with joint composition at one time; some will be in the nuclear, some in the stem, and some in the joint phase at the time of any particular census. In a stem family system, by contrast, one will never find any joint families because the stem form is the maximum complexity allowed by the system.
4. The Genealogical Society's collections are kept by the Latter-Day Saints for ritual purposes, but they may be used freely by outside researchers.
5. For a fuller discussion of the demographic information contained in genealogies, see Telford (1986, 1990) and Harrell (1987).
6. See Telford (1986) for an account of regional and temporal variation in the inclusion of data about wives and daughters. One interesting exception is the imperial clan genealogy (*yudie*), in which daughters rather than wives are carefully recorded (Harrell, Naquin, and Ju 1985; Lee n.d.).
7. *Sui* is a Chinese measure of age indicating the number of calendar years a person has lived in. One is thus one *sui* at birth and gains a *sui* on every New Year's Day throughout life. On the average, a person's age in *sui* is one and one-half years older than that same person's age in the Western count, but the difference varies according to birthday from exactly one year for somebody born on New Year's Day to almost two years for somebody born on the last day of the year.
8. It should be noted that the detailed data presented in the papers in this volume derive primarily from the Lower Yangzi macroregion, with significant contributions also from the Middle Yangzi and North China regions. Insofar as other macroregions experienced other, sometimes phase-incongruent, economic cycles (Skinner 1985),

we might expect demographic rates in these other regions to have followed their own cycles and shown different patterns from those illustrated by the papers here. More research using genealogies and other sources from these other regions is needed. (The Southeast Coast region is represented in Wang's paper on migration, but his data bear only tangentially on the fertility and mortality questions addressed in this section.)

9. A caution is in order here. A few genealogies, and the lineage populations they represent, may be less representative samples of the total population as measures of nuptiality than as measures of fertility or mortality. This is because lineages operate in a marriage market, and the rise or fall of an individual lineage's political and/or economic fortunes may have a drastic effect on the marriageability of the lineage's men. Because he studies a large sample of the lineages in a county, the danger is less in Telford's case than in the cases of Harrell and Pullum and of Liu, whose samples are smaller.

10. But see the rejoinder to Wolf by Ansley Coale (1985a), one of the authors of the original reassessment.

TWO

Marriages among the Song Elite

Patricia Ebrey

Hajnal, in his influential description of the non-European marriage pattern, brought attention to the relatively young age of brides in preindustrial times everywhere but Western Europe. In most of the world virtually all women married and did so at about seventeen or eighteen years of age. Even men generally married by twenty-three or twenty-four (Hajnal 1965). Wolf and Hanley have refined this model for East Asia, confirming that China in recent times was characterized by early marriage, while Japan stood somewhat closer to Western Europe (1985:1–12).

The most common reason for studying age at marriage is its effect on fertility. Women who marry at puberty have more years in which they can bear children and so, everything else being equal, will bear more children than women who marry later. The husband's age at marriage also matters. In societies where mortality in middle age is relatively high, a woman is more likely to be left a widow while still capable of bearing children if her husband is significantly older than she.

An equally valid reason to study age at marriage is to learn about family structure and organization. For China, men's ages at marriage are particularly significant in this regard, given the preference for patrilocal marriage. Generations are short when sons are married young, and short generations increase the incidence of stem and grand families. If their fathers married as teenagers, children are more likely to spend their first years in households that include grandparents, uncles, and cousins. (See chapter 5 by Liu and chapter 6 by Harrell and Pullum for more on the relationship between demographic patterns and household organization.)

For the twentieth century, several surveys have provided information about age at marriage for both men and women. The survey that covered the widest range of localities in China is that conducted from 1929 to 1933 by John Lossing Buck on 38,256 farm families (Buck 1937). The reanalysis of the Buck data by Barclay et al. (1976:609) gives very similar mean ages at first marriage in both North and South China: for men, 21.3 years in the North and 21.4 in the South, for women, 17.2 years in the North and 17.8 years in the South.[1]

Aggregate figures, of course, can obscure all sorts of variation. However, most studies of specific localities in the early twentieth century uncovered ages at marriage close to Buck's figures. These localities include Dingxian in Hebei, two areas in Jiangsu, one in Yunnan, two areas in Taiwan, and Taiwan as a whole (Chen 1946:42; Pasternak 1983:60–62; Gamble [1954] 1968:40–45; Wolf and Huang 1980:133–42). When taken together, these figures indicate that most localities had median ages of marriage for men between 18.6 and 22.0 and for women between 17.5 and 18.6. Outside of this range were Dingxian's low figure for men (17.2) and Taiwan's high figures for men (23.2) and women (19.9).

So far there has been little study of age at marriage for premodern China. Xu Hong compiled data on women's ages at marriage in the Ming from 1309 biographies. From them one can calculate an average age at marriage for women of 16.3 years (Xu 1989:73). Liu Ts'ui-jung, in her study of two clans in Zhejiang during the Qing, estimated ages at marriage of 21.3 for men and 16.1 for women.[2] This figure is fairly low for women, but Liu provided support for its plausibility by calculating age at marriage for women from a local gazetteer, getting a figure of 16.8 years (Liu 1985:23). In chapter 6 Harrell and Pullum estimate age at marriage from age at birth of first son for two lineages in the late Ming and Qing (1550–1850) and arrive at figures that are fairly close to Liu's for men (20.9 and 22.4) but older for women (17.6 and 19.1).

Studies of age at marriage in modern China have also found striking differences according to wealth. Within a specific locality, the richer or higher ranking married their sons at significantly younger ages than other people did, whereas they married their daughters at the same or only slightly younger ages. The most extreme example comes from Dingxian, where sons were married at an average age of 13.2 in families with over 100 *mu* of land, at an average of 15.6 in families with 50–99 *mu,* and at an average of 18.4 in families with under 50 *mu* (Gamble [1954] 1968:41–43). Sophie Sa found a similar situation among Taipei city dwellers, albeit at older ages. In her group nearly one-half the men in the high status group married before twenty; only about one-third in the middle status group and one-quarter in the low status group married before twenty (Sa 1985:298). For the Qing period, Harrell found that men in branches of lineages with more officials (men who were presumably richer) had their first sons a couple of years earlier than men in other branches (Harrell 1985:101–3).

In this essay I will look at vital data concerning marriage in a relatively early period, the Song dynasty (960–1279). In Western Europe, late marriage for women dates back only to the late seventeenth century, though for men it was present much earlier (Hajnal 1965; Herlihy 1985:103–11). What was the situation in China centuries ago? Were spouses usually close in age? How did age at marriage and age differences relate to numbers of children? Was there much variation by class or region in any of these matters? How does this sort of information contribute to our understanding of family organization and family strategies?

The sources needed to answer these questions are, unfortunately, far from plentiful. Unlike other authors in this volume, I have only dozens, not thousands, of cases to analyze. Thus I have not attempted statistical analyses and have usually merely summarized my evidence. Moreover, I base my arguments as much on qualitative evidence as on quantitative evidence.

Epitaphs are my primary source for age at marriage during the Song. Many thousands of epitaphs (*muzhiming*) survive from the Song, preserved in published collections, and a large share of these have been indexed in *Songren zhuanji ziliao suoyin* (Chang 1977). These epitaphs describe people from all over the country but survive in much larger numbers for men than for women.

The information in epitaphs was supplied by the survivors, who would either write the epitaph themselves or ask a friend or relative to compose it for them. Convention called for including the following information: the names and titles of the subject's father, father's father, and often father's father's father; the county the subject came from; the date of death and age at death; the date and location of burial; the name and sometimes the ancestry of the spouse; the names and titles of sons, exluding those who died quite young; and the names and titles of daughters' husbands. For men epitaphs also gave a resumé of their official careers. Epitaphs described the character and personality of the subject in some way, and the value of these descriptions depends on the author's acquaintance with his subject and on his literary ability. When a man remarried after his first wife's death, both wives were listed, and the children were usually distinguished by mother. Sometimes, especially on wives' epitaphs, certain children were listed as born to concubines. Age at marriage is mentioned in approximately two-fifths of the epitaphs for women but almost never on the epitaphs for men. Therefore, since I am interested as much in men's ages at marriage as in women's, I selected epitaphs for this study based on a single criterion: was there also an epitaph for the spouse? Using paired couples also allows me to distinguish first marriages from subsequent ones, since men's epitaphs list all their wives in order, but women's epitaphs sometimes fail to mention that the woman was a "successor" wife.[3]

Altogether, I found 189 pairs of epitaphs for Song couples, 166 of which gave birth dates for both spouses. These epitaphs were written by over ninety separate authors. Of the 166 pairs with complete birth dates, 31 were for a man's second, third, or fourth marriage, and the remaining 135 were for first marriages. Of these 135, 65 explicitly stated age at marriage.[4]

Surviving epitaphs are not an unbiased source. They exist only for the elite and those close to them, that is, families of officials, their relatives, and those they associated with.[5] Moreover, some people's epitaphs were more likely to be preserved. Above all, the friends and relatives of successful writers were favored in this regard. Beyond that, it seems likely that those who lived a full life span were more likely to get epitaphs than those who died young. Neither of these factors, however, has an obvious relationship to age at marriage, and so presumably neither biases the resulting set in that regard.[6] Length of life does, of course, affect total childbearing, but this effect can be taken into account. A more serious limitation is geographical. Writers whose works have been preserved are not spread out evenly around the country, with the result that the surviving paired epitaphs do not cover all regions in proportion to their populations. For the Northern Song, the areas best represented are the Lower Yangtze, the capital region, the Middle Yangtze, the Northeast, Sichuan, and Fujian, in that order. For the Southern Song, the subjects of epitaphs are overwhelmingly from the Lower Yangtze, Middle Yangtze, and Fujian.[7] It should of course be remembered that the late Song did not control the North, and thus there are no epitaphs for men and women from the North in the twelfth and thirteenth centuries.

AGE AT MARRIAGE

Figures 2.1 and 2.2 give the numbers of men and women in these epitaphs marrying at various ages. The same information is given in Table 2.1 in percentages.

As is easily seen from these figures, women married within a fairly short time span. Fifty-four percent married within the four-year time period between fifteen and eighteen, and 89% married within the eight-year time span from fourteen to twenty-one. Thus, 90% of women married by the time they reached twenty-one years. The age at marriage for women thus was certainly young (the mean and the median age were both 18.0). This age at marriage for elite women in the Song is very close to that found in the survey data collected in the early twentieth century. However, it is more than a year older than Xu's figures for the Ming and Liu's for the Qing.

For men the case is different. These Song men spread their marriages over a much longer period, with 52% falling into the six-year period from 16.0 through 21.0 and 92% falling into the sixteen-year period from 14.0 to 29.0. Over half of the men (54%) in this elite sample married as teenagers

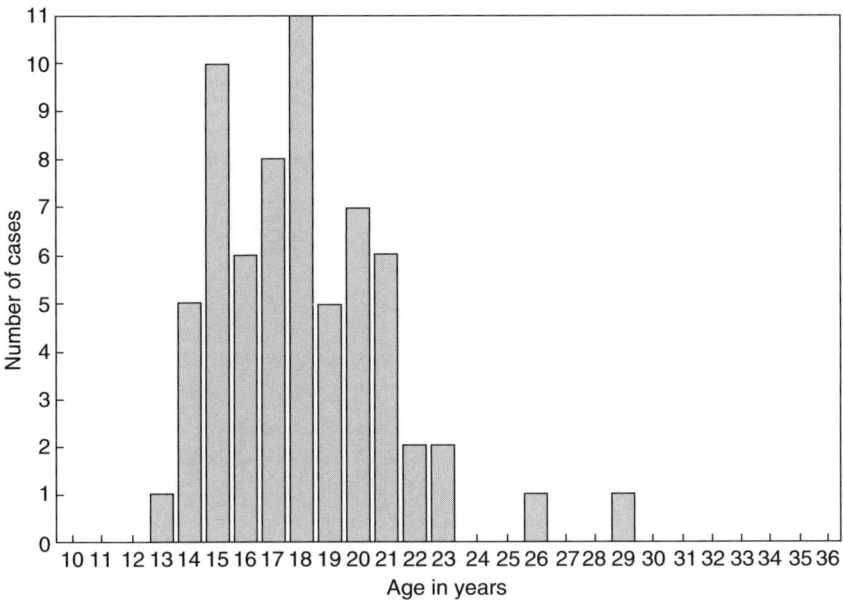

Figure 2.1. Distribution of Women's Ages at Marriage, Set of 65

(at 20.0 or younger). The mean age was 20.8, and the median was 20.0 (21 *sui*). These mean ages at marriage for men also are very close to those from the twentieth-century surveys of farmers referred to above. Compared only to elite men, however, they apparently married somewhat late. Sa (1985: 297–98) and Gamble ([1954] 1968:41–43) both found that well-to-do men married at younger ages than these means.

Why were women married within a shorter time span than men? Biology was probably a major reason. Daughters seem to have been married as close to puberty as possible, but puberty is neither so clear nor so urgent a matter for sons. Biology is of course interpreted through the lens of culture, and the preferred age to marry for women was considerably younger than that for men. According to the classics, women should marry between fifteen and twenty *sui*, or twenty-three if mourning caused a delay, and men should be married by thirty (Legge [1885] 1967, 1:478–79). The law codes in the Song set only minimum ages, thirteen *sui* for women and fifteen *sui* for men (Niida 1937:548–51). Song scholars argued for compromises between the legal minimums and the classical preference for older ages. Sima Guang (1019–86) discouraged marrying at the earlier ages allowed by law in his guide to ritual (ages in the extract have been left as he gave them, in *sui*):

> Boys from 16 to 30 and girls from 14 to 20 may all be married, as long as neither the principals nor their sponsors [generally their fathers] are in

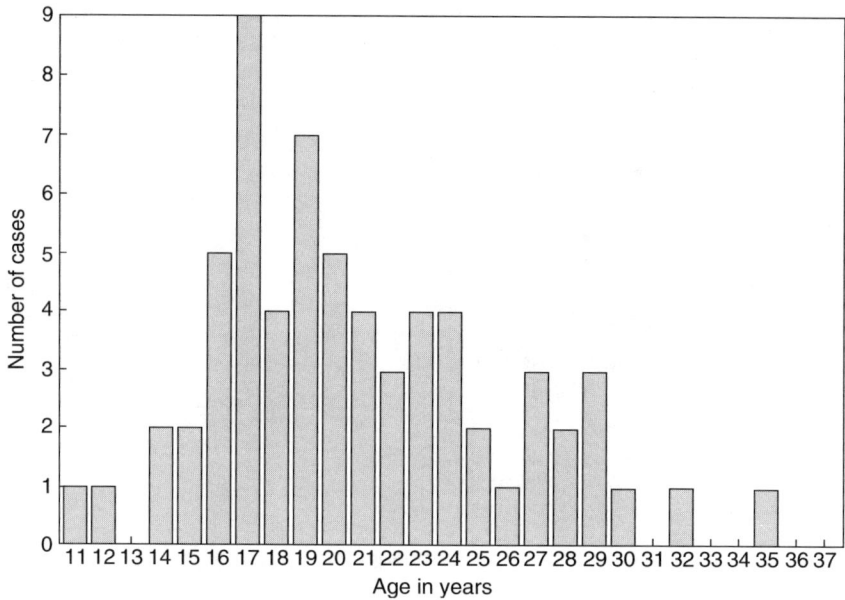

Figure 2.2. Distribution of Men's Ages at Marriage, Set of 65

mourning graded at a year or longer. Note: In the ancient ritual men married at 30 and women at 20. According to the *Jiayu [Family sayings of Confucius]*, Confucius married [a woman of] the Yuanguan family of Song at 19, and a year later begat Boyu. Boyu died at 50, before Confucius did. Thus, not all ancient marriages were at 30. Probably the *Ritual* is referring to the extreme limit; that is, men should not pass 30 or women 20. If they pass these dates they have missed the time. The present law code permits men to marry from 15 and women from 13 and up, probably because the current vulgar custom of early marriage cannot be eradicated. Also sometimes there is an orphan with no one to depend on. Thus it accords with human feelings to set the regulation in this way so that such orphans would not be subject to punishment [if they married early]. (Sima 1936: 3:29)

As mentioned by Sima Guang, the death of a parent, grandparent, uncle, or sibling could delay a marriage of either a man or woman for the length of the mourning period, and in Song times marriages were in fact delayed for these reasons (Ebrey 1984c:426, 433 for two examples).

Sima Guang mentions "missing the time," an idea repeatedly encountered in documents related to marriage, such as engagement letters and contracts. In the case of girls, in particular, the idea that they were "ripe" for marriage at a certain age, much as flowers or fruit are ripe, recurs regularly as a justification for getting a marriage promptly concluded. One

TABLE 2.1. Distribution of Men's and Women's Ages at Marriage

	Men		Women	
Age	Number	%	Number	%
11	1	1.5	0	0.0
12	1	1.5	0	0.0
13	0	0.0	1	1.5
14	2	3.1	5	7.7
15	2	3.1	10	15.4
16	5	7.7	6	9.2
17	9	13.8	8	12.3
18	4	6.2	11	16.9
19	7	10.8	5	7.7
20	5	7.7	7	10.8
21	4	6.2	6	9.2
22	3	4.6	2	3.1
23	4	6.2	2	3.1
24	4	6.2	0	0.0
25	2	3.1	0	0.0
26	1	1.5	1	1.5
27	3	4.6	0	0.0
28	2	3.1	0	0.0
29	3	4.6	1	1.5
30	1	1.5	0	0.0
31	0	0.0	0	0.0
32	1	1.5	0	0.0
33	0	0.0	0	0.0
34	0	0.0	0	0.0
35	1	1.5	0	0.0
36	0	0.0	0	0.0
Total	65	100.0	65	100.0
Mean age	20.8		18.0	
Median age	20		18	
Standard dev.	4.95		2.99	

of the most often cited allusions in marriage documents is a line in the *Book of Songs* that states, "The plum reached its time" (cf. Waley 1937:30).

For recent times, it has been asserted that virtually everyone preferred to see their sons married early in order to have grandsons sooner (Wolf and Huang 1980:141–42). This sentiment was occasionally expressed in the Song, usually by citing the phrase "to see a great-great-grandson," after an anecdote about a man in the Wei period who arranged the marriage of his fifteen or sixteen *sui* great-grandson in order to see the birth of a great-great-grandson (Wei 1974, 58:1302).⁸ Moreover, having to marry late was considered a misfortune. Here the standard allusion was to a poem by Bai Juyi that said that men should be married by thirty and women by twenty, but because of the disorders of the time, many people exceeded these ages, which made childbirth difficult and meant that the parents would be in their decline before their children were full grown (Bai 1965: 2:23).

Nevertheless, there were also arguments in favor of postponing marriage for men. Sima Guang referred to early marriage as a "vulgar custom," using language that suggests he saw an association between early marriage and lower social status or lower educational levels. This possibility is given even greater credibility by a comment in a Song guide for magistrates, which criticized the marriage practices of "inferior people" (*xiaoren*) and objected to cases where the wife was old but the husband young (Li 1976: 9:47b). Perhaps the idea that the elite married earlier because they had the resources to do so was foreign to the Song elite. The scholar Luo Yuan (1136–84), from Anhui, wrote an essay arguing that all men should wait until they were thirty to marry unless they were orphans like Confucius, who had to marry to carry on the ancestral rites. Luo placed particular weight on the need for maturity: "When a man reaches thirty he is knowledgeable and able to lead others" (Luo 1983: 21:13b–16b). The eminent statesman Fu Bi (1004–83), from Luoyang, did not marry until he passed the examination at age twenty-eight *sui*, telling his parents that they should go ahead and marry his younger brothers and sisters before him. He urged late marriage on an unmarried visitor of twenty-four, saying it allowed him to build up his energy and focus his attention on study (Shao 1983: 18:200).

AGE DIFFERENCES BETWEEN HUSBANDS AND WIVES

In this Song elite sample drawn from epitaphs, the difference between the mean age at marriage for men and women is just under three years (2.8 years), well within the range for more recent times. Yet the dispersion of age differences is surprisingly broad. For age differences, it is not necessary to look only at the sixty-five paired epitaphs with age at marriage; the 135 first marriages with complete birth dates can be used. The range of age differences in that larger set are shown in Figure 2.3 and Table 2.2.

As can easily be seen, in almost one-quarter of the cases (23.9%) the wife was older than the husband in *sui* counting (over one-quarter, 27.5%, were older if half those born in the same year are added). In another 31% the husband was five or more years older than the wife, and in 12% he was ten or more years older. These figures at the extremes are high compared to published data from more recent times. In the Qing genealogies Liu analyzed, only about 10 to 12% of the wives were older than their husbands in

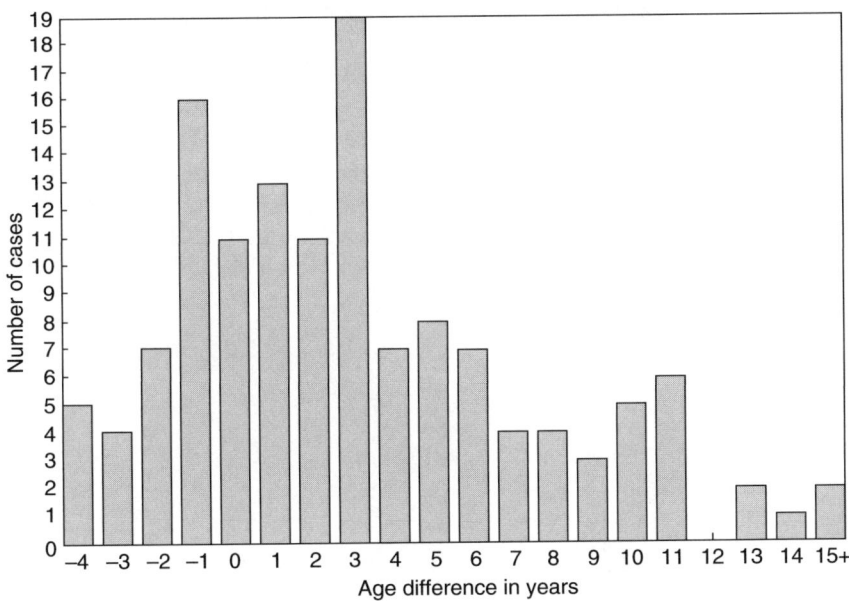

Figure 2.3. Distribution of Age Differences between Spouses, Set of 135 *sui* counting.[9] Telford found only 5.1% of his wives two or more years older than their husbands (chap. 3). Surveys of farmers showed 5 to 12% of wives older, except in Dingxian. The only figures for wives older close to these Song ones are Sa's figures for high-status city dwellers (19%) and Cartier's for Ming officials (22%) (Sa 1985:298; Cartier 1974:1345).

Among the Song elite, women who married relatively young (thirteen through seventeen) were just as likely to be older than their husbands as women who married at nineteen, twenty, or twenty-one. Among men, however, the earlier they married the more likely it was that their wives were older, and the older they married the greater their age superiority over their wives. To put this another way, women's ages at marriage were fairly constant whether the men were fifteen or twenty-one, so that the age difference between them depended primarily on the husband's age at marriage.

LENGTH OF MARRIAGES

The age difference between spouses naturally affects the length of marriages. That is, an eighteen-year-old woman married to an eighteen-year-old man could expect a longer marriage than one married to a twenty-eight-year-old man, given that marriages were almost always ended by the death of one of the parties. If the death of one partner came before the end of the woman's childbearing years, age difference would also affect

TABLE 2.2. Distribution of Age Differences

Age difference[a]	Cases	%
−4	5	3.7
−3	4	3.0
−2	7	5.2
−1	16	11.9
0	11	8.1
1	13	9.6
2	11	8.1
3	19	14.1
4	7	5.2
5	8	5.9
6	7	5.2
7	4	3.0
8	4	3.0
9	3	2.2
10	5	3.7
11	6	4.4
12	0	0.0
13	2	1.5
14	1	0.7
15 or more	2	1.5
Total	135	100.0

[a] The wife's age is subtracted from the husband's age. Negative numbers mean that the wife is older than the husband.

how many children the couple had. In societies where mortality at age forty and fifty is high, as it was in traditional China, a woman has a greater chance of being widowed while still capable of bearing children when her husband is much older than she. Widowhood has the greatest impact on fertility when widows are discouraged from remarrying, as they were in China.

In the set of epitaphs used here, the mean age at death was 58.5 *sui* for women and 61.2 *sui* for men. Considering that we are only dealing with those who lived long enough to marry, this would mean a life expectancy at twenty *sui* of 38.5 for women and 41.2 for men. This is not unreasonable from modern surveys,[10] and so this set of epitaphs may not be too skewed in favor of those who lived long. The distribution of ages at death also seems quite plausible. It is shown in Table 2.3 and Figure 2.4.

Given this pattern of mortality, the lengths of marriages were naturally highly variable. As seen in Figure 2.5 marriages were disrupted at a very regular rate, with close to 20% ending in every decade. In other words, though the curve may have been bell-shaped for life spans, it was not for

TABLE 2.3. Distribution of Ages at Death of Men and Women Who Lived to Marry

Age	Men			Women		
	Cases	%	Cumulative %	Cases	%	Cumulative %
to 20	0	0.0	0.0	3	2.1	2.1
21–25	2	1.4	1.4	6	4.2	6.3
26–30	1	0.7	2.0	6	4.2	10.6
31–35	1	0.7	2.7	8	5.6	16.2
36–40	5	3.4	6.1	6	4.2	20.5
41–45	10	6.8	12.8	4	2.8	23.2
46–50	14	9.5	22.2	14	9.9	33.1
51–55	11	7.4	29.7	10	7.0	40.1
56–60	26	17.6	47.3	17	12.0	52.1
61–65	15	10.1	57.4	9	6.3	58.5
66–70	24	16.2	73.6	13	9.2	67.6
71–75	17	11.5	85.1	13	9.2	76.8
76–80	10	6.8	91.9	20	14.1	90.8
81–85	8	5.4	97.3	5	3.5	94.4
86–90	2	1.4	98.6	6	4.2	98.6
91–95	2	1.4	100.0	2	1.4	100.0
Total	148			142		

marriage spans. Marriages that ended within the first fifteen years were more often brought about by the death of the wife, in many cases in childbirth. After the first fifteen years, the man's death was the more likely event.

Did widowhood remove many women from childbearing? It would appear not. In this set of couples, only 52% of the wives ever became widows; the others died before their husbands. Of those who were left widows, only 5.2% lost their husband in their twenties; by age thirty-five this rose to 7.8%, by forty to 12.9%, and by forty-five to 19.3%. (See Figure 2.6.) These figures seem rather low compared to what Liu found. Her examination of genealogies for two clans in eighteenth- and nineteenth-century China showed husbands to be an average of 5.2 years older than their wives and over 25% of the women aged twenty to forty-four to be widows (Liu 1985:27–28). Twentieth-century surveys have generally reported considerably lower proportions of widows than Liu found; the lower proportions apparently reflect a higher rate of remarriage, better survival of husbands, and perhaps smaller age differences between spouses.[11] For whatever reasons, the proportion of these Song elite women living as widows seems closer to that of twentieth-century peasants.[12]

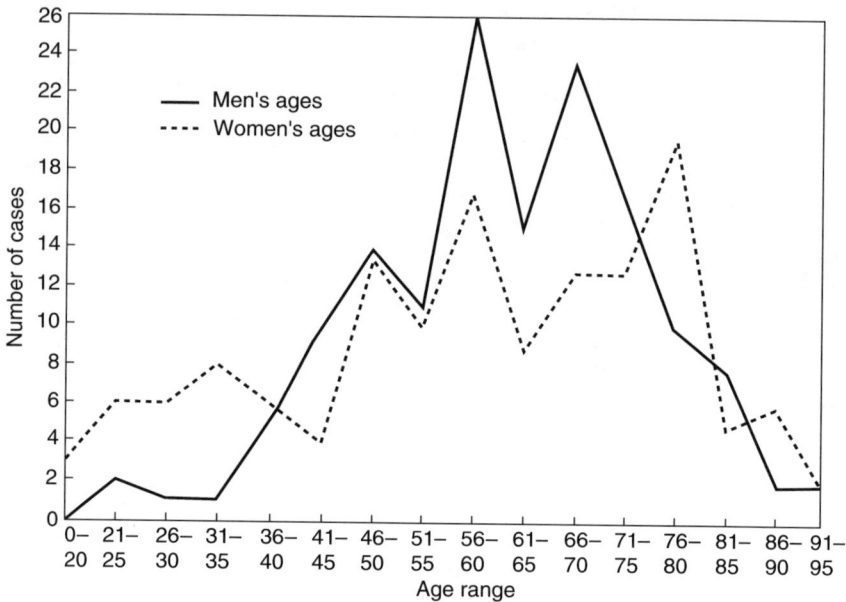

Figure 2.4. Distribution of Ages at Death

NUMBER OF CHILDREN

Whether one wishes to look on these Song marriages as early (compared to Western marriage patterns) or late (compared to well-to-do families in more recent China), they did lead to lots of children. The couples described in these epitaphs generally averaged 5.41 children, the overwhelming majority of whom survived long enough to marry (in the case of daughters) or receive some sort of title (in the case of sons). (If we consider only marriages that lasted through the wife's reproductive span, to forty-five *sui*, the average number of children was 6.13.)[13] Naturally some families had more children than others. Nineteen percent of the couples had eight or more children, and only 3.9% were childless (generally because one spouse died soon after the marriage). See Figure 2.7.

Since some of the children listed on epitaphs (even wives' epitaphs) may have been born to concubines, it is impossible to say with any certainty how many children were born per wife (rather than per husband). But we can say that when a woman had the good fortune to live to forty-five without losing her husband, she was likely to see about six children grow up, some of whom may have been her husband's children by concubines. The epitaphs used here give little evidence for the practice of female infanticide by the Song elite, for they record nearly as many daughters as sons.[14]

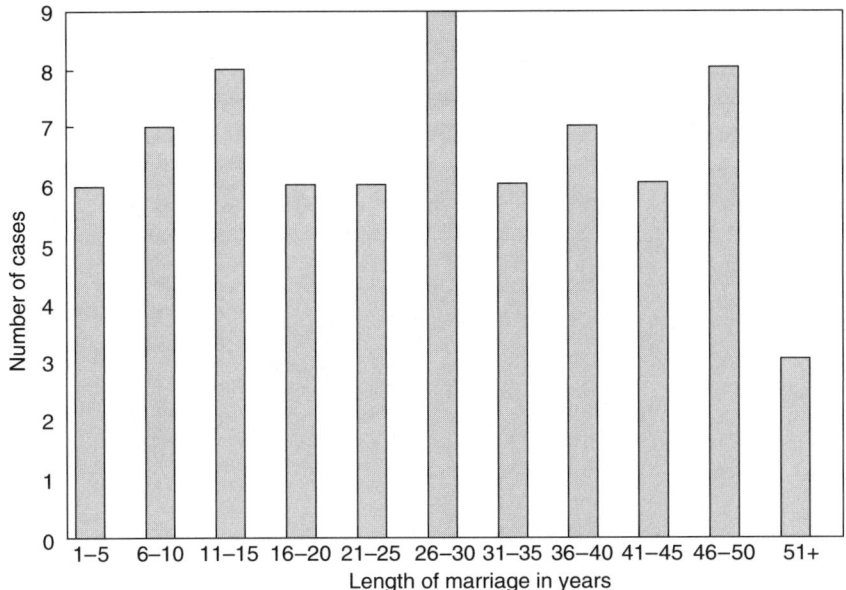

Figure 2.5. Distribution of Lengths of Marriages

China is often thought of as a pronatalist society, that is, one in which families adopt strategies that will lead to more children and grandchildren. But how did people know what strategies would work? Did they think it made much difference whether they found a bride for their son when he was eighteen or twenty or twenty-two, or that they might have one less grandchild if the bride was nineteen rather than sixteen? I have found no textual evidence that people thought these small differences in age at marriage would prove significant to total numbers of children. If these 135 couples studied here are typical of the couples an elite family would have known, it would be difficult for them to infer that early marriage was a pronatalist strategy. Among the 135 first marriages, there was very little correlation between later marriage and fewer children unless the wife was over twenty-three or the husband over twenty-four. Perhaps the presence of concubines obscured any simple relationship between age at marriage and numbers of children, or perhaps so few children were born to couples in their teens that older couples could easily catch up.

IMPLICATIONS FOR UNDERSTANDING ELITE FAMILY STRUCTURE IN THE SONG

The epitaphs examined here provide a plausible group portrait of Song elite families. The educated class as a whole grew rapidly in the Song (Chaffee

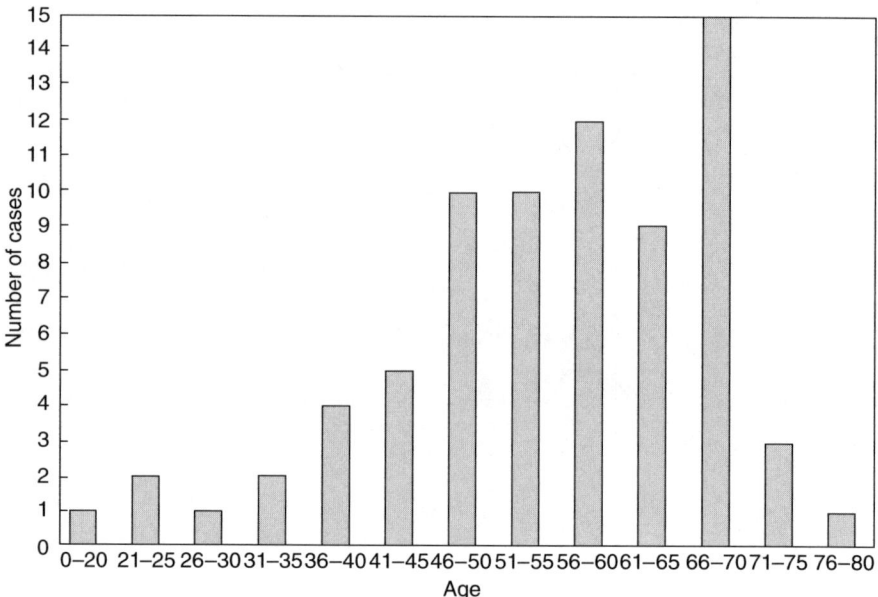

Figure 2.6. Distribution of Women's Ages at Widowhood

1985:35–41), and it would appear that much of this increase came from within, from elite families raising an average of three sons to adulthood. Even if families did not follow entirely pronatalist strategies in deciding ages at marriage (marrying some daughters and many more sons several years after puberty), they took other steps that led to numerous children, especially remarriage of widowed men and acquisition of concubines in addition to wives.

From these epitaphs there is every reason to think most men in the Song elite spent much of their lives in complex families. Marriages of sons were early enough so that many children would have grown up with grandparents, for the younger their fathers the greater the likelihood that their paternal grandparents would be still alive and living with them. Children would also be more likely to live with aunts and uncles and cousins, since the younger the senior generation the less likely they would be to permit their sons to divide the property. And children had uncles and cousins to live with because only sons were relatively uncommon (of the 449 sons listed on these epitaphs, only 27 were only sons).[15] Or, to change the perspective, three-quarters of the couples had two or more sons and over one-half had three or more. We cannot always assume that grand families resulted from such cases, since division soon after the parents' death was considered normal in the Song elite, and many parents would have died

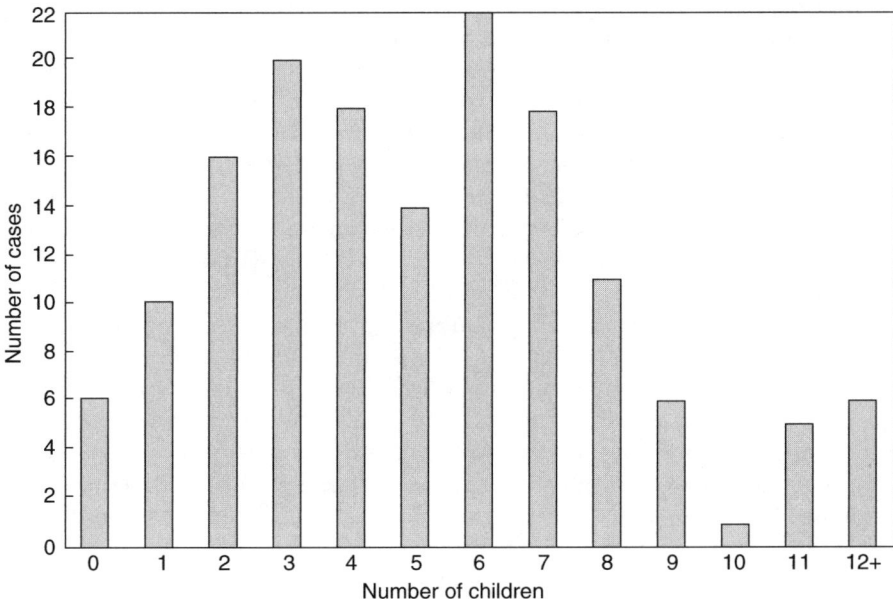

Figure 2.7. Distribution of Number of Children per Marriage

before all their children were married. Nevertheless, about 20% of the epitaphs for wives make specific reference to large complex families, such as noting that a wife obeyed the eldest sister-in-law as if she were her mother-in-law (Yu 1946: 19:22b–23a), or that she led the children every day to pay respects to her husband's elder brothers (Zhu 1929: 19:15a). There is every reason to think many more brides started their marriages in such grand families.

The structure of particular families is always shaped by the accidents of demography: how many children are born and survive, how long parents and grandparents live. Moreover, generations are always variable in length, since a father is much older at the birth of his last son than he was at the birth of his first. One inference that can be drawn from these epitaphs is that parents' choices in deciding when to marry their sons added to the diversity of family forms among the elite. They did not consider it necessary to marry all their sons at very nearly the same age (as they did their daughters).

Marrying sons young not only keeps generations short but also reinforces the authority of the older generation. One often hears of family strategies and family decisions; but the interests of all family members were not identical, and major events such as marriage and property division were marked by tensions of several sorts (Cohen 1976). Marriage of sons in their teens probably benefited parents more than sons, as early marriage allowed the parents to establish a pattern of directing the younger couple. That half of the men in this set of epitaphs married as teenagers tended to reinforce this pattern of parental authority.

Ages of spouses could also affect another dimension of authority in the family. A wife as old as or older than her husband would plausibly have a better chance to avoid being dominated by him, even if she married as a teenager. When a girl of seventeen married a man in his mid-twenties or older, she would have much less chance to assert herself in dealing with him, and he might well look on her as a child. What is notable in this regard is, again, the wide dispersion of age differences. In about one-quarter of the cases the wife was older, but in 12% the man was ten or more years older than his wife. There is no way to know whether these age differences were a major element in the relationships between particular husbands and wives, since epitaphs would never describe a wife as domineering or a husband as oppressive. But it would appear that many families in the elite were confident that the ideology of male superiority would assure appropriate husband-wife relations no matter what their age differences, and so were ready to choose brides who were older than their sons.

MARRIAGE DECISIONS IN THE CONTEXT OF ELITE SOCIAL AND POLITICAL LIFE

As a social historian looking at the evidence of sons' ages at marriage in the Song elite, I am more impressed by the dispersion than by the mean. Compared to sons in Western Europe in the eighteenth and nineteenth centuries, sons married young, but within the Song elite some men married at fifteen, others at twenty-seven.

Cultural notions of preferred ages at marriage are not enough to explain why people chose the ages they did. Parents may well have thought it was best for a son to marry at twenty-two but may have speeded up or delayed his marriage because other considerations outweighed age. After all, marrying a son accomplishes other things besides the birth of grandsons (Watson and Ebrey 1991). In many cases control over wealth changes hands through betrothal gifts or dowry or both. Marriages create ties to affines who extend a family's social and economic network. Indeed, marriages are often referred to as alliances in China and elsewhere. Each marriage is a chance to gain or lose economically or socially, and thus it provides an occasion for thinking tactically. A family head need not make similar matches for each son; in one case he may seek useful affines, in another case a large dowry, in another a quick wedding. Marriage choices can be compared to market choices, with the various decision makers weighing an assortment of factors, including the age and attractiveness of their children, the supply of potential spouses, the other demands on their resources, and so on.

Given what has been reported of elite family behavior in more recent times, it is more surprising that so many sons in the Song elite were married "late," at twenty-four, twenty-five, twenty-six, than that some were married young, at fourteen, fifteen, and sixteen. Accidental circumstances (especially being orphaned) would have delayed specific marriages. Beyond that, however, certain patterns can be noticed. Late marriage was not common in the Northeast or in the imperial family.[16] Elite men in the Northeast during the Northern Song were married early (median age nineteen), with a small age difference between spouses (2.3 years), and the wife was older than the husband over one-third of the time. The imperial clan married men very young (median age fifteen) and often to quite young women.[17] Later marriage was common, however, in the Lower Yangtze area (median age twenty-two), especially in the Northern Song. In this region it was fairly rare for the wife to be older than her husband (only 5%), and on the average the man was 3.5 years older than his wife. Men from the Middle Yangtze married even later (median age twenty-four) and had greater age differences (average 5.0 years), with 55% of them five or more years older than their wives.

Are these regional patterns of any historical importance? Do they reflect different political strategies? Different cultural values? Different relations between the official elite and other members of the local society?[18] Robert Hartwell (1982) and Robert Hymes (1986) have discussed a shift in strategies away from cross-prefectural marriages from Northern to Southern Song, but this shift does not explain the regional differences already visible in the Northern Song. Nor does a preference for cross-prefectural marriages seem to be related to men's ages at marriage. In the Northeast marriages were young and in all but one case joined families across prefectural lines. But in the Lower and Middle Yangtze the 43% of marriages that crossed prefectural lines averaged two years *later* than those within a single prefecture.

Could it be that the men from the Yangtze regions in this set of epitaphs are from lower levels of the elite and, therefore, had different marriage practices? This possibility can be examined by comparing the evidence found in epitaphs with that found in genealogies. Genealogies that include birth dates back to the Song for both men and women are rare for any areas but the Lower and Middle Yangtze. In this discussion I will use data from nine genealogies from these areas.[19] These genealogies were published in the Qing, but the details provided for Song ancestors must have been based on Song sources, probably recopied and reedited a dozen times. The lineages whose genealogies were used are listed below in Table 2.4. Altogether they provide information on 189 couples.

TABLE 2.4. Lineages Whose Genealogies Were Used for Birth Dates of Couples

Name	Province (Modern)	Circuit (Song)	No. of Couples	Social Status
Wang	Jiangsu	Liangzhexi	12	started as officials
Sun	Jiangsu	Liangzhexi	10	officials
Hang	Jiangsu	Huainandong	15	officials
Song	Jiangsu	Liangzhedong	24	started as officials
Zhan	Anhui	Jiangnandong	24	non-officials
Zhang	Zhejiang	Liangzhexi	23	non-officials
Li	Jiangxi	Jiangnanxi	24	have officials late
Wei	Jiangxi	Jiangnanxi	38	officials
Gong	Jiangxi	Jiangnanxi	22	officials

NOTE: "Started as officials" means some officials are recorded for the early generations but none are recorded for the later generations.

The major advantage of genealogies is that they describe a more diverse social stratum than epitaphs. The compilation of genealogies was not nearly as common in Song times as in Qing times and probably was done only when the descent group had some highly educated men to take the lead (Ebrey 1986:35–37, 44–50). Still, some genealogies are for descent groups that produced no officials, and even those that produced a good number of officials also have many men with no close relatives in office.

The major drawback to genealogies is that they do not give date of marriage. Nevertheless, from genealogies one can make some broad estimates of age at marriage based on age at birth of first recorded son. This estimate is more useful when the genealogy shows the birth of a son fairly early, at age twenty or less, which undoubtedly means the parents married in their teens. Table 2.5 lists some basic statistics on the couples found in these nine genealogies, divided according to region.

From the total column of this table and Figure 2.8 it is clear that late marriage for men was not the general custom in the Lower and Middle Yangtze areas.[20] Compared to the couples from this area known from epitaphs, the couples known from genealogies had a smaller age difference, were more likely to have the wife older in *sui* counting, and were much less likely to have the husband significantly older than the wife. Early marriage of men must have been quite common, since over 30% of men had a surviving son by age nineteen. On the average, such men must have married about six years earlier, since half of the first children will be daughters, and many children do not survive to be recorded.[21] By contrast, the epitaphs for the Lower and Middle Yangtze show only 3.3% of the men had married by fifteen. There are some status differences within the ge-

TABLE 2.5. Age Differences of Spouses in Genealogies

Region	No. of Couples	Avg. Age Difference (in sui)	% of Wives Older	% of Husbands 5+ Yrs. Older	% Husbands w/ Sons by Age 19.0 (20 sui)
Lower Yangtze officials	61	2.10	16.4	11.5	23.9
Lower Yangtze non-officials	47	.54	38.3	10.6	42.9
Middle Yangtze	81	.84	35.8	8.6	29.6
Overall average		1.2	30.2	10.3	31.3
Total	189				

nealogy set, and they also suggest that in this area higher status groups married sons later.[22]

Why were the high elite of the Lower and Middle Yangtze areas more inclined to delay their sons' marriages than the high elite of the Northeast? Late marriage for men was apparently not a general custom of the Lower and Middle Yangtze areas. But there are many other possible explanations. There could have been regional differences in attitudes toward age differences between spouses, status differences between spouses, or the propriety of a man's remarrying a never-married woman of his own class after the death of his first wife. If such differences reduced the pool of women considered most suitable as wives, it would take men longer on the average to find wives.

Late marriage for men in the Lower and Middle Yangtze areas could also have been encouraged by local attitudes toward examination success and possibly by regional differences in the intensity of competition. The texts of epitaphs show that marriages were sometimes delayed to wait for progress in gaining official credentials. Epitaphs offer evidence that over one-half of the men marrying at twenty-five *sui* or later married women from families richer or better connected than their own, often after passing the *jinshi* or at least entering the Imperial University. For instance, Jiang Bao (1069–1117), from Xinan in Zhejiang, was the son of a low official. He entered the Imperial University before being "capped" and at twenty-five or twenty-six *sui* received a *jinshi* degree. At this point the high official Zeng Bu (1036–1107) offered him three hundred thousand cash as an engagement present to marry his daughter by a concubine. Jiang Bao declined the large gift, but did marry the daughter (Cheng 1929: 31:3a–6a; 13b–15b). Another example is Hu Quan (1102–80), from Luling in Jiangxi. His father had taken the examinations but did not pass. Hu entered the Imperial University and received *jinshi* credentials in 1127 at twenty-six *sui*. Liu Mincai, a regional official in Hu's home area whose father had also

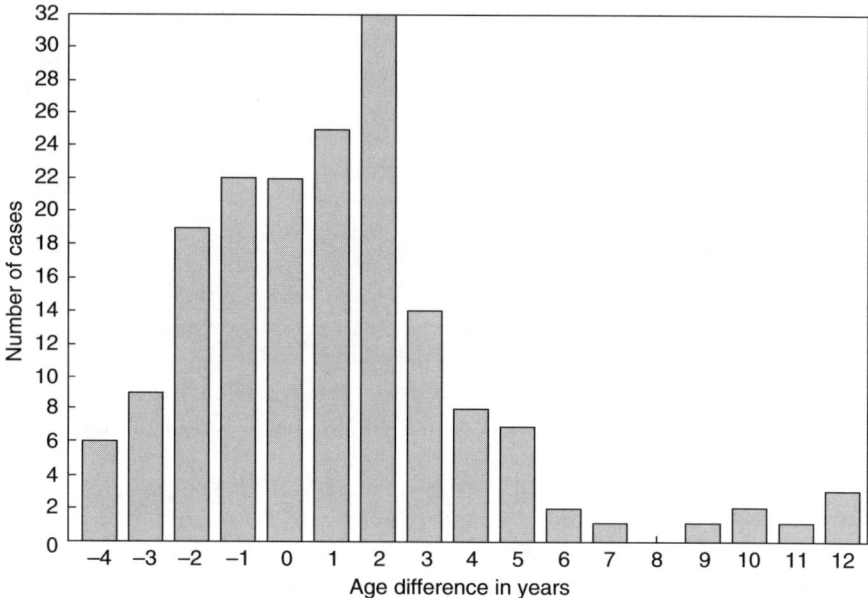

Figure 2.8. Distribution of Age Differences between Spouses, All Genealogies

been an official, was then looking for a scholar for a son-in-law. Hu's reputation from the examinations led Liu to choose him (Zhou Bida 1971, 30:10b–21b; Wang 1972, 42:8a–10a). Another case is Xu Jingheng (1072–1128), from Ruian in Zhejiang. His epitaph lists no immediate relatives who were officials, but he passed the *jinshi* examination in 1094 at age twenty-three *sui*. At twenty-five *sui* he married a girl from Yuezhou in Zhejiang whose father had been an official and who brought a dowry large enough to use for Xu's brother's expenses in studying at the Imperial University (Hu 1983, 26:1a–7b; Xu 1975, 20:8b–10a). A similar case is provided by Zhang Wei (1112–1181) from Nanjianzhou in Fujian. Again no immediate ancestors were officials, and his father died while he was still a child. Yet he passed the *jinshi* in 1138 at twenty-seven *sui*, and the next year married a girl from the same prefecture who used her dowry to help in getting Zhang's younger sister married (Zhu 1929: 90:15a–16a; 93:13b–20a).

From these accounts it is clear that delaying marriage until passing the examinations might bring not merely affines of official status but also a large dowry. Indeed, there were several complaints in Song times of the ways new *jinshi* would offer themselves as sons-in-law to the highest bidder. Dowries of land are mentioned quite frequently in Song sources, especially in women's epitaphs and in lawsuits over inheritance (Ebrey 1991). Perhaps the contrast between the elites of the Northeast and the Lower and Middle Yangtze was that between an older and more established elite and a newer and more open one in which wealth played a larger role in the choice and timing of marriages.

CHANGES OVER TIME IN ELITE STRATEGIES

The evidence from epitaphs and genealogies shows that Song men sometimes had their marriages delayed as part of a strategy aimed at advancing their careers and making better matches, and that in some areas at least families with official connections married their sons later than families without them. This finding is at odds with what Liu and Harrell found for the Qing and with what Sa and Gamble found for the twentieth century. Is the difference a function of the sources I used, or did something change? If elite practice changed, when and why? To pursue answers to these questions, I collected epitaphs for Ming couples comparable to those of my Song couples.[23] As in the Song, in the Ming virtually all of the subjects of the epitaphs are from families that produced officials. Moreover, they were selected to give a comparable geographical spread. And yet the age at marriage for both men and women in the Ming epitaphs is about a year younger than that in the Song, making it closer to estimates of age at marriage reported in other studies of the Ming and Qing. See Table 2.6.

These Ming figures from epitaphs come closer to Ming and Qing figures from biographies and genealogies than to Song figures from epitaphs. What changed from Song to Ming times? Certainly the examination system did. In Song times over half of all bureaucrats entered the civil service through means other than success in the exams, and the close relatives of officials had facilitated access to the exams in the Song in ways that they did not in later periods (Chaffee 1985:27, 95–115; Ebrey 1988). Thus, in the Song families of officials who expected to depend on privileges could marry sons young without worrying about the effect on their careers, whereas those who wished their sons to attempt the examinations could wait a few years to see if they could enhance their prospects by gaining a degree, always able to fall back on privileges if necessary. By Ming times this was no longer a reasonable strategy because privileges were greatly curtailed and examination success was too risky to wait for.

Another change that occurred from the Song to the Ming concerned dowries. The curtailment of wives' legal claims to their dowries after the Song made transmission of property through daughters less attractive (see Holmgren 1986). In Ming and Qing times it was riskier to wait for progress toward office before getting married, and perhaps the potential financial gain through dowries was not so tempting.

TABLE 2.6. Distribution of Ages at Marriage from Ming Paired Epitaphs

Age	Men		Women	
	Number	%	Number	%
10	1	1.5	0	0.0
11	0	0.0	0	0.0
12	0	0.0	0	0.0
13	2	3.0	3	4.5
14	2	3.0	7	10.6
15	4	6.1	10	15.2
16	8	12.1	14	21.2
17	7	10.6	8	12.1
18	9	13.6	9	13.6
19	13	19.7	5	7.6
20	3	4.5	4	6.1
21	2	3.0	3	4.5
22	6	9.1	3	4.5
23	3	4.5	0	0.0
24	0	0.0	0	0.0
25	3	4.5	1	1.5
26	1	1.5	0	0.0
27	2	3.0	0	0.0
28+	1	1.5	0	0.0
Total	67	100.0	67	100.0
Mean age	19.05		16.99	
Median age	18.5		16.5	
Standard dev.	4.22		2.49	

The relative decline in the significance of dowries could also explain why elite women's ages at marriage also went down after the Song. Some men's families may have delayed a marriage several years looking for an attractive dowry. Others, however, tempted by the financial gain offered by even ordinary dowries, married their sons quickly. The woman's family, no matter what their financial status, needed time to put together a suitable dowry. In the Song, local officials sometimes complained that poor people were having a hard time marrying their daughters promptly because of the difficulties of raising dowries (e.g. Cheng 1981:504). The rich, who felt compelled to raise much larger dowries, also felt similar time pressures. Yuan Cai argues that parents should begin planning for a daughter's dowry as soon as she is born so that she will not "miss the best time" (Ebrey 1984b:266). Just as the need to provide large betrothal gifts could delay marriages of men in the twentieth century, so may the need to prepare large dowries have delayed women's marriages in the Song.[24]

CONCLUSIONS

This essay has three aims. One is to provide evidence of age at marriage for a relatively early period of Chinese history to determine the extent of change over time. The evidence presented is consistent with a hypothesis of relatively modest change from the tenth to the twentieth century. The women and men described in epitaphs had median ages at marriage of eighteen and twenty, respectively, figures that are typical of twentieth-century peasants but a little old for elite groups.

My second purpose is to use the basic demographic data in these epitaphs to add to our understanding of upper-class family life in the Song period. In other essays I have examined the ideas, ideals, and conventions governing family organization and marriage in the Song (1984a, b, and c; 1991; 1993). In this paper I have been able to give a quantitative glimpse at family practice and to show the diversity of family forms that resulted from the wide variation in the length of marriage and numbers of children.

The third purpose of this essay is to place parental decisions about the ages at which to marry their sons in the context of elite life more generally. Given academic specializations, demographic historians have tended to interpret acts that have demographic consequences in terms of these consequences. Thus since early marriage of sons leads to fewer widows, more grandchildren, shorter generations, more stem and grand families, and so on, age at marriage has been interpreted in terms of preferences for these family forms. Here I have suggested that dowries and career paths were also considerations. The prospects of better dowries and more useful affinal connections for those who had made progress toward office led some families to wait before marrying their sons.

NOTES

1. All of the ages given here are in chronological years unless they are explicitly given in *sui*.

2. Liu's age at marriage for men is an estimate based on the proportion of men single at age fifteen to nineteen and twenty to twenty-four; "high" and "low" figures were determined and then averaged. The high figure was 25.02 years, the low 17.58, and the average 21.3. Women's ages were reached by subtracting 5.2 years from the men's, since wives were on the average 5.2 years younger than their husbands.

3. For translated examples of epitaphs for women, see Ebrey 1984c. The problem of "successor" wives is probably why Bettine Birge (1985) found a different

mean age at marriage for Song women than I did, even though she also used epitaphs. She gets a second peak at about twenty-six years; the women marrying at twenty-five or twenty-six were probably often second wives, and their ages bring up the average.

4. The ninety-odd books in which these epitaphs were found are not listed in the References. Many are included in the Sources Cited in Ebrey 1993. Epitaphs do not give exact age at marriage; they give instead the woman's age in *sui* when she married, without saying the month of the year the wedding occurred. For instance, an epitaph might state that a woman married at nineteen *sui* and died at seventy-one *sui* in 1102. From these data we can see that she was born in 1032 and married in 1050. If her husband died in 1099 at sixty-nine *sui*, he was born in 1031 and, therefore, married at twenty *sui*. The actual difference in age between the husband and wife could be anywhere from a day to a day less than two years but would average 1.0 years. Their actual ages on the day of the wedding would depend on the day each was born and on the day the wedding took place. Thus if the wedding took place on the first day of the sixth month, and that day also happened to be both of their birth dates, the woman would be 18.0 years old that day and the man 19.0. If the wedding took place on the first of the third month, she would be 17.75 and he 18.75; on the first of the ninth month, 18.25 and 19.25; and so on. Here, for the sake of averaging, I will assume midyear births and midyear weddings.

5. Hymes's (1986) description of the elite of Fuzhou, Jiangxi, provides a good sense of the social status of those portrayed in epitaphs.

6. That those who lived a full life span are more likely to get epitaphs does, however, mean that the ages recorded are often fairly high (sixty or over), and older people may have a greater tendency to err in remembering ages. Mistaking the woman's age by one year would affect the calculation of the man's age at marriage by a year. Given that the group represented by these genealogies was a highly literate one, and given that birth dates are recorded to the day in many genealogies, I tend to think that misreporting of age on these epitaphs is probably not a major problem.

7. To give exact figures, the set of 135 first marriages included 16 from the capital and its east, west, north, and south circuits (14 born before 1100, 2 after); 9 from elsewhere in the Northeast (Hedong and Hebei circuits) (7 born before 1100, 2 after); none from the Northwest (Yongxingjun and Qinfeng circuits); 48 from the Lower Yangtze (Liangzhe, Huainan, and Jiangnan East) (19 born before 1100, 29 after); 20 from the Middle Yangtze (Jiangnan West and Jinghu) (10 born before 1100, 10 after); 23 from Fujian (7 born before 1100, 16 after); 6 from the Sichuan area (all born before 1100); none from Guangnan; and 13 from the imperial family (11 born before 1100, 2 after). The places and birth dates used here are the husbands'.

8. Some sources garble this story, making the great-grandson ten *sui*. See Liu 1307: *i*, 4:8a.

9. Liu (1985:23) gives 18% for one clan and 10% for the other, but these figures need to be reduced by about 15 to 20% to be comparable to the figures here, since Liu's figures include wives who are the same age in *sui* but are actually older by days or months.

10. Chen Ta (1946) found in Yunnan in the early 1940s a life expectancy at twenty of 39.3 for women and 35.6 for men. James Lee (chap. 7) reports a life expectancy of about 34 for women eighteen to twenty and 34.5 for men twenty to twenty-five in Liaoning in 1796–1840. The physical circumstances of the Song elite (availability of food, health care, and so on) may well have been a little better than either of these groups, so the Song elite could plausibly have lived a year or two longer on the average.

11. Barclay (1954:217) found that from 2 to 3% of women in their twenties and from 6 to 13% of women in their thirties were widows, with the percentage decreasing from 1905 to 1935. Buck (1937:378–79) found 2 to 3% of women in their twenties widowed and about 6% in their thirties.

12. Epitaphs for first marriages are not a good source for widows who remarried. If a widow who remarried had an epitaph at all, it would match her with her second husband not her first. Moreover, there was enough of a stigma attached to remarriage to suppose that remarriage may have been underreported. That eleven epitaphs for "successor" wives show their ages at marriage to be six to seven years older than those of wives in first marriages suggests that a significant number may have been young widows, though this is rarely stated explicitly.

13. Of the 105 cases where the marriage extended through the full reproductive span, there are 2 that must include quite a few children of concubines. One gives the names and titles of thirty-five children, the other twenty-five children. If these 2 cases are excluded from the calculation, the couples married throughout the reproductive span had an average of 5.77 children.

14. These epitaphs show altogether 449 sons and 377 daughters. This is an average of 2.96 sons and 2.45 daughters per couple. The resulting sex ratio of 119 can easily be accounted for by the greater interest families took in sons than in daughters. Daughters who did not live to marry are very rarely mentioned. Some of the many sons listed as "died young" may not have reached the age to marry. Moreover, the number of sons may include some who were brought in by adoption but not labelled as such, but the number of daughters probably does not.

15. These only sons may include some adopted sons. The epitaphs only explicitly state that three couples remedied their lack of sons by adoption. Probably some other only sons were adopted sons but were not labelled as such.

16. For the definitions of the regions discussed in the text, see note 7.

17. My contention that the imperial family followed a distinct pattern is not based solely on the six cases of men from the imperial family cited here. I am also relying on the M.A. essay by Bettine Birge (1985), who found that fifty-nine women who married into the imperial family did so at an average of 17.0 *sui*, significantly younger than other women.

18. I have only sixty-five couples whose age at marriage is known, and once these are divided by region and the imperial family separated out, there are not very many cases for each region. As Telford shows (chap. 3) families within one region can vary considerably in such matters as age at marriage. But it is not implausible that the elites of different regions might have married their sons at different ages because families from these different regions seldom intermarried. From 73% to 85% of the marriages of men in the four main regions were to women in these regions. This

is true even in the Northeast where people largely chose spouses from a different prefecture.

In looking for patterns in age at marriage, I also found a difference over time; men married significantly younger in the eleventh century than in the twelfth, but this difference turns out to be largely a product of the shift in the geographical source of the evidence. The cases for the imperial family, Sichuan, and the Northeast, where marriage was earliest, were predominantly eleventh century. Only the Lower and Middle Yangtze were about equally split between early and late Song (with birth date before 1100 as the dividing line). In the two Yangtze regions, there was a later age of marriage in the first half of the Song than the second (24.0 to 21.0), the opposite of the overall figures.

19. The genealogies were chosen by going through over a hundred genealogies that were listed as having a first ancestor in the Song or earlier in the index to genealogies compiled by Telford, Thatcher, and Yang (1983). Only genealogies that had at least ten couples from Song times and that showed signs of being accurately compiled were selected. Evidence for accurate compilation included such matters as giving birth dates to the day, not including data for everyone (suggesting that the editors were willing to leave out data when they had no evidence), and having prefaces that showed that earlier versions of the genealogy had been compiled in the Song. The genealogies did not need to have all three signs of accuracy; generally two were enough.

20. Another possibility that must be considered is recording biases. That is, did the Ming and Qing editors of genealogies fudge the data to make them look better? I see no reason why they would have made women a little older, since by Qing times the type of families in this region that produced genealogies do not seem to have had an exceptionally high proportion of wives older (Liu 1985:23). If anything, one would expect the editors to have fudged the data the other way. Would Song writers of epitaphs have understated women's ages, making them appear younger than their husbands more often than actually was the case? Since epitaphs for husbands and wives were written separately, usually years apart, the authors were unlikely to have even known whether the age given indicated that the wife was older or younger than her husband. And it is very unlikely that families, in giving data to the authors of epitaphs, would have understated a woman's age, since achieving an advanced age brought honor. Are the genealogies so full of random errors that the tabulations are of little value? Random errors might be the explanation if a single genealogy were used. For five of the nine genealogies to show over 30% of the wives older and one-quarter or more of the men married very young suggests that they reflect a common social reality.

21. On intervals between births and average age at first child and average age at birth of all children, see Harrell and Pullum (chap. 6) and Lavely 1984:377.

22. The four lineages in Jiangsu, all of whom had officials, had the highest average age difference between husbands and wives, 2.10 years. These lineages also had the lowest average percentage of men with sons by the time they were 19.0 years and the lowest proportion who were younger than their wives.

23. Collecting the appropriate Ming epitaphs proved to be considerably harder than collecting the Song epitaphs, in part because the standard bibliographical

dictionary is not as complete, and in part because age at marriage is given on a much smaller percentage of women's epitaphs (20% rather than 40%). Most of the epitaphs used here are joint epitaphs for couples found by reading through Ming collected works, especially ones in the *Siku quanshu zhenben* series. I would like to thank Bau Hwa Sheieh for her help in locating these epitaphs.

24. On the relationship of age at marriage and the size of dowries in Renaissance Florence, see the study by Kirshner and Molho (1978:430–33).

THREE

Fertility and Population Growth in the Lineages of Tongcheng County, 1520–1661

Ted A. Telford

During the Ming and throughout the Qing, the Jiangnan area underwent rapid population growth, growth that even outpaced China's overall rates of natural increase.[1] That the growth of lineage groups in the Lower Yangzi macroregion paralleled overall population trends in the region has already begun to be documented (Liu 1985; Harrell 1985), and this paper extends similar research to another county in the region. At the same time that lineages in the Lower Yangzi regional core (parts of Jiangsu and Zhejiang Provinces) were experiencing high rates of natural increase and consequent growth in their numbers, peripheral counties like Tongcheng in Anhui Province may have grown at even more rapid rates. Peripheral counties in the Lower Yangzi region, if they were anything like Tongcheng, would have had more undeveloped agricultural land, into which growing populations could expand, until mid- or even late Qing times (Beattie 1979:34, 48). Thus, growth rates in such peripheries would have been less subject to the usual agrarian constraints on reproduction. Although the birth rates of lineage populations in both the core and periphery of the Lower Yangzi region may have varied only slightly, it is still possible that rates of natural increase differed considerably because natural increase is the excess of births over deaths in any population.[2] Because mortality is a key component of population growth, rates can vary dramatically between locales, time periods, social classes, or individual families, even where birth rates are constant. Because the findings reported here are basically a continuation of earlier research on marital fertility levels in the lineages of Tongcheng County during the late Ming–early Qing period, the details on the lineage sources, their biases, the rationale for their inclusion in this study, and the methods used to generate standard demographic measures will not be recounted here (see Telford 1992a, 1985). But the first order of business will be the documentation of possible differentials in fertility between the forty-one lineage groups in thirty-nine genealogies included in this data set, which has not previously been done. This examination of fertility levels will then be extended through a study of intergenerational growth in these lineages, and the growth in these lineages will be used to generalize about population growth in the area.

Accurate estimates of fertility or any other demographic variable based on records created by corporate lineage groups are unavoidably complicated primarily because of the absence of complete information on female children. All fertility indexes as well as measures of population growth must necessarily be derived on the basis of one-sex, that is, male-only, indicators. Liu Ts'ui-jung (1985) and James Lee and Robert Eng (1984) have generated age-specific marital fertility rates from male births, and Stevan Harrell (1985) has successfully constructed male-only indicators of lineage population growth. The techniques applied here are similar to these approaches with regard to fertility levels but have an added adjustment for unrecorded infant mortality that is never included in these sources and a further adjustment for incomplete recording of males who died as children or migrated from the area. The procedures used to make these adjustments to recorded son-only fertility levels involve first the application of the known sex ratio at birth and second, the application of a uniform set of assumptions regarding infant mortality levels and missing births due to bad records. Basically, these adjustments assume a "moderate" infant mortality rate (IMR) of 250 deaths within the first year per 1,000 live births, a 10% rate of underrecording of male children, and the known sex ratio at birth of 105 males per 100 females (Telford 1992a; 1985). Second, an index of the intergenerational reproduction of males (analogous to Harrell's index of population growth) is also calculated (Harrell 1985). Finally, this measure of population growth is analyzed with a standard multiple regression approach to examine various factors thought to explain the rates of population increase.

FERTILITY IN THE TONGCHENG LINEAGES

One standard indicator used to index the fertility of married women is the age-specific marital fertility rate (ASMFR), which is a measure of the number of children a woman in a particular age category will have if she survives to that age in a married state; that is, if the death of either spouse, separation, or divorce does not intervene. ASMFR therefore takes into account both the marital status and the age structure of any given population and in doing so creates a truly comparative measure of the fertility experience of very different populations. Two additional fertility indexes can be calculated based on any set of ASMFRs: M, the abbreviation for an accepted index of the level of natural fertility, and the total marital fertility rate (TMFR). Natural fertility is defined as childbearing in the absence of deliberate family limitation (Henry 1961) and was typical of nearly every premodern agrarian society. M measures the level of natural fertility in terms of the ratio of observed fertility at age twenty to twenty-four to a model schedule of natural fertility at age twenty to twenty-four (Coale and Trussell 1974, 1975, 1978). This model schedule of natural fertility, abbreviated by n(a), does not refer to any real population but was derived for use as a comparative device by taking the mathematical average of twelve well-documented natural fertility populations. TMFR is the sum of age-specific fertility rates for married women across the childbearing years of fifteen to forty-nine (Shryock, Siegel, and Stockwell 1976). Simply, TMFR is a measure of the total number of children each woman will have if she survives to age forty-nine in a married state and is based on the fertility actually observed for those women who do live to age forty-nine.[3]

Table 3.1 reports ASMFR, TMFR, and M by lineage group and for the population as a whole for the entire time period of study. Lineages with fewer than 150 cases were aggregated into a lineage category called small, since very small numbers of cases will always result in extreme variations. In order to pinpoint lineages whose age patterns of fertility deviate significantly from each other or from the model schedule, fertility curves (graphic displays of ASMFR for ages twenty to forty-nine) by lineage are plotted in Figures 3.1–3.4 together with the curve for the entire aggregated population (total) and n(a), the model natural fertility curve.

Lineages have been grouped rather arbitrarily for the figures because of the large number to be drawn on a single graph. Elite lineages are reported in Figure 3.1. These are lineage groups in which more than 10% of the wives have gentry husbands (see Table 3.5 for proportions of wives with gentry husbands). The remaining lineages are grouped on the basis of the number of cases involved—a case being a single conjugal marriage. Small lineages (Figure 3.2) are those with 150–299 cases; medium lineages (Figure 3.3) are those with 300–499 cases; and large lineages are defined as those with 500 or more cases (Figure 3.4).

With a few important exceptions, the fertility curves fluctuate around the aggregated curve. The most extreme variations in both level and age pattern appear in the small lineages (Figure 3.2), most likely as a result of the relatively small number of cases from which to calculate ASMFR. Bizarre curves for some medium to large lineages, on the other hand, are almost certainly due to poor records either with abnormally large numbers of missing sons or with especially fragmentary vital dates that have been estimated using mean values.[4] Genealogies with poor records of vital dates are indicated by an asterisk in the tables and figures. The Gan (Figure 3.3) and Cheng1 (Figure 3.4) genealogies had some of the poorest data of any of the

TABLE 3.1. Fertility Measures by Lineage Group, Tongcheng Lineages, 1520–1661

Lineage Group	(N)	TMFR	M
Small	(898)	8.35	.74
Hu*	(348)	8.13	.66
Ma*	(156)	7.57	.69
Ye	(241)	7.24	.71
Gan*	(417)	6.78	.43
Li	(279)	7.92	.88
Pan	(457)	8.49	.82
Rao	(349)	9.56	.84
Sun	(269)	7.85	.78
Wu	(197)	7.15	1.07
Yao*	(516)	7.78	.61
Yu	(333)	7.55	.75
Zou*	(605)	8.15	.61
Zuo	(594)	8.82	.71
Chen2*	(358)	8.03	.68
Cheng1	(605)	7.87	.89
Gao*	(1085)	8.13	.65
Huang	(182)	5.77	.82
Jiang2	(290)	7.78	.89
Miao	(358)	7.01	.72
Tang1*	(158)	7.45	.64
Tang2	(171)	7.78	.99
Tang*	(844)	8.44	.64
Wang1	(227)	6.77	.75
Wang2	(344)	8.67	.87
Zhang1*	(317)	7.03	.69
Zhang2	(305)	7.62	.86
Zheng	(160)	8.55	.81
Zhong	(196)	9.11	.83
Zhou2	(545)	9.19	.87
Total	(11804)		
All lineages		8.21	.75
n(a)		11.05	1.00

*Genealogies having much poorer than average recording of vital data for individuals in the late Ming portions of the documents.

documents included in this data set, especially for the late Ming portion of the records. In spite of their poor records, these lineages were included in an effort to get more complete geographic coverage of the county. Consequently, the resulting fertility curves are very aberrant. Some of the lineages also have odd curves with an unusual dip at age 30–34, a pattern

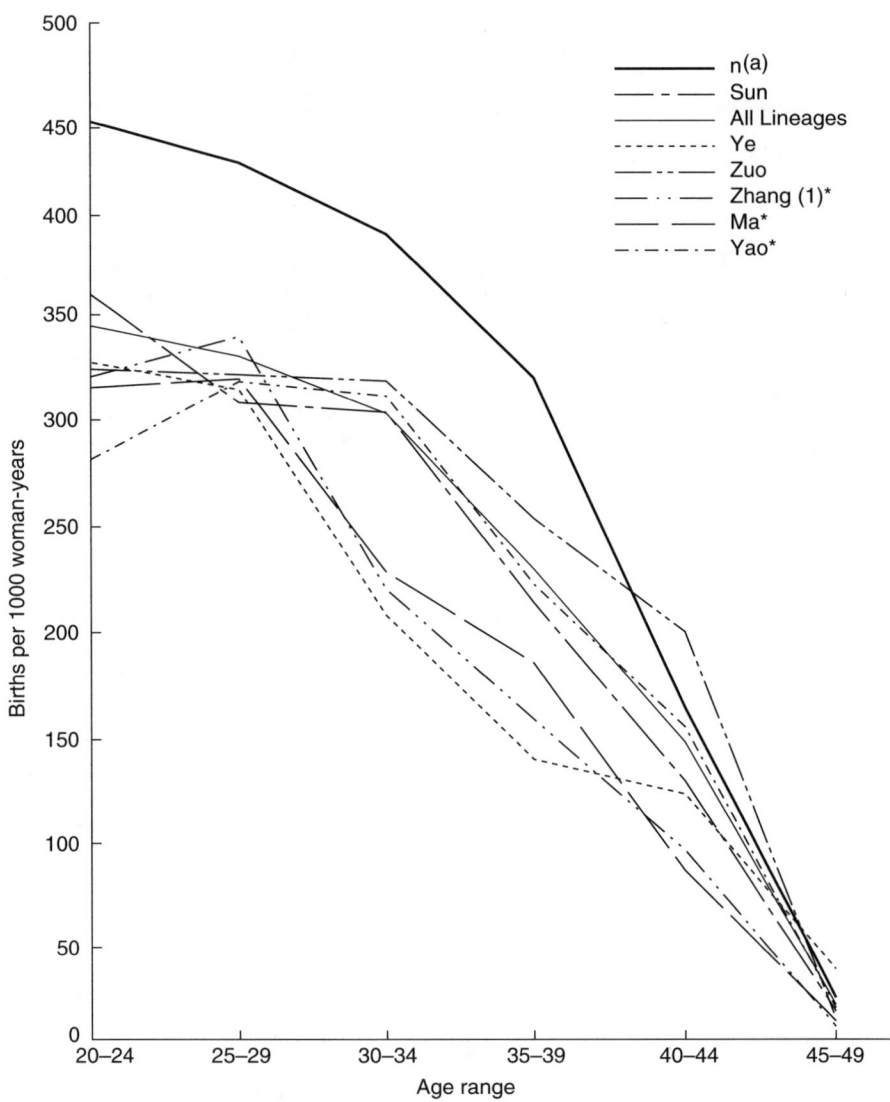

Figure 3.1. Fertility Curves for Elite Lineages, Tongcheng County, 1520–1661
*Genealogies having poorer than average recording of vital data for individuals in the late Ming portions of the documents.

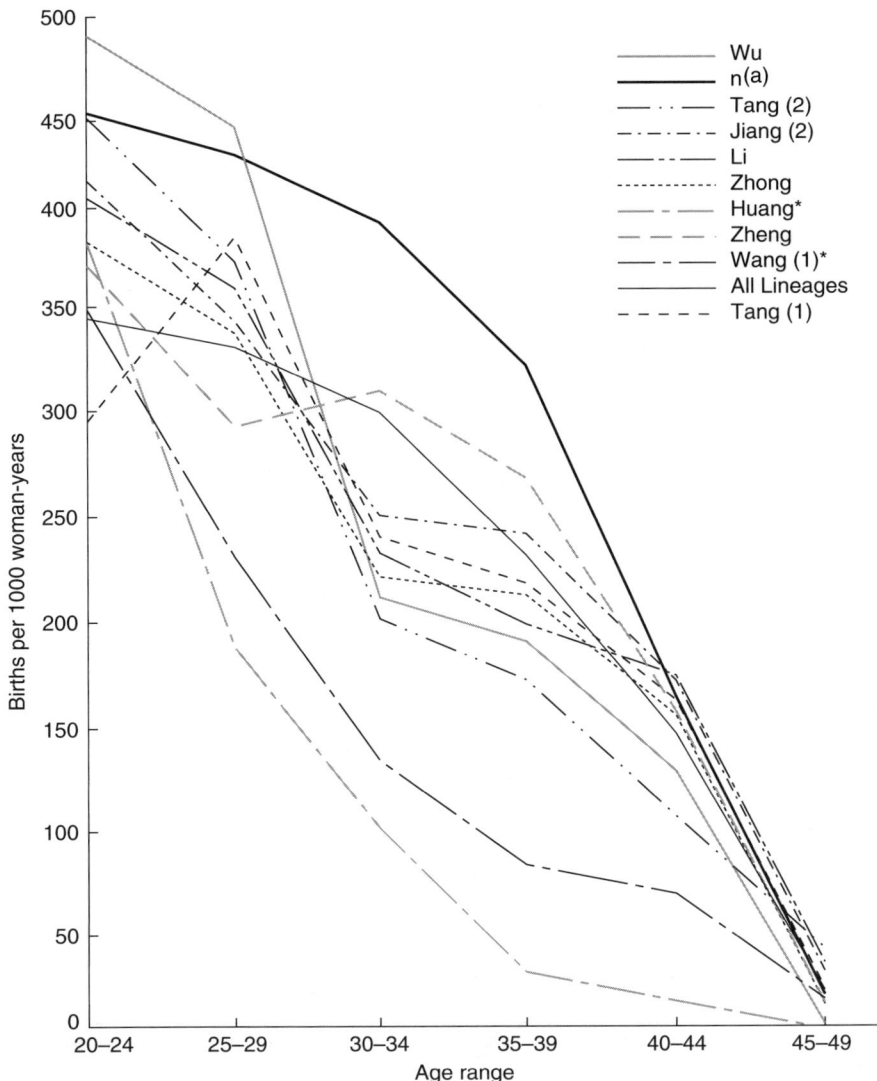

Figure 3.2. Fertility Curves for Small Lineages (150–299 Cases), Tongcheng County, 1520–1661

*Genealogies having poorer than average recording of vital data for individuals in the late Ming portions of the documents.

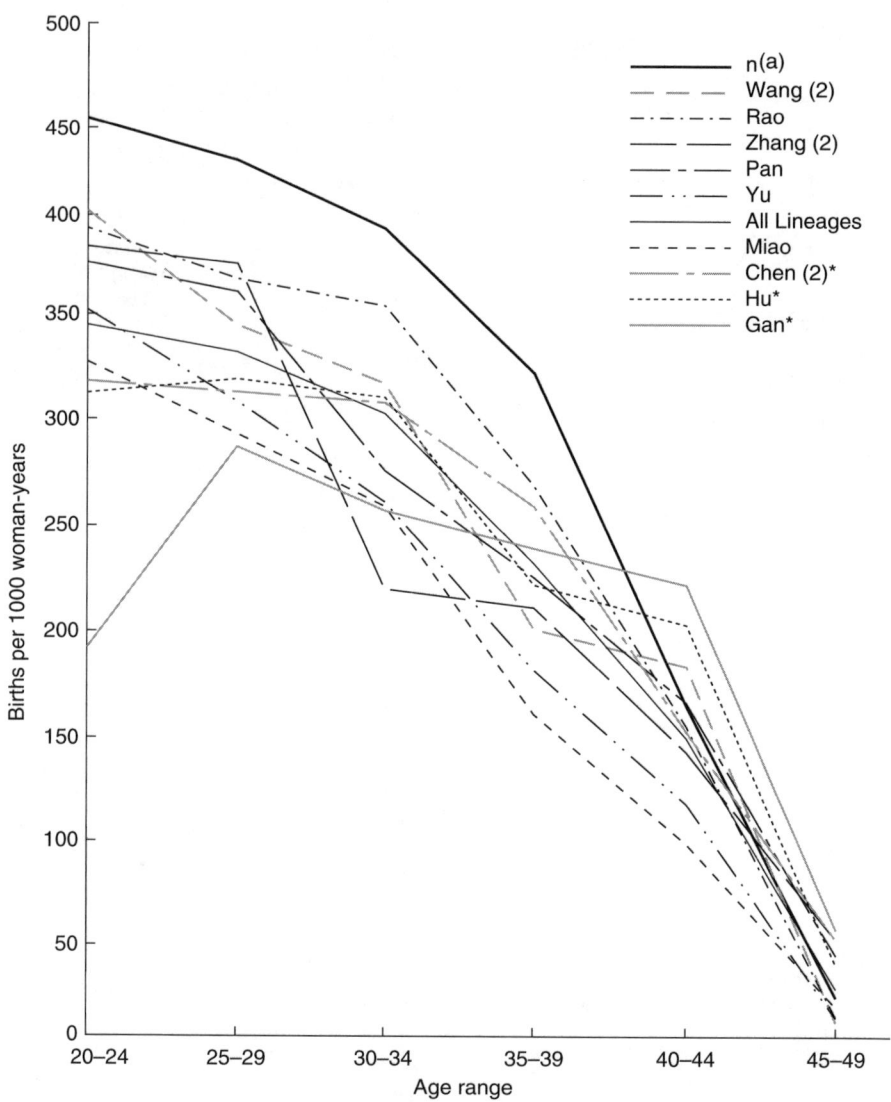

Figure 3.3. Fertility Curves for Medium Lineages (300–499 Cases), Tongcheng County, 1520–1661

*Genealogies having poorer than average recording of vital data for individuals in the late Ming portions of the documents.

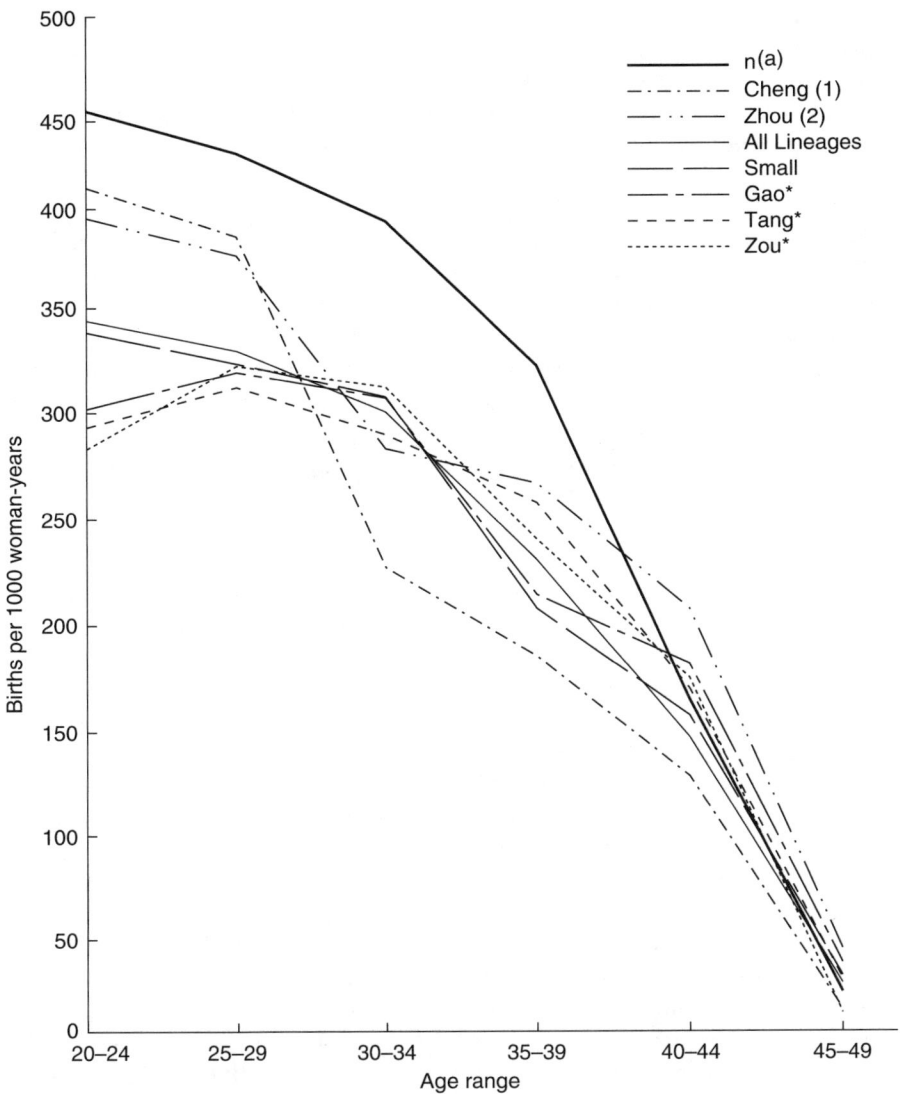

Figure 3.4. Fertility Curves for Large Lineages (500+ Cases), Tongcheng County, 1520–1661

*Genealogies having poorer than average recording of vital data for individuals in the late Ming portions of the documents.

that the elite lineages tend not to display. This dip is most likely due to disturbances caused by a combination of incomplete records and significant numbers of remarrying widows among non-elite families. These effects will always be more pronounced in lineages having very small numbers of cases and large proportions of in-marrying widows, many of whom will be involved in such remarriages around age 30–34. In addition, the convex shape of the curves for the Huang and Wang1 lineages in Figure 3.2, a shape that is usually taken as an indication of deliberately controlled fertility, is also explainable in terms of very poor or otherwise incomplete records resupplied through all-too-crude estimation techniques (Telford 1990b). One advantage in studying fertility levels by lineage group is that it is possible to evaluate the effects of incomplete records on the results. From this analysis, it appears that the 10% adjustment factor used here for several of the lineage groups in this data set is completely inadequate and that far more than 10% of their surviving sons who died unmarried or migrated from the area went unrecorded.

If the widely divergent age patterns of fertility of the extreme cases can be dismissed as artifacts of the poor records created by those lineages, then it is safe to say that minimum fertility levels among the lineage groups of Tongcheng were moderate to high (TMFR for the entire data set was 8.21 children). Furthermore, the overall pattern is one of natural fertility at about 75% of the model schedule (M = .75). Should the genealogies with the poorest records be eliminated from the overall calculations, in almost every case we would be dropping the lineages with the lowest recorded fertility levels (see Table 3.1), and TMFR could easily run as high as 9.50 children and M as high as 85% of model fertility. Such fertility rates are among the highest documented anywhere for any historical Chinese population and adjust upward my previous estimates of marital fertility levels in these populations to support even more strongly Wolf's argument regarding prerevolutionary Chinese fertility (Wolf 1985b; Hanley and Wolf 1985). Examining fertility by lineage has permitted a more refined estimate of minimum fertility levels in these populations by taking into account the relative quality and completeness of the different lineage sources, which I did not previously do when social classes and residential groupings were studied (Telford 1985). However, in lineages with relatively complete records, there is not a great deal of variation in their overall moderate to high levels of marital fertility. If we are to explain differential reproduction and varying population growth rates among these lineage groups, we will have to look at something other than the age-specific fertility of married couples. Mortality is the other side of the population growth equation, and it will have to be taken into account in any discussion of China's historical rates of natural increase (Telford 1990a). In addition, marriage variables, representing exposure to intercourse, may also help to explain differences in reproduction rates.

ONE-SEX MODELS OF POPULATION GROWTH

A number of difficulties with the nature of the Chinese lineage data can be rather easily circumvented by focusing on relative population growth and intergenerational reproduction of males, as Harrell (1985) has done, rather than on fertility or mortality as conventionally defined. Given a demographic regime characterized by high rates of female infanticide (Dickeman 1975), and by female death rates that in most age categories up to age thirty to thirty-five exceed those of males (Telford 1990a), unbalanced sex ratios in the marriageable age groups will result. In addition, upper-class polygyny will further exacerbate the shortage of females in the marriageable ages. Both patrilineages and families not organized into lineage groups would only have been able to grow when male members brought in females from other families and lineages to produce offspring for them. Surviving female children were married out or occasionally sold in a marriage system that was fundamentally patrilocal and strictly surname exogamous. Women born into the lineage reproduced for the larger community only in the case of illegitimate births or uxorilocal marriages (those in which the husband joined the wife's family); neither of these cases, it is thought, ever represented anything but the most insignificant contribution to population growth in most Chinese populations.

The actual reproduction of males is therefore of more interest than age-specific fertility levels, since ASMFR indicates only the fertility that women *would* have at each age *if* they survived to that age. It is clear that not all couples had both spouses survive until the wife reached menopause. Thus, the focus of research on rates of growth must be the actual reproductive success of married couples. It will thus be differing marriage and mortality factors that will result in high or low rates of natural increase. It is therefore appropriate to treat the total reproduction of males as central to an analysis of relative population growth among these Chinese lineage populations. ASMFR and TMFR have already been calculated for lineage groups, and some variation is observed; but in these sources the best available measure for actual completed marital fertility, equivalent to the conventional children ever born (CEB) index, is the total number of surviving sons ever born per *wife*. However, the best measure of intergenerational population growth is the number of total surviving sons ever born to each *husband*, in effect a paternal rate summing all sons ever born to the wives and concubines of each married male. Such a measure is easy to generate from the reconstituted lineage records.

This latter measure of intergenerational population growth is a measure of the gross reproduction of males and is analogous to the standard gross reproduction rate (GRR) usually calculated for females and the reproduction of their daughters (Shryock, Siegel, and Stockwell 1976). This gross rate is then adjusted by subtracting 1.00 to account for replacement of fathers; further subtractions account for sons who never marry, sons who leave the lineage through out-migration and adoption, sons who join Buddhist religious orders, and sons who otherwise do not contribute to intergenerational reproduction. The paternal net intergenerational growth rate that results is an index of net growth analogous to the net reproduction rate (NRR) normally calculated for females (Shryock, Siegel, and Stockwell 1976). Use of this measure of net intergenerational reproduction of males will allow the study of the growth rates of lineages, lineage segments, birth cohorts, status groups, and residential groupings.

Conversion of these intergenerational measures to estimates of annual rates of population growth is also possible. Assuming that the microlevel processes that account for the growth of conjugal families are the same processes that account for the macrolevel growth rates of the lineage groups and communities to which they belong, it is reasonable to take the paternal net intergenerational growth rate and divide it by the mean length of generation to arrive at approximations of average annual rates of population growth based on the reproduction of males in the population. Generation length is defined here as the mean age of fathers at the birth of their surviving male children and is equivalent to the standard calculation of generation length based on the average age of mothers at the birth of their female children (Shryock, Siegel, and Stockwell 1976:31). For this particular data set, the mean age of fathers at the birth of their sons is just over thirty-two years. The formula used to calculate annual growth rate is as follows:

$$r = \frac{\ln(1 + NRR)}{T},$$

where r is the annual rate of growth; NRR is the (male) net reproduction rate; and T is time—in this case, the mean length of a (male) generation; and ln is the natural logarithm. One had to be added to each NRR to account for replacement of fathers and so that negative logarithms would not result from the use of fractions in the calculations. This formula has been used to create estimates of average annual growth rates reported in the following tables.

LINEAGE GROWTH AND POPULATION GROWTH

The usefulness of studying intergenerational growth for males may be evident for lineage groups, but the same approach should also be appropriate for indexing the natural increase of whole communities, as already indicated. Marriage markets already tight because of higher female mortality rates would have been further aggravated by the absorption of disproportionate numbers of marriageable women by upper-class males, who tended to have more than one wife or concubine. The males of the larger community, whether organized into lineage groups or not, would have been subject to intense competition in the same marriage markets for a generally short supply of marriageable women. Under such conditions, virtually all women will marry and, because of traditional Confucian norms, will do so at relatively early ages. Many women will be child brides, and some will marry more than once as they are widowed (Telford 1992a, 1992b). Most of these processes typical of the general population should also be reflected in the demographic characteristics of its lineage groups.

Contrary to culturally determined expectations, some men who survive to a marriageable age will be unable to marry at all, or they will be forced to postpone marriage and take widows or girls much younger than themselves as wives (Telford 1992a, 1992b). Thus, various social groups will differ in their ability to produce sons, to see that sons survive long enough to marry, to replace wives who die, and to minimize out-migration. In terms of important social-demographic categories, social class—as indicated by examination degree and bureaucratic-office-holding status—is believed to be one of the key variables expected to affect various demographic processes resulting in variations in net growth rates. To the extent that different status groups concentrate in towns or villages, social class may also be one factor in the spatial distribution of growth. Spatial-ecological factors such as high population density and land productivity may affect growth rates, but these are not hypothesized to be major factors in Tongcheng during the time period of this study. The only spatial factor assumed to be important during this time period is residence in a geographic area that may have been seriously affected by the period of crisis in Tongcheng during the Ming-Qing wars. Several other factors are thought to affect growth rates as well, and concentrations of families affected by these factors in specific lineages might also account for some of the observed differences.

MULTIPLE REGRESSION ANALYSIS

The net growth index is an interval-level ratio measure and is the main dependent variable of interest in this analysis. Since all explanatory/independent variables are measured at the ordinal or interval level, or as recoded dummy variables, standard multiple regression analysis is an appropriate statistical method for estimating the relative strength of the effects of such variables (Hull et al. 1975:320–67). Lineage group is the only explanatory factor measured at the nominal level, and therefore it could not be included in the regression analysis. The number of categories for this variable (forty-one) was far too large to create a set of dummy variables, and there was no theoretically sound way of grouping lineages into meaningful ordinal- or interval-level categories. Certainly there are significant differences in rates of growth between lineage groups, but it is difficult to see how lineage as a variable could be independent of the effect of the number of high-status families, the number who married early and often, or lineage members who died at higher or lower rates, etc. In fact, the inclusion of lineage group as a variable, which is possible when using other statistical methods (Telford 1992a), is not significant at all in explaining anything apart from the effect of incomplete records, which does vary by lineage group independently of other factors. In other words, the inability to include lineage group as an explanatory variable in the regression analysis causes no serious harm to this study of population growth rates.

Given that paternal net intergenerational reproduction of males can be used to measure the growth rates of these lineage populations, the focus of the balance of this paper will be the distributional and correlational characteristics of this basic measure of population growth. First, the descriptive aspects of the measure of net growth and the social-demographic factors assumed to affect its levels will be examined. Finally, a multiple regression analysis of the net growth index will follow.

EXPLANATORY VARIABLES AND DESCRIPTIVE STATISTICS

The variables thought to have had some effect on population growth rates are as follows: husband's social status, time period (birth cohort), total number of wives, wife's status, wife order number, degree of formal lineage organization, total surviving sons per wife, age difference of spouses, residence (standard market areas affected by crisis conditions), lineage group, major lineage segment, husband's birth order, wife's age at birth of first son, wife's age at birth of last son, proportion of sons unmarried, and proportion of sons out-migrated. The fundamental question asked in this analysis is which variables have the greatest impact on population growth rates when all the others are statistically controlled for?

Husband's Social Status (HSTAT)

Three status categories are used for analytic purposes here. These three categories are derived by grouping husbands according to the wealth, education, examination degree, and bureaucratic-office-holding information detailed in Appendix 3.A. The top level, educationally qualified elites of traditional Chinese society, is referred to as "gentry." However, the vast majority of cases in this data set are "nongentry," or "peasantry," and even though occupational data are very sketchy, this category must represent a large population of peasant farmers, tenants, small traders, and craftsmen. An intermediate category referred to as "near gentry" includes well-to-do landowners or merchants, educated men not qualified to hold office by virtue of success in the examinations, and sons of men who were degree- or officeholders. This intermediate category constituted a group of privileged, local elites that should be quite distinguishable from the bulk of the nongentry population. All three categories are found in representative proportions in these lineage populations.[5]

As defined here, the husband's social status variable is essentially a measure of household or family wealth and status. It is concentrations of high-status families in specific lineages, segments, or locales that make any given lineage or segment "wealthy" or "poor." Access to income from any extensive lineage-owned estates should also be reflected in this measure of social status just as wealth and status derived from other sources are reflected. Because high-status groups were more likely to have had adequate nutrition, some insulation from the demographic crises of the times (protection behind city walls, temporary migration to safer areas, etc.), better access to efficacious medical treatment, and the essential economic resources to get their sons married off, there should be large zero-order correlations (bivariate correlations) between these factors (see Appendix 3.B), as well as a strong positive correlation between high status and rapid rates of growth.

Table 3.2 represents the distributional characteristics of variables of interest including the net growth rate by husband's social status. Note that the magnitude of differences in gross reproduction per husband are considerable between gentry and nongentry categories, perhaps because of the tendency of the gentry to have multiple wives. But, as expected, the numbers of sons born to gentry and nongentry wives are virtually identical. In other words, fertility levels as measured by the gross number of sons ever born per wife were essentially the same for high- and low-status households. P-values (probability or statistical significance levels) also indicate there are no important differences in gross reproduction per wife between status groups.

However, group differences in net growth rates between status categories are very striking, with the gentry growing at a rate over five times greater than the peasantry. The rich indeed do "get children" in these Chinese lineage populations (Harrell 1985), but not because their wives have higher fertility. Based solely on mean numbers of surviving sons ever born per wife, it appears that total marital fertility did not vary much between status categories and may even have been slightly higher among peasants if we can assume that more children go unrecorded for the uneducated than for the upper classes (Telford 1992a). This leaves mortality and marriage

TABLE 3.2. Family Characteristics by Husband's Social Status, Tongcheng Lineages, 1520–1661

Husband's Social Status	Gross Reproduction[a]		% Somless (N)	% Sons Unmarried	% Sons Out-Migrants	Net Growth Rate/Husband	Average Annual Growth Rate
	per Wife (N)	per Husband (N)					
Nongentry	1.72 (8082)	1.82 (7635)	17.72 (1353)	25.90	2.08	.21	.59
Near gentry	1.67 (3188)	2.09 (2539)	16.10 (409)	14.88	1.52	.65	1.56
Gentry	1.78 (534)	2.80 (338)	11.24 (38)	7.81	1.77	1.47	2.82
Mean	1.71 (11804)	1.92 (10512)	17.12 (1800)	22.10	1.91	.36	.96
SD	1.51	1.55	—	37.10	1.22	1.44	—
P-value	.1295	.0000	—	.0000	.0921	.0000	—

[a]Gross intergenerational reproduction of males per husband and wife.

differentials between status categories as the most likely factors to account for most of the differential growth.

Unlike infant mortality rates in historical European populations, infant mortality rates in these Chinese populations varied dramatically by social status (Telford 1990a). In addition, higher mortality levels for children and potential parents were at least as important in keeping growth rates down among the peasantry.[6] It is not hard to imagine the effects of poor nutrition or the concentration of "high-risk" occupations among low-status families accounting for higher death rates and the consequent low rates of growth. The nature of peasant agriculture, which involved long hours of exposure to parasite- and malaria-infested paddy fields, could easily have made for differences in mortality between the peasantry and the leisured upper classes, even while their fertility varied little or not at all. The vast majority of the population—the nongentry—grew at considerably less than 1%, precisely .59%, annually. The near gentry, on the other hand, grew two and a half times faster at 1.56% annually. The gentry, however, grew at an amazing average rate of 2.82% per year, which is as high as some of the fastest growing contemporary third-world populations. The entire population grew at an annual rate just under 1% (.96%), a rate within the range expected for the Lower Yangzi region during this period.

Total Number of Wives (NWIVES)

If total marital fertility and reproduction did not vary significantly per married woman, the ability of high-status husbands to replace wives who died or to take additional polygynous wives and concubines should be an important factor in the production of sons and thus should help to explain high rates of intergenerational growth. Positive correlations are therefore expected between high status and additional wives or concubines and between having more than one wife and net intergenerational reproduction per husband.

Even though a strong positive correlation between high status and large numbers of wives can be seen as an important factor affecting growth rates, total number of wives may also operate independently of social status, as even relatively poor heads of households may have been able to take additional wives (Lee and Campbell forthcoming). Proportions of each status group having more than one wife vary considerably, with 49.9% of all gentry husbands having more than one wife or concubine. In contrast, 19.7% of near gentry and only 4.6% of nongentry status husbands had, on average, more than a single wife. As already noted, differences in gross reproduction of sons per wife are not statistically significant[7] between status groups, but the differences are significant for husbands (Table 3.2). Since the growth indexes for husbands ascribe sons from all wives to the husband, this difference can only be due to the effects of some men taking more than a single wife or concubine who produced additional male offspring.

Wife's Status Relative to Other Wives (WSTAT) and Wife's Marriage Order (WNUM)

Men who never marry, of course, do not contribute any reproductive capacity to their lineage groups, and since this is a study of reproductivity, only married couples are included. At the same time, the vast majority of married men in this data set had only a single wife. Some took an additional wife upon the death of the first, and a few, who had the means to do so, took polygynous wives and concubines. Polygynous marriages are defined as those in which more than a single wife or concubine is alive at the same time. Thus, marriages involving the remarriage of a widower are still considered to be monogamous. Secondary polygynous wives and concubines were inferior in prestige and status to first wives; and unless they were very much younger than their husbands, they were likely to be remarried widows (Lang 1946). Remarrying widows are rarely indicated in any of the genealogies but were, of course, coming from previous marriages to men in other lineages, where they may well have left several children. Low growth rates for second and higher-order marriages may also involve second marriages as responses to the infertility of first wives (Telford 1985). Because of the manner in which WSTAT data were coded for statistical manipulation, i.e., lower numerical values represent higher marital status (1 = only wife, 2 = first wife of several, 3 = subsequent wife, first wife not living, and 4 = polygynous wife or concubine with the first wife living, etc.), the effects of wife's status relative to other wives and concubines should be reflected in negative correlations between wife's status and net growth rates.[8]

Studies of polygynous marriages have shown that fertility is generally lower for women involved in such unions (Ukaegbu 1977; Smith and Kunz 1976). In a further refinement of the original argument, Bean and Mineau (1986) state that while polygynous marriages tend to have lower fertility than once-married, monogamous couples, one additional factor crucial to the high fertility displayed by some women in polygynous situations is the presence or absence of a rigid status system among the wives. If status within the household and among wives is determined solely by childbearing, women will continue to display high fertility even after polygynous wives are added to the household. If, on the other hand, the status of first wives is fixed and always higher than subsequent wives regardless of the number of children born, high-status wives will tend to cease childbearing and will always have comparatively low fertility.

The status of first wives in prerevolutionary Chinese households was relatively fixed and always higher than that of subsequent wives, regardless of whether they had sons or not. The wife-status variable included in these analyses is intended to measure this factor. Since each wife's status is fixed in these lineage populations, there should be a negative correlation between polygynous marriage and reproduction of sons.

Similarly, the order in which these women were taken should also be a related but highly autocorrelated factor. For WNUM only three categories are used: first wives, second or subsequent wives, and third and higher-order wives and concubines. The second and higher-order wives should include most of the remarrying widows, and women with higher-order marriages are certain to have low reproductive rates, as children born to previous marriages in other families are unobserved and uncounted. Thus, wife's marriage order should be negatively correlated with net growth rates—first wives will have higher rates, and second and higher-order wives will have lower reproductive rates.

Degree of Lineage Organization (ORG)

The degree of formal lineage organization is expected to have a positive correlation with high rates of growth, not necessarily because formal lineage organization enhanced the prospects of demographic success independent of household wealth and status but because formally organized lineage groups were more able to keep accurate and complete records. The formal organization of any lineage usually involved the compilation of genealogies, construction of lineage halls, and endowment of lineage estates, which constituted the institutional machinery and motivational impetus for more complete recording of lineage-related vital events.

One possible indicator of the degree of formal lineage organization is the use of a personal name element common to the males born in each generation, a "generation name." Lineages or segments conforming to rules regarding the use of specific generation characters are also likely to be those with well-organized procedures for the formal registration and recording of male births to lineage members, even if those sons subsequently die as children or move away. For periods prior to the formal organization of the lineage group or for unorganized descent lines and ritual segments that only became part of the lineage after the initial compilation of the genealogy, there may have been no way of consistently recording new male births, out-migrations, or sons who never married. This inconsistent recording would tend to exclude from the "non-lineage" portions of the genealogies all but those males who actually survived to marry and produce surviving sons. The exclusion of these males should result in positive correlations between the degree of lineage organization and high gross reproduction rates but should have little or no effect on net rates because unmarried males and out-migrants are subtracted in the derivation of the net rates.

Poor record quality should not only tend to reduce apparent growth rates but might also tend to overestimate numbers of sons who record no wives. At the same time, poor records will underestimate the numbers of sons who actually migrated from the area. Deficient recording in some genealogies can be spotted partly by what is clearly missing. For example, the Zhang1 lineage was the most prominent in the area but had one of the worst recorded genealogies incorporated into the data set until about 1600, when the lineage was formally organized and began to keep consistent records. The relatively large number of cases generated by this lineage (N = 317) do not include the record of a single out-migrating son (See Table 3.5), a good indication that something is clearly missing. Just how atypical the oft-studied Zhang1 lineage is (Ho 1962; Beattie 1979; Ebrey 1983) even among the Tongcheng lineages can also be illustrated by the whopping 23.9% of wives who have gentry husbands (Table 3.5). Along the same lines, lineages with abnormally low proportions of sons without spouses must also be taken as an indication that bad records are at least partly to blame, as with the Tang1 lineage, in which only 8% of all sons have no spouse. Lineages or segments with extremely low or no recording of out-migrants or sons without wives clearly have seriously incomplete records. The incorporation of an index of formal organization might help to measure the effects of this factor on growth rates. Unfortunately, this measure cannot be used to evaluate how many sons are left out of the genealogies because their descent lines became "socially extinct." One of the few sanctions lineage groups had against grossly deviant members was exclusion from the genealogy and "excommunication" from the lineage, resulting in the loss of whatever benefits of lineage membership there were. Some believe this practice accounts for many biases in the genealogies, as not only deviant individuals but also "poor cousins" are thought to have been eliminated (Meskill 1970). The tiny proportion of elite families in this data set from Tongcheng County militates against the idea that very many low-status families are lost in this manner. Furthermore, the genealogies for this part of China give very little evidence for the prevalence of such practices.

Even in the genealogies from Guangdong, where powerful dominant lineages are purported to have "socially exterminated" many descent lines, the practice was in fact quite rare. In South China genealogies where lineage members were punished for serious crimes, such as the murder of a clansman, by elimination of their names from the genealogy, usually only the offending individual's name was blotted out, and all his sons' and grandsons' names, if there were any to record, were left intact. Even though the name and other vital data for the offending clansman are missing, the essentials can be easily reconstructed based on his parents', siblings', or sons' vital dates. I am convinced that a vast majority of "social extinctions" even in the South China sources can be accounted for by the real extinction of descent lines before good records began to be kept and by out-migrations to areas distant enough to be beyond some effective range of communication with the main body of lineage members. In any event, the focus on net growth rates of males circumvents most of these problems.

Total Surviving Sons Ever Born per Wife (TOTSONS)

Although TOTSONS tends to confuse the effects of unrecorded infant and child mortality and actual fertility, total surviving sons ever born per wife can be taken as a crude measure of total completed fertility. For this entire data set, the average number of surviving sons is only 1.71 per married woman, and women with high fertility as indicated by the birth of several sons are sure to display high rates of net growth. Because this variable is so highly autocorrelated with the net growth index (see Appendix 3.B), it cannot be used as a measure of overall fertility in the multiple regression analysis. When it is included as one of the independent variables, it alone explains 95% of all variance in net growth; that is to say it only explains itself.

Age Difference of Spouses (AGEDIFF)

If marriageable women are generally in short supply, some men will be forced to delay marriage; but when they eventually do marry, they will marry relatively young women just coming into the marriage market. Furthermore, if average male life expectancy is only about thirty to thirty-five years (Telford 1990a), delaying marriage means that many years of potential reproductivity will be lost. Under such conditions, there should be some difference in net growth rates for husbands who are many years older than their wives. Wide age gaps between husbands and wives may have had some effect on the reproduction of sons in other ways as well. For example, aversion to intercourse or even reduced male virility may have played some minor role in marriages where an older husband was married to a much younger wife.

In addition, cases where the wife is older than the husband might indicate minor marriages of child brides or adoptions of "little daughters-in-law." At the least, minor marriages may constitute a sufficient number of marriages where the wife is older (two years or more) to cause significant effects on net growth rates.[9] It is known that minor marriage resulted from distinct strategies of both wealthy and poor families, and these strategies are sometimes indicated by wives who are older than their husbands. Poorer families in some parts of China "adopted" young girls to "lead in" the birth of a son, to marry a son at some later time, or to avoid the expense of a formal betrothal and marriage (Wolf and Huang 1980). Wealthy families also arranged for child brides, primarily to provide for the earliest possible marriage of their sons.

In this study, age difference of spouses is defined in terms of the *wife's* age; that is, negative values indicate that the wife was younger than the husband, and positive values indicate that the wife was older than the husband. The number of cases in which a wife was older than her husband was relatively small—only 610 women or just 5.17% of all wives were two or more years older than their husbands. Such marriages seem not to have been preferred in this part of China during this period of time, in contrast to the large proportions appearing in some other locales.[10] Given the numerical coding of the age difference variable (1 = husband and wife approximately same age, 2 = husband much older than wife, 3 = wife older than husband), net growth rates and age difference should be negatively associated. That is to say, higher values for the spouses' age difference variable should lead to lower rates of net growth.

Time Periods (TIME)

Table 3.3 indicates there are statistically significant differences in both gross and net reproduction rates by ten-year birth cohorts of wives. The effects of the Ming-Qing wars are described in more detail in the following section, but they would have been felt to varying degrees by different birth cohorts. The cohorts of women born 1595–1624 would have been the most seriously affected by crisis conditions at the end of the Ming Dynasty (1368–1643) and, as expected, have the lowest gross reproduction and net growth rates for the entire time period of study. One cohort, 1595–1604, even has a negative net growth rate; that is, net reproduction of males fell below replacement levels. "Normal" Ming-period net growth rates—those of the 1494–1594 cohorts—averaged less than 1% per year. However, postcrisis early Qing rates, those of the 1625–95 cohorts, dramatically rebounded to over 1.5% per year, almost uniformly doubling the average Ming growth rates. For the entire study period, average annual growth rates of .96% are high for preindustrial populations but are within the realm of possibility and consistent with the notion that early and mid-Qing population growth rates were exceptional, even for South China.[11]

For the regression analysis, the time period categories have been arranged to isolate the effects of the Ming-Qing transition period on net growth rates. For this analysis, birth cohorts have been grouped and recoded as a dummy variable: 0 = cohorts exposed to crisis conditions; 1 = cohorts born before and/or after the crisis period. Given this coding in the regression analysis, positive correlations between time period and net growth rates are expected. Grouping and recoding of wives' birth cohorts for the time period variable into two categories—those unaffected and those seriously affected by crisis conditions—also had the beneficial result of forcing the independent variable time period into a linear relationship with the

TABLE 3.3. Family Characteristics by Wife's Ten-Year Birth Cohort, Tongcheng Lineages, 1520–1661

Birth Cohort	N Wives	Gross Reproduction[a] per Wife	Gross Reproduction[a] per Husband	% Sonless	% Sons Unmarried	% Sons Out-Migrants	Net Growth Rate/Husband	Average Annual Growth Rate
1494–1524	251	1.76	1.97	11.44	23.89	1.59	.38	1.00
1525–1534	489	1.71	1.91	15.69	25.10	1.11	.35	.94
1535–1544	560	1.68	1.84	17.18	23.10	2.81	.26	.72
1545–1554	636	1.63	1.81	15.61	23.07	1.84	.24	.67
1555–1564	655	1.71	1.90	12.97	30.41	2.39	.18	.52
1565–1574	719	1.77	1.97	14.64	26.51	1.97	.30	.82
1575–1584	725	1.68	1.84	19.36	26.02	2.08	.23	.65
1585–1594[b]	785	1.60	1.73	19.86	28.07	2.79	.03	.09
1595–1604[b]	892	1.37	1.53	24.30	23.16	2.68	−.01	−.03
1605–1614[b]	950	1.31	1.56	21.56	21.34	2.76	.04	.12
1615–1624[b]	944	1.36	1.63	23.92	16.72	1.56	.22	.62
1625–1634	947	1.88	2.11	18.04	16.24	1.36	.63	1.53
1635–1644	700	1.96	2.19	13.48	18.31	.68	.69	1.64
1645–1654	1014	2.04	2.23	13.71	17.83	1.45	.75	1.74
1655–1695	1537	1.99	2.31	11.90	20.93	1.63	.68	1.62
Total	11804							
Mean		1.71	1.92	17.12	22.10	1.91	.36	.96
SD		1.51	1.55	—	37.10	1.22	1.44	—
P-value		.0000	.0000	—	.0000	.0062	.0000	—

[a] Gross intergenerational reproduction of males per wife and per husband.
[b] Cohorts experiencing some portion of their reproductive years during crisis period of 1635–45.

dependent variable of net growth. This linear relationship was essential for the multiple regression analyses.[12]

Standard Market Area of Residence (RESIDENCE)

Most variables of interest also vary by standard market area (Skinner 1964) of residence (see Table 3.4). Ecological factors having a spatial component, such as overcrowding in older areas of settlement, are not postulated to have been a factor in Tongcheng at this time, since new land was available in various parts of the county well into the Qing (Beattie 1979:48). In order to study possible geographic variations in growth rates, standard market areas of residence have been grouped on the basis of an estimate of the degree to which each was affected by the warfare and turmoil of the 1635–45 crisis period described in earlier studies (Beattie 1979; Telford 1992a).

An estimate of the increased mortality for the crisis period of 1635–45 for each standard market area was derived as follows: assuming that all infant and much child mortality is systematically excluded in these sources, a decline in the mean number of sons ever born per married woman is taken as an indication of increased mortality rather than decreased fertility. Crisis mortality due to warfare, rebellion, crop failure, and famine would affect the total numbers of surviving sons not only by increasing infant and child mortality but also by shortening the life spans of parents. In other words, decreases in the mean number of surviving sons ever born to women in specific birth cohorts can be taken as a crude indicator of increased general mortality. As already noted, specific birth cohorts of women experienced different portions of their reproductive lives during just such a period of turmoil. Whereas the birth cohorts of 1590–1594 experienced only their final years of fecundability during the first few crisis years, the 1610–1614 cohort would have been in their prime childbearing years at the height of the crisis. Finally, the 1630–1634 cohorts would only have come into their childbearing years after the end of the crisis period in 1645.

The differences between the mean number of sons ever born to birth cohorts of women from 1590–1630 and the number of sons born to those in cohorts from 1631 on (reflecting more "normal" mortality conditions) in each standard market area ranged from −.95 to +.13. The largest difference, −.95, represents a nearly 60% decline in the mean number of surviving sons ever born to married women, who had an average of only 1.71 sons per wife for the entire data set. This continuous variable was grouped and classified in the following way: areas with values from +.13 to −.40 were considered to be *unaffected* by the crisis conditions; the crisis conditions were considered to have had a *low* effect in areas with values from −.51 to −.58, a *medium* effect in areas with values from −.62 to −.74, and a *high* effect in

TABLE 3.4. Family Characteristics by Standard Market Area of Residence, Tongcheng Lineages, 1520–1661

Standard Market Area	N Husbands	Gross Reproduction[a] per Wife	Gross Reproduction[a] per Husband	% Sonless	% Sons Unmarried	% Sons Out-Migrant	Net Growth Rate/Husband	Average Annual Growth Rate
County City	986	1.61	2.10	14.70	14.76	2.04	.65	1.56
Suburbs	794	1.68	1.82	16.50	21.87	3.18	.26	.72
Cungyang	454	1.81	2.05	10.79	18.88	3.80	.58	1.43
Guanfouqiao	283	1.75	2.05	17.31	23.08	1.72	.36	.96
Huigong	342	1.58	1.72	22.80	28.79	.97	.01	.03
Yijinqiao	133	1.75	1.83	39.09	31.39	.96	.11	.33
Pogeng	114	1.66	1.73	14.91	15.55	2.31	.32	.87
Lojiashan	225	1.59	1.76	22.67	11.58	1.60	.42	1.10
Tangjiagou	154	1.87	2.28	11.03	19.77	1.29	.75	1.75
Shiqi	966	1.80	2.00	15.11	24.53	1.59	.37	.98
Yuanzijiang	127	2.12	2.58	6.30	14.29	1.16	1.14	2.38
Hengfouhe	239	1.78	1.98	18.41	22.89	1.07	.42	1.10
Zhoujiatan	483	1.96	2.17	9.94	23.99	1.25	.55	1.37
Yangjiashi	347	1.68	1.82	14.41	28.91	4.14	.27	.75
Kongcheng	651	1.66	1.82	18.89	27.23	1.93	.20	.57
Qianjiaqiao	919	1.50	1.62	23.50	31.55	2.00	−.08	−.03
Beixiaguan	348	1.76	1.86	16.09	31.14	1.25	.17	.49
Lutingyi	614	1.48	1.53	22.80	18.55	1.61	.14	.41
Liantan	612	1.83	2.09	16.67	18.18	2.16	.54	1.35
Xin'andu	497	1.88	2.24	16.90	18.27	1.99	.62	1.51
Guachehe	423	1.86	1.97	9.46	22.13	1.19	.43	1.12
Taochongyi	177	1.67	1.96	19.20	23.72	1.82	.34	.91
Tianningzhuang	216	1.62	1.78	20.37	15.13	2.53	.30	.82
Jinshentun	415	1.64	1.81	18.31	17.94	2.34	.38	1.00
Total	10512							
Mean		1.71	1.92	22.10	17.12	1.91	.36	.96
SD		1.51	1.55	37.10	—	1.22	1.44	—
P-value		.0000	.0000	.0000	—	.0318	.0000	—

[a] Gross intergenerational reproduction of males per wife and per husband.

areas with values from −.77 to −.95. When the grouped values are plotted on a map of the county (Map 3.1), interesting spatial patterns that generally coincide with what is known about the demographic crisis in Tongcheng county from 1635–45 emerge in these differences.

It is known from historical accounts that villages in the mountainous western part of the county were less affected by the devastation of various campaigning armies that crisscrossed the county. In fact, many of the genealogies report that the western hills were an area to which local families fled in an attempt to escape the general destruction of the period. Only the extreme eastern part of the county, also bounded by mountainous areas to the north and the Yangzi River to the south, escaped completely unscathed.[13] These are the same areas that show very small or no differences in the mean number of sons ever born. In fact, two standard market areas in the extreme southeastern part of the county even had positive values for this index. That is, average total number of sons ever born per married woman was slightly higher during the crisis period than afterward. Also, by this index, the residents of the walled county city seem to have fared somewhat better than those in surrounding areas, in spite of the terrible conditions described during repeated seiges of the city (Beattie 1979:46).

Other fascinating patterns also emerge with regard to the most seriously affected areas. All these areas appear to lie along the primary transportation, and therefore invasion, routes running southwest from Lujiang Prefecture in the north to the county city of Tongcheng and on south to the prefectural capital of Anqing—precisely the route taken by various rebel and imperial forces (Beattie 1979:45, 47). A second fork of seriously affected areas runs south from Lujiang Prefecture in an almost direct line toward Gueichi Prefecture just across the Yangzi River—a second natural invasion route from the north across Tongcheng County to another important prefectural capital south of the Yangzi River.

It is assumed that residence in areas seriously affected by crisis conditions should be negatively correlated with growth rates, if for no other reason than low reproduction rates were used to define areas most affected. What will be of interest is how and to what degree these autocorrelations are affected when other factors are controlled. Are high-status families able to avoid the effects of crisis conditions, or do they suffer at the same rate as low-status families in the same area?

Since each lineage group tended to concentrate in relatively few places in the county, those lineages that were unfortunate enough to be resident in the areas most seriously affected are also those most likely to have low rates of growth because of elevated mortality rates. To illustrate how lineage groups tend to concentrate residentially, Map 3.2 details the dispersion of two groups over the county: the Zuo lineage in the extreme eastern part of the county, which was least affected by crisis conditions, and the large Gao

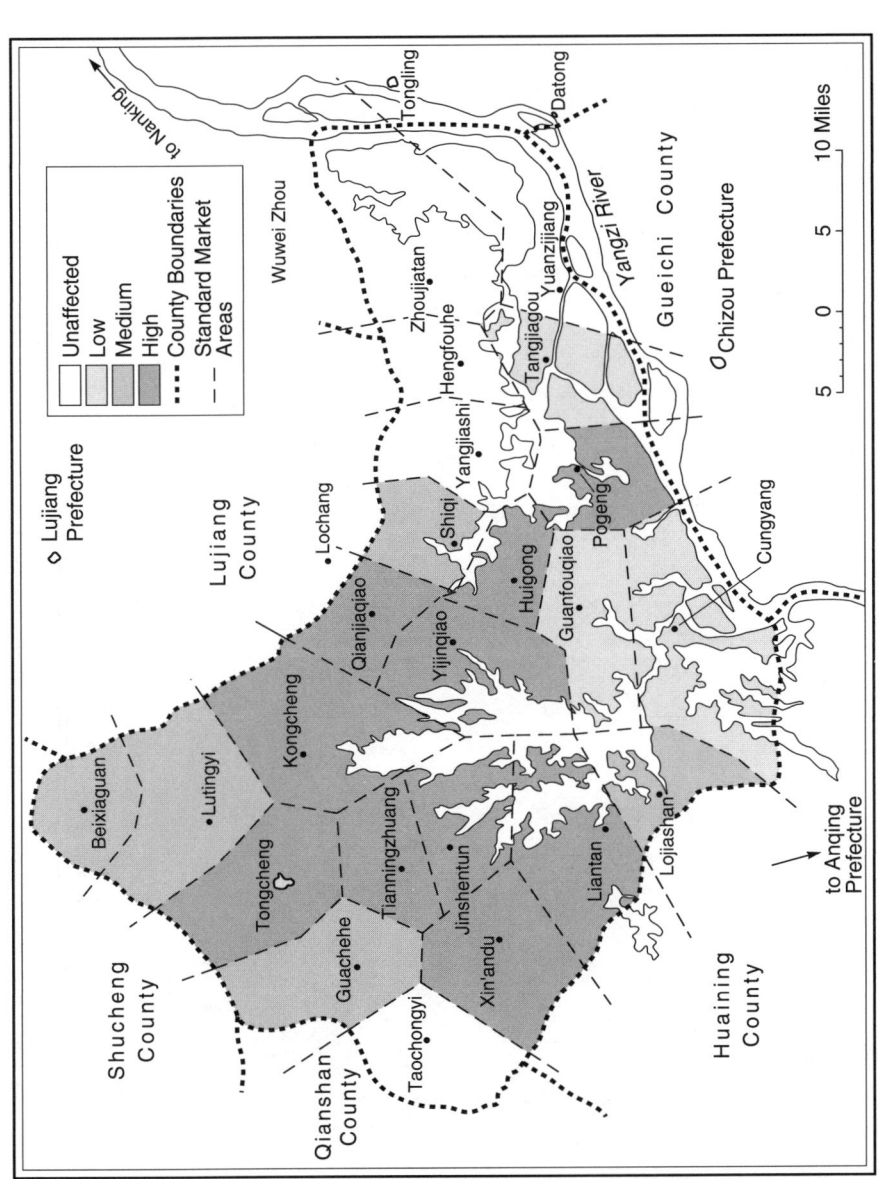

Map 3.1. Standard Market Areas Affected by Ming-Qing Wars and Rebellion, Tongcheng County, 1635–45

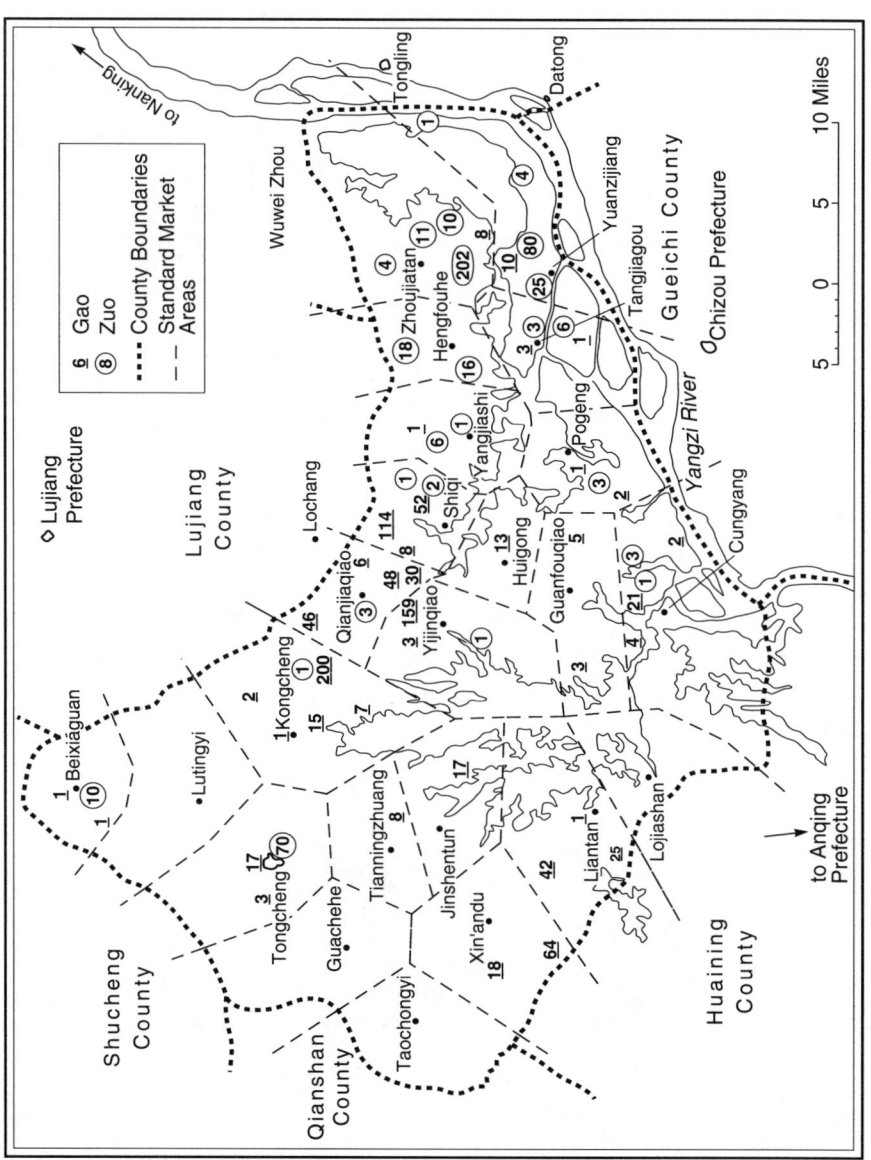

Map 3.2. Geographic Distribution of the Zuo and Gao Lineages, Tongcheng County, 1520–1661

NOTE: Gao lineage numbers are in boxes; Zuo lineage numbers are in circles.

lineage, which had the misfortune of having its segments concentrated in the Kongcheng and Qianjiaqiao areas and in the southwestern part of the county—all seriously affected locales. Consequently, the net growth rates for these two lineages illustrate the drastic extremes that are possible (Table 3.5). The Gaos actually have a negative net growth rate, whereas the Zuos have a very high positive rate, part of which must have been a result of their place of residence.

Lineage Group

As already indicated, some lineages even have negative rates when averaged over the entire time period of study, indicating males were unable to replace their numbers in subsequent generations (Table 3.5). Unfortunately, lineage group could not be included as an explanatory variable in the multiple regression analysis of net growth rates because of the large number of nominal categories involved. If the coefficients for lineage group obtained using other statistical techniques are any indication of the effects of lineage group apart from other factors (Telford 1992a), then the addition of lineage group to the regression analysis would not have lent any additional explanatory power when other key variables were taken into account. The coefficient for lineage group in that earlier analysis, though statistically significant, was so small when other factors were controlled that it simply added nothing to the analysis, regardless of which other variables were included.

This finding is nonetheless important for studies of lineage populations for at least this part of China, as it indicates that membership in a specific lineage group is unimportant when other social-demographic factors are taken into consideration. Statistically significant differences between lineage groups will be found for some demographic measures, but it appears that lineage group is only important if other factors are ignored. If significant differences are revealed between lineage groups, they will invariably be due to the concentration of high- or low-status individuals, the time of birth, or the place of residence rather than to membership in a specific lineage or ritual segment.[14] The association of lineage group with net growth and other variables evident in the P-values of Table 3.5 will disappear when other social-demographic variables are included.

Ritual Segment (SEGMENT)

Almost every Chinese lineage is segmented into ritually defined subgroups tracing patrilineal descent from one or another early progenitor. Depending on theoretical emphasis and research purpose, ritual segment can be conceptualized as a nominal-, ordinal-, or interval-level variable. As a nominal-level variable, segment might be treated as a "sublineage" to examine how

TABLE 3.5. Family Characteristics by Lineage Group, Tongcheng Lineages, 1520–1661

Lineage Group	N Wives	% Wives with a Gentry Husband	Gross Reproduction[a] per Wife	Gross Reproduction[a] per Husband	% Sons Unmarried	% Sons Out-Migrants	Net Growth Rate per Husband	Average Annual Growth Rate
Hu*	348	1.1	1.67	1.91	20.20	1.15	.36	.96
Ma*	156	25.0	1.50	1.93	16.19	1.50	.55	1.37
Ye	241	19.9	1.40	2.01	13.26	2.43	.53	1.33
Cao	85	0.0	1.88	2.46	34.80	.59	.37	.98
Gan*	417	1.4	1.69	1.83	23.56	.59	.34	.91
Li	279	3.2	1.72	1.90	22.66	4.95	.32	.87
Pan	457	1.8	1.85	2.01	20.21	2.64	.45	1.16
Rao	349	0.0	2.16	2.32	25.38	1.44	.62	1.51
Sun1	259	23.9	1.54	1.84	23.67	1.35	.21	.60
Sun2	10	0.0	1.40	2.00	18.33	0.00	.29	.80
Wu	197	2.0	1.96	2.04	38.06	1.09	.20	.57
Yao*	516	15.1	1.58	1.90	17.59	1.52	.46	1.18
Yu	333	3.6	1.84	1.96	19.50	1.92	.50	1.27
Zou*	605	0.0	1.63	1.74	30.46	1.90	.08	.20
Zuo	594	13.9	1.85	2.28	15.82	.74	.83	1.89
Chen1	32	0.0	2.47	2.47	32.40	3.13	.56	1.39
Chen2*	58	9.8	1.76	1.88	21.24	2.08	.33	.89
Cheng1	605	4.9	1.72	2.07	21.64	1.46	.42	1.10
Cheng2	112	.9	1.87	2.09	21.49	2.31	.44	1.14
Fang	138	1.4	1.82	2.06	24.58	1.09	.37	.98
Gao*	1085	1.1	1.52	1.72	31.93	1.94	−.05	−.16
Huang	182	0.0	1.19	1.20	13.69	2.84	−.06	−.19
Jiang1	93	0.0	1.84	1.97	24.33	.54	.41	1.07
Jiang2	290	.3	1.64	1.86	16.89	1.59	.35	.94
Mao	49	6.1	1.73	1.81	18.20	0.00	.32	.87

Miao	358	5.8	1.59	1.64	13.44	1.52	.30	.82
Tang1*	158	4.4	1.57	1.68	8.09	3.35	.41	1.07
Tang2	171	.6	1.91	2.05	28.28	2.68	.38	1.00
Tang*	844	.1	1.69	1.87	26.46	.70	.27	.75
Wang	52	1.9	1.63	1.73	16.03	11.86	.41	1.07
Wang1	227	2.6	1.58	1.70	12.25	4.82	.37	.98
Wang2	344	0.0	1.81	2.10	15.34	.98	.64	1.55
Yin	87	3.4	2.07	2.28	28.03	5.56	.57	1.41
Zhan	40	0.0	1.93	2.03	29.00	5.00	.40	1.05
Zhang1*	317	23.9	1.48	1.95	24.30	0.00	.35	.94
Zhang2	305	.9	1.60	1.64	19.94	2.21	.20	.57
Zheng	160	1.9	2.08	2.49	10.89	2.51	1.06	2.26
Zhong	196	1.0	1.58	1.72	15.62	2.67	.29	.80
Zhou1	76	3.9	1.61	1.79	12.52	14.69	.28	.77
Zhou2	545	0.0	1.99	2.15	24.30	1.29	.54	1.35
Zhu	134	5.2	1.78	1.82	19.13	1.11	.31	.84
Total	11804							
Mean		3.0	1.71	1.92	22.10	1.91	.36	.96
SD		—	1.51	1.55	37.10	1.22	1.44	—
P-value		—	.0000	.0000	.0000	.0000	.0000	—

[a] Gross intergenerational reproduction of males per husband and wife.
*Genealogies having much poorer than average recording of vital data.

status or other categories are distributed within a larger lineage group. As an interval-level variable, segment could be thought of as a measure of the degree of lineage segmentation. Some lineages are highly segmented, with dozens of important ritual segments and subsegments, while other lineages distinguish only a few ritual subdivisions. Segmentation into large numbers of ritual divisions is thought to always accompany growth in the size of the lineage.[15] Therefore, highly segmented lineages are likely to be those with the fastest rates of growth. As an ordinal-level variable, a segment can be distinguished as *senior* or *junior*. Ritual segments descended from elder sons of early ancestors are senior or major segments (*dafang*), and junior or minor lines (*xiaofang*) descend from subsequent sons of those early ancestors. According to some conceptions of Chinese lineage organization, senior descent lines not only have ritual preference but, more importantly, benefit more than junior segments from control of lineage property (Eberhard 1962:206–9). Because of such presumed advantages, senior segments are expected to grow more rapidly than junior ones and are more likely to have above average concentrations of high-status, wealthy families.

For this regression analysis of net growth rates, ritual segment is defined, coded, and interpreted as an ordinal-level variable. If senior segments (code = 1) grow at higher rates than junior segments (codes = 2 or higher), negative coefficients should result. There should also be negative bivariate correlations between senior segment and high social status, if senior segments benefit more from preferred ritual positions in lineage organizations. However, as with lineage group, the effect of ritual segment is expected to be negligible when other factors are controlled.

Husband's Birth Order (BIRTHORD)

Even though distinctions between junior and senior branches of lineages may not be significant in explaining differential growth rates, preference given to older sons might still have been an important factor for individual families. Preference may have been given to first sons in providing for marriage, preventing out-migration, or dividing property, which by law and custom was supposed to have been divided equally amongst the sons but may have included a larger share for the eldest. If preference was given to older sons in these lineages, birth order would account for some portion of the variance in net growth rates. Preferences should thus be indicated by a negative correlation between birth order and net growth.

Proportion of Sons Unmarried (%UNMARR)

Not all sons who survived early childhood would have lived to age twelve or thirteen—a marriageable age in these populations; and not all of those surviving into adolescence and adulthood would have been able to find wives. In fact, in these lineages an average of 22% of all sons surviving into adolescence and beyond never married. Given the incomplete recording of several of the genealogies included in this study, this 22% is probably an underestimate. Furthermore, there are significant variations in proportions of sons unmarried by social status, time period, residence, and lineage group, as reported in Tables 3.1–3.5. Families with large proportions of unmarried sons are certain to have low rates of net growth. This relationship should be indicated by negative correlations with the rate of net intergenerational growth.

In calculating the proportion of unmarried sons, no attempt has been made to distinguish between sons who died prior to marriage and sons who survived into adulthood but never married. For this particular time period the selected genealogies largely prevent such discrimination, as those who do not marry and produce sons are the same persons who tend to be neglected in the documents, especially where complete recording of death dates is concerned. Assuming that high-status families have the necessary resources to acquire wives for all sons who survive into their teens, then the proportion of gentry sons unmarried (7.8% in Table 3.1) represents the proportion of sons who did not survive long enough to marry, say to about age fifteen. If mortality for the other status categories from about age one through fifteen was approximately 8% but was balanced by poor recording of unmarried males (assuming that low-status families will be those most often neglected in the records), then 15% of near-gentry sons and an amazing average of 26% of all nongentry sons were unable to find wives. For analytic purposes, the proportion of sons unmarried will be interpreted primarily as a marriage variable, even though it combines important effects of mortality.

Proportion of Marriages with No Sons (%SONLESS)

For the entire data set, an average of 17.12% of all marriages produce no sons, but there is wide variation by status group, time period, and residence, as reported in Tables 3.2, 3.3, and 3.4.[16] The wide variances in these proportions generally conform to expectations and are sometimes interesting indicators of hard times, but the occurrence of marriages that do not produce surviving male children is not conceptualized as a possible explanatory variable. In fact, the below-replacement reproduction represented by these cases is part of what is being explained by the overall regression analysis and therefore cannot be treated as an independent explanatory variable.

Proportion of Sons Out-Migrated (%OUTMIG)

Some reproductive potential is lost to lineages as well as the larger community as sons migrate out of the area. Out-migration in this study is defined as a permanent change of residence to a place outside the administrative boundaries of Tongcheng County. An average of only 2% of all sons recorded such moves (Tables 3.2–3.5), and most of these recorded moves were to counties adjacent to Tongcheng. An additional 2% of all sons were involved in permanent changes of residence within the county but continued to be included in the records. Even though nongentry sons migrated at a higher average rate than gentry sons, the differences are not statistically significant (Table 3.2). The out-migrations recorded for these sections of the genealogies are almost certainly incomplete and, as with most of the genealogies, can be assumed to be more complete for high-status families and for some lineages. At least some of the surviving sons missing from the records are certain to have been out-migrants from low-status families. Were the records more complete, as they seem to be for later time periods in the documents, the differences would surely have been even more important.

In spite of the incomplete recording of migration, differences in out-migration rates of sons for different birth cohorts of mothers, standard market areas of residence, and lineage group are all statistically significant (Tables 3.2–3.5). Some of the smaller lineages, specifically the Wang and Zhou1 lineages, have relatively large proportions of sons who leave the area (see Table 3.5). Many members of some lineages had occupational specialties such as trade or military service that necessitated permanent out-migration. For some lineage groups, out-migration must have been an important factor in explaining low net growth rates. For example, the Zhou1 lineage described itself as belonging to a military family-status category. During the Ming such families were required to register and provide quotas of sons for military service, many of whom left the area never to return. Significantly, the Zhou1 lineage group has one of the highest reported rates of out-migrating sons, 14.69% of all sons.

In general, out-migration is not likely to be a major explanatory variable for net population growth of most lineages or of the county as a whole, at least for this period of study.[17] Some "return" migration of lineage members is recorded in the genealogies, but these return migrations occur at a level much lower than total out-migrations. If out-migration is an important factor influencing growth rates, negative correlations should result between proportions of sons out-migrating and net growth rates.

Age at Birth of First Son (WFIRST, HFIRST)

Given the lack of actual marriage dates in these sources, the best available indicator of age at first marriage is wife's age at birth of first surviving son (Telford 1992a). As a proxy for age at marriage, ages of both wife and husband at first son's birth are included as independent variables in the multiple regression analysis. Age at birth of first son is expected to have a strong inverse relationship with net growth rates. Simply put, women and men who marry early are also the most likely to produce large numbers of children.

For the multiple regression analysis, calculation of this variable depends on the existence of at least one surviving son for each case. In fact many couples have only female children or have no surviving sons recorded at all. These cases cannot be dropped from the analysis without seriously distorting the overall results, as couples without male children account for the very slow or negative rates of some social-demographic categories. So that no cases would be dropped as "missing" because this single variable could not be calculated, the wife's median age at birth of first son (age twenty-two) and the husband's median age at birth of first son (age twenty-five) were substituted whenever a couple did not have a recorded surviving son. Substitution of such median values should not disturb the expected association between early age at marriage and high rates of growth, although it might attenuate the size of the actual coefficient and underestimate the real strength of the relationship between early marriage and high rates of net growth.

Age at Birth of Last Son (WLAST, HLAST)

The ages at which men and women bear their last surviving son are probably the best available proxy for marriage duration in these sources. As divorce and desertion were very rare in these Chinese populations, the primary factor influencing marriage duration must have been the death of one or another spouse. The ages of mother and father at last son's birth, when included in the multiple regression analysis as independent variables, will be interpreted as marriage-duration cum mortality factors and should reveal very strong positive correlations with net growth rates.

Two technical problems arose when this variable was included in the regression analysis. First, couples for whom only a single son's birth was available to calculate both the birth of first and last son presented a relatively minor problem. The use of an only surviving son to indicate both age at marriage and marriage duration is far from a sensitive indicator of either but should approximate both if aggregated with large numbers of cases having more complete information. At the very least, the use of this approximation should not entirely eliminate the expected relationship between long marriage durations and high rates of reproduction. At the same time, such a practice is likely to underestimate the actual strength of the effect of mortality on net reproduction.

Cases where missing death dates were coupled with no sons were more difficult to deal with. On the assumption that many of the married couples with no sons and missing death dates married at the same average age as other couples but died early, the wife's median age at birth of first son (age twenty-two) and the husband's median age at birth of first son (age twenty-five) were substituted for couples with no recorded male births and no dates of death rather than trying to use median age at birth of last son as a proxy. It is reasonable to think of an early age at last male birth as equivalent to short marriage duration due to the death of a spouse. By doing this, all couples can be included in the regression analysis without disturbing an expected positive relationship between older age at birth of last son (long marriage duration) and high rates of population growth.

MULTIPLE REGRESSION ANALYSIS OF NET INTERGENERATIONAL GROWTH

Table 3.6 summarizes the expected signs of the correlations of the social and demographic explanatory variables with the index of net growth together with the reported signs of the correlation coefficients from the actual regression analysis. Three variables—wife's status, ritual segment, and husband's birth order—do not have the expected sign; that is, the direction of the relationship is not that hypothesized between net growth rates and these three explanatory variables. The sign of the wife's status variable, given its ordinal numerical coding, indicates that the high-status wives (only wives and first wives in polygynous households) have lower net growth rates, when everything else is controlled. This relationship may seem somewhat contradictory but is consistent with the practice of taking additional (low-status) wives and concubines as a response to low (or no) fertility of first (high-status) wives. It is also consistent with the stopping or slowing down of childbearing by older wives as younger wives and concubines are brought in. Furthermore, it is certainly consistent with Bean and Mineau's (1986) notion that continued high fertility is not characteristic of rigid systems ascribing high status to first wives. The unexpected signs of ritual segment and husband's birth order indicate that senior lineage segments and older sons within families have no demographic advantage in terms of net intergenerational growth.[18] In addition, neither of these values are statistically significant.

One variable, residence in seriously affected areas, has the expected sign but is not statistically significant at the .05 level; that is, the probability is high that the relationships observed occurred by chance. The reason why residence has no significant effect is probably the fact that standard market areas seriously affected by the Ming-Qing turmoil were not continuously affected throughout the time period of study, only from 1634–45. Any effect of residence has most likely been dampened out by analyzing all residents of those places rather than only those cohorts living there during the crisis period.

TABLE 3.6. Summary of Expected Relationships, All Variables with Net Growth Rate, Tongcheng Lineages, 1520–1661

Acronym	Operational Definition	Expected Sign	Reported Sign
HSTAT	Husband's social status	+	+
NWIVES	Total number of wives	+	+
WSTAT	Wife's status relative to other wives	−	+
WNUM	Wife's marriage order	−	−
ORG	Degree of lineage organization	+	+
TOTSONS	Sons ever born per wife	+	+
AGEDIFF	Age difference of spouses	−	−
TIME	Birth cohorts affected by crisis conditions	+	+
RESIDENCE	Residence in areas affected by crisis conditions	−	−[a]
SEGMENT	Senior ritual segments	−	+[a]
BIRTHORD	Husband's birth order	−	+[a]
%UNMARR	% of sons unmarried	−	−
%OUTMIG	% of sons out-migrated	−	−
WFIRST	Wife's age at birth of first son	−	−
WLAST	Wife's age at birth of last son	+	+
HFIRST	Husband's age at birth of first son	−	−
HLAST	Husband's age at birth of last son	+	+

[a] Not significant at .05 level.

As already emphasized, the bivariate cross-tabulation of husband's status with net growth rates (Table 3.2) indicates exceptionally large differences between low- and high-status groups. However, an adequate description of the relationship between status, or any of the other social-ecological variables, and net reproduction requires the inclusion of demographic mechanisms through which high status produced high or low rates of net growth. Several possible mechanisms have already been discussed and are included in the regression analysis as explanatory variables. It is difficult to conceive of a way in which wealth or high status, not to mention place of residence or birth cohort, could influence growth rates except through some effect on demographic variables such as length of life, infant mortality rates, number of wives, age at marriage, marriage duration, out-migration, and proportion of sons unmarried.

In terms of causal models, the usual way of thinking about such demographic variables is to treat them as "proximate determinants" (Bongaarts 1983) standing between net growth on the one hand and the social-ecological factors on the other. The primary purpose of the multiple regression analysis is to determine the relative strength of the direct effects of each variable when all of them are taken into account. Standard multiple regression techniques are not intended to measure and account for the

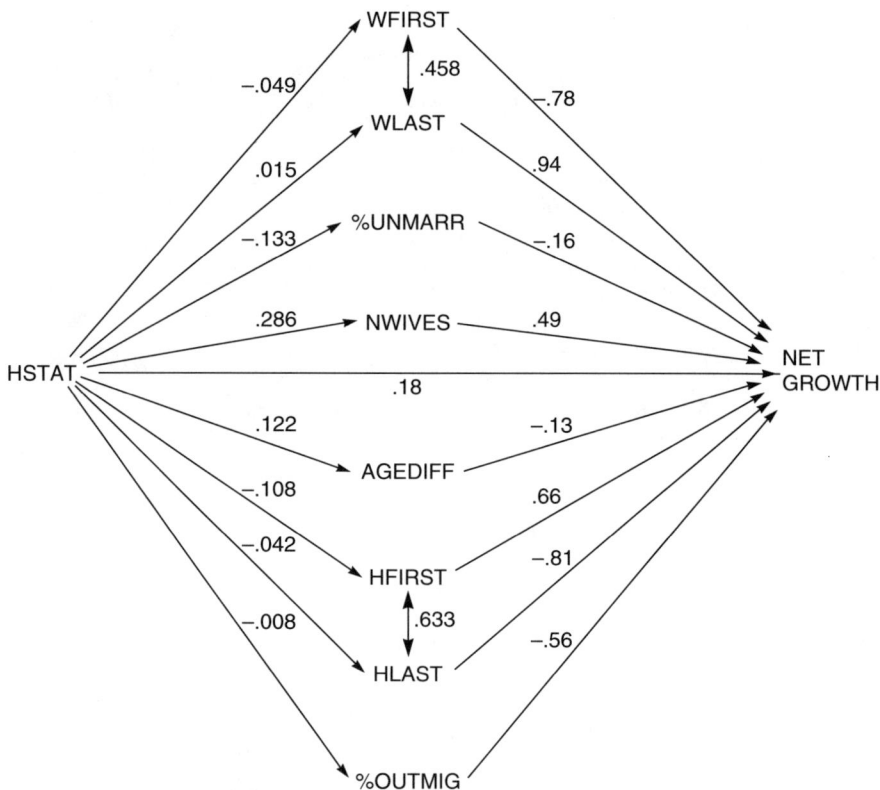

Figure 3.5. Path Diagram of the Relationship of Husband's Social Status to Net Intergenerational Growth

indirect effects of one variable on a second, through which the first affects a third (see Figure 3.5). Multiple regression coefficients are the raw material for an even more sophisticated statistical technique called path analysis, which sorts out the direct and indirect causal influences of many variables that are related to each other in complicated ways. Figure 3.5 is a path diagram that lays out in graphic form the possible causal relationship between a single independent variable (husband's social status) and the dependent variable of net intergenerational growth. Standing between the two are several intermediate or "proximate" demographic variables through which status must operate to have an effect on net growth. The coefficients included on the diagram indicate the direction and strength of that particular relationship as derived from the multiple regression analysis or from the bivariate correlation matrix for this data set (Appendix 3.B).

Even when only one social variable and a few intermediate demographic variables are included, the possible causal "paths" through which the social variable could operate multiply rapidly and make such an analysis beyond the scope of this paper. If the important connections between demographic variables—for example, the high correlation between the husband's and wife's ages at first and last sons' births—are also included, the analysis becomes impossibly complicated. In other words, the effect of social status may be small when the size of the correlation of any two variables is examined, but the total effect of status may be very large, as it operates indirectly though many channels (Figure 3.5). Two of the key paths, as judged from the size of the coefficients, are the relationship between status and number of wives and the relationship between number of wives and net growth, but other causal paths are important as well. From the multiple regression analysis there remains a significant direct effect of social status on growth rates, which is indicated by an arrow running directly from status to growth in Figure 3.5, with a coefficient of .18. What the presence of this coefficient indicates is that there is at least one unmeasured variable through which status affects growth rates that has not been included in this analysis. Any number of things might account for this association, perhaps something like nutrition or even the high value placed on having sons in high-status families. In any event, no set of social-demographic variables however numerous will ever account for all variation in net growth rates because of the limitations of the data or of the creativity of the researcher. The ability to explain as much as 80% of the variance in any multiple regression analysis (as is accomplished here) is to achieve a great deal, since most social research is considered successful when far less variance is explained.

The goal of multiple regression research is to discover which of any set of independent variables that can be measured (and that should be included for sound theoretical reasons) accounts for the most variation in the dependent variable of interest. To that end, alternative regression models that incorporate different sets of explanatory variables can be conceived. The following three regression models have been run: Model I includes only the social-ecological variables, Model II incorporates only the proximate demographic variables, and Model III includes both sets of variables to explain as much variation in net growth index as possible. Table 3.7 summarizes the results of an ordinary least-squares multiple regression analysis for the three proposed sets of variables. In terms of amount of variance explained (Multiple R^2), Model III is only slightly better than Model II. As expected, the sizes of the direct effects of the social-ecological factors, though statistically significant, are negligible when the demographic determinants are included.

Model I measures the relative strength of the direct effects of the social-ecological variables, which alone account for only 28.5% of explained variance (Multiple R^2 = .285). Of these, husband's social status has the largest effect (with a B, or standardized coefficient, of .51) and is followed

86   TED A. TELFORD

TABLE 3.7. Multiple Regression of Social Demographic Variables on Net Growth Rate, Tongcheng Lineages, 1520–1661, Models I–III

Variables	Model I			Model II			Model III		
	B	b (Beta)	F	B	b (Beta)	F	B	b (Beta)	F
HSTAT	.51	.18	395.84				.18	.07	109.85
ORG	.24	.17	328.77				.82	.06	90.76
TIME	.31	.10	124.29				.11	.03	41.03
RESIDENCE	−.06	−.04	26.19				−.96	−.007	1.46
SEGMENT	.014	−.02	6.22				.47	.007	1.72
BIRTHORD	−.006	−.005	.40				−.21	−.002	.13
WLAST				.94	4.95	1187.93	.94	4.95	1217.61
%UNMARR				−1.62	−.42	5015.09	−.16	−.41	4745.05
WFIRST				−.77	−2.91	754.16	−.78	−2.95	786.90
NWIVES				.55	.15	214.83	.49	.12	169.50
HLAST				−.80	−4.99	879.19	−.81	−5.01	905.73
HFIRST				.65	3.18	542.36	.66	3.23	572.15
AGEDIFF				−.13	−.42	547.59	−.13	−.40	514.37
%OUTMIG				−.58	−.05	73.84	−.56	−.05	71.99
WIFENUM				−.18	−.03	8.52	−.15	−.02	6.07
WSTAT				.11	.04	8.42	.95	.03	6.24
(Constant)	−1.15			−.84			−.13		
Degrees of Freedom	6			10			16		
Multiple R²		.285			.799			.801	
Sum of Squares		1799.91			14051.29			14236.84	
Mean Square		299.98			1405.12			889.80	
F		155.88			1852.59			1200.46	

in importance by time period, with a B of .31. Degree of lineage organization is also important, but husband's status stands out as the key social factor. Residence and ritual segment have statistically significant effects (F values larger than 2.00), but the extremely small coefficients mean these variables have little or no effect on net growth rates when considered with the other variables. Finally, husband's birth order is neither statistically significant nor important in its effect on net growth.

When the variables in Model III are analyzed in a stepwise regression, which allows the variables to compete with each other in explaining the most variance, four demographic variables account for virtually all of the explained variance, even though several other variables have large and statistically significant coefficients. Furthermore, only three of these account for the vast majority of the explained variance (.746), as Table 3.8 indicates. These three demographic variables—wife's age at birth of last son, proportion of sons unmarried, and wife's age at birth of first son—are the key factors accounting for differences in growth rates. Clearly, the single most

TABLE 3.8. Stepwise Regression of Model III on Net Growth Rates, Tongcheng Lineages, 1520–1661

Variables	Multiple R	Simple R	B	b (Beta)
WLAST	.485	.485	.94	4.96
%UNMARR	.626	−.359	−1.58	−.41
WFIRST	.746	−.123	−.78	−2.94
NWIVES	.762	.158	.49	.13
HSTATUS	.765	.193	.17	.07
ORG	.767	.174	.82	.06
HLAST	.769	.403	−.81	−5.01
HFIRST	.790	−.102	.66	3.23
AGEDIFF	.801	−.062	−.13	−.40
%OUTMIG	.803	−.099	−.57	−.05
TIME	.804	.646	.11	.04
WSTATUS	.804	.156	.09	.03
WIFENUM	.804	.126	−.15	−.02
SEGMENT	.804	.013	.005	.008
RESIDENCE	.804	−.080	−.001	−.007
BIRTHORD	.804	.002	−.002	−.002
(Constant)			−.131	

NOTES: Multiple R = Total amount of variance explained as each variable is added "stepwise" from top to bottom.
  Simple R = Amount of variance explained by each variable separately.
  B = Standardized regression coefficient (comparable strength of effect when controlling for other variables).
  b = Unstandardized coefficient (size of coefficient not comparable to others in the same model).

important variable resulting in high rates of net growth in these populations is age at birth of last son, which in these data is a proxy for long marriage duration due to low mortality of wives. Alone, this single variable accounts for 48.5% of all variance in net growth. This analysis indicates that adult mortality levels had a much greater effect on rates of population growth in these lineage populations than did marriage factors. However, a fertility variable—proportions of sons unmarried—is the second most important factor and is negatively correlated with net growth rates as expected. Naturally, the more sons who survive to marry, the higher the net reproduction rate. A second fertility factor—mother's age at first son (early marriage)—is the third most important variable in explaining high rates of growth. If fertility varies little within marriage, the age at which childbearing begins is certain to be crucial to the reproduction of large numbers of sons and consequently to high net growth rates for some lineages and for the population of the county as a whole. Low-status males in fact do marry at significantly later ages than their high-status contemporaries (Telford

1992a). But together, these variables measuring exposure to marriage account for only 36.1% of the variance in net growth, and it must be remembered that both of these (age at first marriage and duration of marriage) as coded here have important mortality effects incorporated in them. Essentially, most of the variation is explained by mortality variables, but two marriage variables, which technically belong to the fertility side of the population growth equation, also play a role in accounting for differential reproduction. Finally, the dramatic differences in growth rates between status categories can be explained by the large zero-order correlations (correlations between two variables without controlling for any others) between high status and these three factors (see Appendix 3.B). The final conclusion that can be drawn from all of this data is that in these particular lineage populations at this particular time, fertility factors were less important in explaining differential growth rates than mortality. The factors that appear to explain varying rates of natural increase are mortality factors, and future research on this and other related topics should concentrate more on differential mortality and less on fertility and marriage.

CONCLUSION

The notion that mortality rather than fertility constituted the primary constraint on population growth in these lineages points to striking differences between the agrarian societies of Western Europe and China and has a number of interesting implications for Chinese history in general. It is generally accepted among demographic historians that with rare exceptions, even very high mortality levels are incapable of slowing population growth in the long run. Populations subject to severe famines or other forms of crisis mortality are very quick to recover and suffer few long-term effects (Watkins and Menken 1985). Only reductions in birth rates will result in long-term stability of population size, and it was premodern Western Europe's unique marriage system that effectively reduced fertility and allowed the homeostatic balancing of population growth with availability of land and other resources (Hajnal 1965). Many believe this European marriage system was an important factor that helps to explain why it was Western Europe that led the world into the Industrial Revolution. With the only significant restraint on population growth being death rates, the historical Chinese demographic system's only response to worsening balances between resources and numbers would have been increases in mortality—some deliberate, as with infanticide, and some involuntary, as with increases in adult mortality during times of crop failure and famine. Without effective restraints on marriage and fertility, the only possible result of China's historic rapid population growth could have been serious economic stagnation, agricultural involution, and more peasant rebellion rather than innovation, economic growth, and the flowering of the "sprouts of capitalism" (Huang 1985:298–304).

The implications for the fate of the elites of traditional Chinese society, with their dramatically higher rates of growth, are even clearer. With a state bureaucracy that hardly grew in size from the beginning of the Qing to the end of the dynasty (Skinner 1964) and the explosive rates of population growth in the families of the elite, it was a wonder the whole system of elite recruitment did not collapse long before 1905. The abolition of the examination system came only after centuries of intensified competition and reduced rates of upward mobility that must have resulted from such high rates of population growth among the elite. As the Qing dynasty wore on, rather than delay marriage or reduce the number of offspring among whom available resources had to be distributed, as characterized the Western European system, both the gentry and peasantry alike seemed to intensify their efforts to produce more children by marrying as many off as early as possible. In fact, the response to demographic crisis, and the increasing imbalance between numbers and resources, seemed to be earlier rather than later marriage as in Western Europe (Telford 1992a). Furthermore, growth rates would have been even higher but for the endemic shortage of marriageable women in these populations (Telford 1992a). Given increased death rates as the only possible restraint on growth in numbers, it would have taken truly catastrophic mortality with the magnitude of Europe's Black Death to divert China's path from one of increasing stagnation, the extreme intensification of labor in agriculture, the ensuing general decline in living standards, and the general lack of economic "development." For reasons as yet unclear, China never experienced a widespread and devastating mortality crisis that altered the value of peasant labor and stimulated technological innovation as the Black Plague seems to have done in Western Europe. Nevertheless, this lesson seems not to have been lost on China's current leadership in its efforts to win prosperity through forced reductions in fertility and population growth.

NOTES

1. Ho (1962) and Marme (1981) document population growth rates for the Ming and Qing in excess of 1% per year. Rates of natural increase in South China, especially the Lower Yangzi, were in excess of the average while North China's rates were below average.

2. The terms *population growth* and *natural increase* are often used interchangeably when populations are either "closed" to migration or where in- and out-migration rates are thought to be balanced. Technically, natural increase is used only in reference to the excess of births (fertility) over deaths (mortality) and does not incorporate any migration component. For the period in question for China's

population taken as a whole, the migration component of growth was negligible, and natural increase accounted for the vast majority of population growth.

3. ASFMR calculates the rate at which married women bear children, conventionally for five-year age groups from 15–19, 20–24, etc., through the childbearing years. TMFR is derived by summing the five-year age-specific rates and dividing by five (the size of each age category). These standard measures are used because they give the most accurate possible comparisons to the fertility experience of other populations.

4. For this study only missing birth years have been estimated, but it is also possible to fill in the missing death years by using other techniques (Telford 1990).

5. Chang (1955:114, Fig. 2) estimates his "upper gentry" and "lower gentry," corresponding to all holders of the first-level degrees and up, at less than 2% of the total population. By approximately the same definition, "gentry" accounts for 3.2% of the cases analyzed here—not far out of line considering Tongcheng's reputation for extraordinary success in the civil service examinations. On the other hand, Fei (1946) estimates the whole of the "leisured classes" or "gentry" to have been about 20% of the population. If we take the top two gentry categories here together (near gentry and gentry), which are comparable to Fei's definition of "gentry," we have 26.6%, again, not far from that expected.

6. Sharlin (1978) cites a number of studies primarily of historical European populations that indicate mortality schedules are relatively invariant among social classes. Therefore, the discovery of mortality differentials by social class in Chinese historical populations is completely unexpected (Lee forthcoming; Telford 1990a). Explanations for this phenomenon are pure speculation at this point, but variations in mortality across all age groups by social status may have something to do with the nature of traditional Chinese medical practices and other class-specific cultural practices that may have had some hygienic effect. It is widely accepted that Chinese medical practices were far less "harmful" than the traditional European medicine of the time and may have actually been helpful in some situations. Thus, access to medical care may have actually benefited the upper classes who could afford it. Also, advanced medical technologies such as smallpox virulation in China, known to have been practiced by the elite, may also have been able to reduce mortality for specific diseases. The Chinese upper class bathed frequently (compared to the unwashed European upper classes) and drank tea instead of unboiled water; these class-specific cultural practices may have had tangible effects in the lowering of death rates for the elites of Chinese society.

7. Whether variables are statistically significant or not is indicated by a probability value (P-value). The lower the P-value of any variable, the less likely the observed correlation could have occurred by chance. Variables with P-values over .05 are usually considered not to be statistically significant, that is, the correlation could have occurred by random chance. F-scores or F-tests reported in several tables also indicate statistical significance levels. A crude rule of thumb is that any F-statistic larger than 2.00 is significant at the .05 level.

8. Negative (or inverse) and positive relationships between two variables are conventionally indicated by negative and positive signs, respectively. A negative

relationship is one in which the value of one variable increases as the value of the second decreases.

9. Arthur Wolf presents much data to support the hypothesis that children raised together as brothers and sisters and then expected to live as husband and wife will have a very strong sexual aversion to each other, and that this aversion will result in lower fertility rates for couples in these types of marriages. If wives older than husbands indicate such marriages, their fertility level and consequent reproduction rate will be lower than marriages where husbands are about the same age or somewhat older than wives (Wolf and Huang 1980: 161–70).

10. Liu (1985) reports that as many as 34% of marriages in her lineages have wives older than their husbands, although she does not specify how much older these women were.

11. Lee (1982:731–32) describes the high rates of population growth for the Qing in comparison to more moderate rates for the Ming.

12. Ordinary least-squares regression techniques can only measure linear relationships between variables. Breaking the time period variable into three divisions—before, during, and after the crisis period—results in curvilinear relationships between the values of the variable, as conditions were very similar before and after the crisis period. Grouping the cohorts living before and after the crisis period and comparing them with the crisis-period cohorts makes the relationship linear and results in overall higher coefficients for the time period variable than when three divisions were used.

13. Beattie cites *Tongcheng xian zhi* (1807), 23.21a–b, in her discussion of the areas left untouched by crisis conditions (Beattie 1979:25, 47).

14. Harrell (1985) found important differences between lineages and segments. Although he did not control for social status, he did note that high-status families were concentrated in certain lineages and segments.

15. Harrell (1985) spends a good deal of time discussing the relationships between lineage growth, segmentation, and population growth in general for his Zhejiang province lineages. Also, Emily Ahern makes similar observations for her Taiwan lineages (Ahern 1976).

16. Liu (chap. 5) reports proportions-heirless for five lineages from 17.3% to 24.3%. Assuming by "heirless" she means "sonless," a remarkable consistency is seen in these proportions between two very different sets of lineage genealogies.

17. James Lee (1982) details the importance of in-migration to rapid growth rates in China's southwestern provinces. In-migration was an important component in the documented rapid population growth of other frontier areas such as Manchuria and Taiwan. But Tongcheng was not such a frontier area during the time period of study, although out-migration might have been significant from time to time.

18. In most of his work on Banner populations James Lee finds a strong relationship between reproductive success and a son's birth order. This relationship must be explained by the unique character of his population, where hereditary Banner privilege is passed to the eldest son (Lee and Eng 1984; Lee and Campbell forthcoming). The lineage populations of Central China studied here are mostly peasant farmers who seem to have given little or no preference to eldest sons.

APPENDIX 3.A. Husband's Social Status Variable Coding

Raw Data Code	Type of Information
Nongentry	
00	No title, degrees, office, evidence of wealth, etc.
01	Honorary or posthumous titles; Main Guest at the county banquet
02	Multiple wives (two or more not at the same time)
Near gentry	
03	Father a *shengyuan*, minor official, official student, evidence of wealth, *jiansheng*, expectant official
04	Grandfather a *juren, gongsheng, jinshi*, or official
05	Father a *juren, gongsheng, jinshi*, or official
06	Educated, scholar, no degrees or office (editor of the genealogy, refused office, prepared for but did not pass examinations)
07	Concubinage, polygyny (two or more wives or concubines at the same time)
08	Other evidence of wealth, property (ancestral estates, large donations, wealthy farmer, landowner or merchant, philanthropy)
09	Official students (*xiangsheng; yixiang; junxiang; wu xiangsheng*)
10	Military *shengyuan* (*wu shengyuan*); minor military office
11	Purchased *jiansheng* and/or purchased office
12	Students of the Imperial Academy (nonpurchased) (*taixue sheng; guoxue sheng*)
Gentry	
13	Civil *shengyuan* (*shengyuan; lingsheng; fusheng; zengsheng; xiucai*); minor civil office; Ming period *jiansheng*
14	Expectant official (*houxuan*), no degrees
15	Expectant official, with one of the lower degrees
16	Military *juren, jinshi;* major military officer
17	Civil official, no degree, minor or purchased degree
18	*Juren, gongsheng* with no office
19	*Juren, gongsheng* with office or expectant official
20	*Jinshi,* no office
21	*Jinshi,* with official provincial post or expectant official
22	*Jinshi,* with top-level post in the Imperial bureaucracy (Hanlin Academy, Grand Secretariat, Five Boards, etc.)
23	Hereditary princes, Imperial Clan

APPENDIX 3.B. Zero-Order Correlation Matrix

	SEGM	BIRTHO	HSTAT	AGED	RESID	NWIVE	WSTAT	WNUM	TIME	%UNMAR
SEGMENT	1.000									
BIRTHORD	.009	1.000								
HSTAT	−.004	.087	1.000							
AGEDIFF	−.025	−.018	.122	1.000						
RESIDENCE	.088	−.027	−.117	−.045	1.000					
NWIVES	.008	.029	.286	−.051	−.067	1.000				
WSTAT	−.001	.017	.239	−.134	−.068	.807	1.000			
WNUM	.006	.004	.136	−.225	−.046	.513	.724	1.000		
TIME	−.007	−.016	.014	−.022	−.010	−.018	−.006	−.004	1.000	
%UNMARR	−.039	.008	−.133	−.040	.021	−.047	−.041	−.015	.014	1.000
%OUTMIG	−.017	−.017	−.008	.013	.007	−.012	−.012	−.009	−.029	.116
ORG	−.025	−.048	−.009	−.067	−.063	−.011	−.013	−.014	.027	−.034
WFIRST	.004	−.025	−.049	−.068	−.040	−.048	.028	.015	−.034	.001
WLAST	−.008	−.015	.015	−.138	−.079	−.052	−.002	.079	.078	.074
HFIRST	−.021	.001	−.108	−.621	−.002	.005	.067	.115	−.024	−.005
HLAST	.007	.002	−.042	−.563	−.043	−.011	.068	.172	.068	.058
NETGROWTH	.013	.002	.193	−.062	−.080	.159	.156	.127	.112	−.359

APPENDIX 3.C. Zero-Order Correlation Matrix

	OUTMIG	ORG	WFIRST	WLAST	HFIRST	HLAST	NETGRO
%OUTMIG	1.000						
ORG	−.010	1.000					
WFIRST	.014	.069	1.000				
WLAST	.004	.180	.458	1.000			
HFIRST	−.006	.068	.796	.391	1.000		
HLAST	−.010	.166	.407	.880	.633	1.000	
NETGROWTH	−.099	.174	−.124	.485	−.102	.403	1.000

FOUR

A Comparison of Lineage Populations in South China, ca. 1300–1900

Liu Ts'ui-jung

INTRODUCTION

Chinese genealogies are indispensable, though not the only, source materials for the study of Chinese historical demography. There are thousands of genealogies kept in the world's major Chinese-language library collections; these genealogies belonged to lineages residing in various parts of China, but mostly in the southern provinces. Some genealogies are voluminous, containing records of many branches of a lineage; some are rather small and record only descendants of a single line. Whether a genealogy is useful for the study of historical demography depends on its completeness in recording vital dates of persons involved. Earlier preliminary studies have told us that a genealogy that provides birth dates for about 80% of the people recorded and death dates for about 50% can be quite useful in estimating the fertility and mortality rates of its subject population.

This paper presents vital statistics taken from five lineage genealogies. The five lineages are the Jiangdu Zhu in Jiangsu, the Tongcheng Zhao in Anhui, the Wuchang Xu in Hubei, the Shaoyang Li in Hunan, and the Xiangshan Mai in Guangdong. These lineages were chosen primarily because of the relative completeness of the vital data they record. Moreover, these genealogies all recorded multiple lineage branches, and they each came from a different province. They could thus serve for comparison across branches in a lineage, as well as for interprovincial comparison. This chapter is mainly concerned with demographic characteristics related to fertility and mortality in these five lineage populations. In some cases, data are arranged by birth cohorts so that changes through time can be examined. This chapter shows that demographic trends demonstrated in these genealogies can be interpreted in terms of the general social and economic conditions of the provinces studied.

FERTILITY

When we use the vital records from a Chinese genealogy to estimate fertility, we have to keep in mind that there are some defects that certainly make the results only approximate, not exact. The first of these defects, the almost total lack of birth dates for daughters of the lineages, requires that fertility be estimated from recorded male births only. Even in the case of male births, those who died young were usually recorded without vital data or not at all. Since Chinese genealogies did not all follow the same rules in recording sons who died young, and were often not even internally consistent in this regard (though in general those who died within three months of birth were not recorded at all), it is rather difficult to estimate a specific percentage of underrecording (Liu Ts'ui-jung 1978:867). The problem of missing birth dates can be ameliorated to some extent by the process of family reconstitution, through which parents and children of a conjugal family are brought together with their vital dates in order to trace the parents' ages at the birth of each child. Family reconstitution is an important method that was developed by European historical demographers for the study of parish registers (Henry 1967:78–105; Wrigley 1966:96–159). In applying the family reconstitution method to Chinese genealogical data, however, we can only use male births. If a son's date of birth is missing, it can be interpolated or extrapolated with the help of his brothers' birth dates, if these are available (Liu 1978:857–60; 1983:284–86). Yet we still have to note that those not recorded at all are beyond our observation, and we do not attempt to adjust our estimates to account for them.

Moreover, because the recorded cases do not include those persons who were at reproductive ages but were not married, the genealogical data are not suitable for estimating the general fertility rate. The genealogical data may be used to estimate the marital fertility rate, but even within this limitation, there are still defects to be overcome. First, that Chinese genealogies did not record dates of marriage makes it difficult to determine the starting point of the time unit used to calculate marital fertility. Moreover, not every death date is recorded. The lack of death dates, in turn, makes it rather difficult to decide the terminus of the at-risk period in calculating marital fertility. Thus, if we begin the at-risk period with the youngest age group at which a male birth was recorded (fifteen to nineteen for a woman or even twenty to twenty-four for a man), then the marital fertility estimates for the lowest age group will be too low, since not everyone in the recorded population was married at those young ages. Moreover, if the observation ends with the birth of the last son (at least for those whose end of marriage cannot be dated precisely), then the estimates of marital fertility in the higher age groups will be too high, especially when there are many cases for which the end date is unknown. Here we can look at the Jiangdu Zhu lineage as an example.

In Table 4.1, three sets of male-based fertility rates are listed for this lineage. There were 1739 conjugal families reconstituted from the Zhu genealogy, with husbands' birth dates ranging from 1517 to 1877. Among these 1739 families, only 813 had a known date of end of marriage. In the first panel of Table 4.1, the husbands with unknown dates of end of marriage were distributed according to the age at birth of the last son, and thus the number remaining at each age group was derived by subtracting both the number with a known date of end of marriage in that interval *and* the number whose last son was born when they were at the age in question from the number remaining at the end of the previous age interval. For example, at age 15–19, the number remaining in observation was $1739 - 0 - 1 = 1738$. In the second panel, only the cases with a known date of end of marriage were subtracted for each age interval, and the cases with an unknown date of end of marriage were assumed to have remained married until age sixty. In the third panel, proportions of cases with the end of marriage date known were used to distribute the cases with end of marriage unknown into each age group, and the number remaining was calculated by subtracting both the known and unknown cases from the number remaining at the end of the previous age interval. For example, at age 20–24, $1739 - 1 - 1 = 1737$. After the number of fathers remaining in each age interval is calculated, the number of person-years may be calculated by multiplying the number of fathers remaining by five. The age-specific fertility may then be computed by dividing the number of sons born in each age interval by the number of person-years lived in that same interval. The age-specific fertility rate calculated in this way indicates the average number of sons born per father per year in a particular age interval. Thus the total fertility of male births (the average number of sons per father) can be calculated by a summation of age-specific fertility rates times five. In Table 4.1, the total fertility rate of husbands was calculated either by including all age groups or by using only age groups from twenty to fifty-nine. The former figure does not represent marital fertility in a strict sense, since not everyone was married in the early ages of this range; for this reason the latter figure may be preferable, though even it is not precise.

In Table 4.1, the three sets of estimates derived using the different calculation methods described above yield estimates of total male fertility of husbands (average number of sons per father) from ages twenty to fifty-nine as 2.74, 2.03, and 2.13. The first estimate is highest because a larger number of husbands are excluded from observation after their last

TABLE 4.1. Male-Based Fertility Rates, Zhu Lineage

Panel 1

		N Fathers				
Age	N Sons (N = 3553)	End of Marriage (N = 813)	Birth of Last Son (N = 926)	Remaining (N = 1739)	Person-Years	Age-Specific Fertility
10–14	3	0	1	1739	8695	0.0003
15–19	133	1	31	1738	8690	0.0153
20–24	569	7	93	1706	8530	0.0667
25–29	799	13	165	1606	8030	0.0995
30–34	775	39	184	1428	7140	0.1085
35–39	636	68	216	1205	6025	0.1056
40–44	381	107	135	921	4605	0.0827
45–49	172	109	71	679	3395	0.0507
50–54	49	120	15	499	2495	0.0196
55–59	27	141	9	364	1820	0.0148
60+	9	208	6	214	1070	0.0084
Total fertility, ages 10–60+						2.86
Total fertility, ages 20–59						2.74

Panel 2

		N Fathers			
Age	N Sons (N = 3553)	End of Marriage (N = 813)	Remaining (N = 1739)	Person-Years	Age-Specific Fertility
10–14	3	0	1739	8695	0.0003
15–19	133	1	1739	8695	0.0153
20–24	569	7	1738	8690	0.0655
25–29	799	13	1731	8655	0.0923
30–34	775	39	1718	8590	0.0902
35–39	636	68	1679	8395	0.0758
40–44	381	107	1611	8055	0.0473
45–49	172	109	1504	7520	0.0229
50–54	49	120	1395	6975	0.0070
55–59	27	141	1275	6375	0.0042
60+	9	208	1134	5670	0.0016
Total fertility, ages 10–60+					2.11
Total fertility, ages 20–59					2.03

(*continued*)

TABLE 4.1. (*continued*)

Panel 3

| Age | N Sons (N = 3553) | N Fathers | | | Person-Years | Age-Specific Fertility |
		End of Marriage (N = 813)	Cases Unknown (N = 925)	Remaining (N = 1739)		
10–14	3	0	0	1739	8695	0.0003
15–19	133	1	1	1739	8695	0.0153
20–24	569	7	8	1737	8684	0.0655
25–29	799	13	15	1722	8609	0.0928
30–34	775	39	44	1694	8471	0.0915
35–39	636	68	77	1611	8054	0.0790
40–44	381	107	102	1466	7330	0.0519
45–49	172	109	124	1257	6285	0.0274
50–54	49	120	137	1024	5120	0.0096
55–59	27	141	161	767	3835	0.0070
60+	9	208	237	465	2325	0.0039
Total fertility, ages 10–60+						2.2221
Total fertility, ages 20–59						2.1235

sons were born, and this exclusion causes the estimates of age-specific fertility from ages thirty upwards to be much higher than those derived using the other two methods of calculation. It is also notable that the difference between the second and third estimates is almost negligible. Moreover, even with a difference of about 0.6 between the high and low estimates, all methods of calculation yield estimates that show a rather low total fertility rate for the men of the Jiangdu Zhu lineage.

Calculated by means of the first method discussed above, the fertility of husbands and consorts (including both wives and concubines) of the five lineages are listed in Table 4.2. A few points should be noted here. The data used to calculate the estimates in Table 4.2 cover a wide time period, as indicated by the birth years of fathers (i.e., husbands) listed right below the name of each lineage. Thus these estimates provide us only a rough idea of the levels of fertility and do not indicate changes through time. There are a larger number of mothers than fathers, since many men remarried or took concubines. But it should also be noted that the total numbers of sons used to calculate the number of sons per father were not the same as the totals used to calculate sons per mother, since mothers whose vital dates were not available were not included in the calculation.

The age-specific fertility rates are estimated with male births only, but the total fertility rate is estimated including both sons and daughters on the

TABLE 4.2. Fertility of Husbands and Consorts, by Lineage

	Jiangdu Zhu	Tongcheng Zhao	Wuchang Xu	Shaoyang Li	Xiangshan Mai
		Husbands			
Birth years					
of father	1517–1877	1462–1864	1627–1912	1296–1864	1435–1869
N fathers	1739	1620	1611	2626	1791
N sons	3553	3871	3615	6284	4024
Age-specific fertility rate (male births)					
10–14	0.0003	0.0010	0.0002	0.0011	0.0009
15–19	0.0153	0.0250	0.0113	0.0217	0.0065
20–24	0.0667	0.0800	0.0741	0.0760	0.0689
25–29	0.0995	0.1068	0.1132	0.1065	0.1007
30–34	0.1085	0.1198	0.1220	0.1121	0.1037
35–39	0.1056	0.1159	0.1135	0.1098	0.0911
40–44	0.0827	0.0810	0.0797	0.0788	0.0746
45–49	0.0507	0.0476	0.0444	0.0519	0.0440
50–54	0.0196	0.0184	0.0202	0.0280	0.0309
55–59	0.0148	0.0123	0.0100	0.0106	0.0210
60+	0.0084	0.0038	0.0039	0.0080	0.0180
Total fertility rate (male births)					
10–60+	2.8612	3.0580	2.9627	3.0229	2.8018
20–59	2.7409	2.9091	2.8854	2.8689	2.6752
Total fertility rate (both sexes, sex ratio = 105)					
10–60+	5.8655	6.2689	6.0735	6.1969	5.7437
20–59	5.6188	5.9637	5.9151	5.8812	5.4842
		Consorts (Wives and Concubines)			
N mothers	1784	1654	1625	2670	1917
N sons	3518	3861	3612	6274	3884
Age-specific fertility rate (male births)					
10–14	0.0021	0.0019	0.0012	0.0020	0.0017
15–19	0.0298	0.0472	0.0289	0.0434	0.0222
20–24	0.0964	0.1152	0.1124	0.1163	0.1087
25–29	0.1176	0.1297	0.1293	0.1348	0.1251
30–34	0.1200	0.1300	0.1271	0.1255	0.1061
35–39	0.1170	0.1078	0.1115	0.0991	0.0820
40–44	0.0703	0.0567	0.0704	0.0567	0.0427
45–49	0.0150	0.0096	0.0132	0.0086	0.0059
Total fertility rate (male births)					
10–49	2.8404	2.9902	2.9698	2.9317	2.4728
15–49	2.8297	2.9805	2.9637	2.9216	2.4645
Total fertility rate (both sexes, sex ratio = 105)					
10–49	5.8228	6.1299	6.0881	6.0100	5.0692
15–49	5.8009	6.1100	6.0756	5.9893	5.0522

assumption that the sex ratio at birth is the human norm of 105, the same assumption made by Telford in chapter 3. These estimates show that the total fertility in these lineage populations over a long period averaged around six children per family. It is notable that there was not a great difference between the fertility rates of husbands and of consorts, except in the Xiangshan Mai lineage, which had a considerably larger number of consorts than husbands. This finding confirms my earlier finding (Liu Ts'ui-jung 1983:301) that women married into elite families, where concubines were more common, had lower fertility than women married monogamously.

Following the first method described above, but with the slight difference that age ten to fourteen was not included in the estimation, a previous study of mine used data on conjugal families from fifteen lineage genealogies from Jiangsu, Zhejiang, Anhui, Hubei, and Hunan to estimate age-specific fertility and total fertility rates in terms of male births. This study found that the pattern of age-specific fertility was quite similar among the fifteen lineages studied (Liu Ts'ui-jung 1983:295–301). When fertility rates were plotted against the age of parent, a lopsided bell-shaped curve emerged, revealing a pattern of natural fertility, in which there was no apparent use of birth-limitation methods to cause any sharp fertility decline after the peak. For the husband, the peak of fertility occurred at ages twenty-five to thirty-four; for the first wife, the peak was at ages twenty to twenty-nine. Moreover, the husband's curve was somewhat flatter and wider than that of the first wife, since his reproductive period was longer. The total number of sons averaged from 2.24 to 2.92 for the husband, and from 2.18 to 2.95 for the first wife. These figures could be augmented to account for births of both sexes (again assuming a sex ratio at birth of 105), in which case the figures would be 4.59 to 5.99 for the husband and 4.47 to 6.05 for the first wife. It is notable that lineages in Jiangsu (the Jiangdu Zhu lineage was not included in that earlier study) were at the lower extreme, those in Hunan were at the upper, and those from Zhejiang, Anhui, and Hubei fell in between. If the lower estimate of Jiangdu Zhu fertility from Table 4.1 is used, it fits in with the other Jiangsu lineages studied earlier. Reasons for the difference in fertility between Jiangsu and Hunan lineages are discussed below.

One might argue that a total fertility of less than three sons, or about six children per conjugal family, seems too low for a traditional society such as Ming-Qing China. Of course, some of the aforementioned defects in genealogical recording might cause underestimates. The above estimates were derived from age-specific fertility rates, which required the data from each conjugal family to include quite complete vital dates for each member, and those families with no sons were not included in the observation. If the requirement for complete vital dates is relaxed somewhat—if only the birth

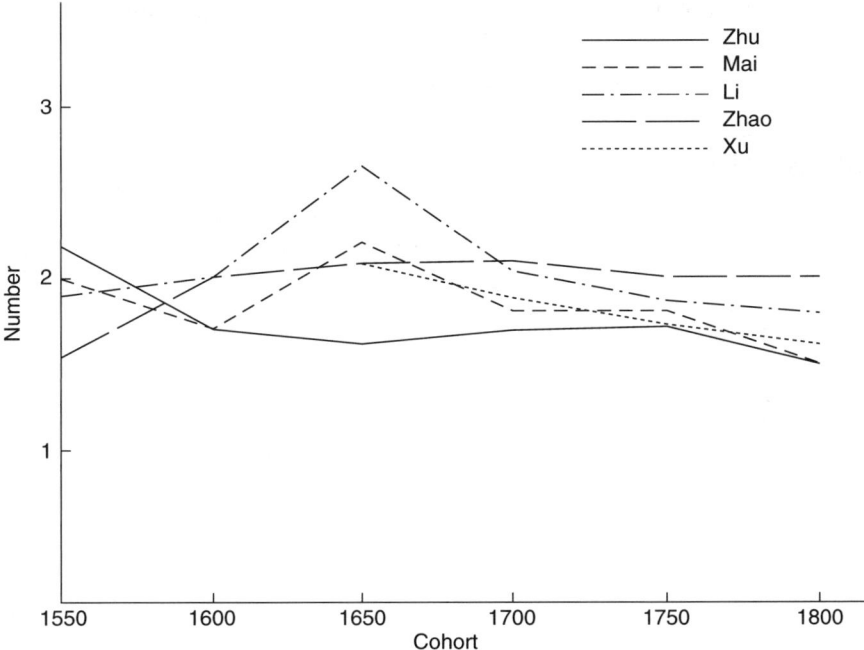

Figure 4.1. Average Number of Sons per Family

date of the father is required—then more conjugal families can be taken into observation, and total fertility can be estimated simply in terms of average number of sons per father, without going through the intermediate step of calculating age-specific fertility rates. Calculated in this way, the average number of sons per family was even lower than the estimate calculated on the basis of families with complete records only. This outcome can be seen from Table 4.3, in which the same five lineages used in Table 4.2 are taken as examples. In this table, the observed data are first arranged according to birth cohorts of fathers into six fifty-year cohorts from 1548 to 1847. The ten rows of the table are self-explanatory, except for row nine, which counts each remarriage once. Thus, for example a man who had three wives would be counted as two remarriages.

From Table 4.3 we may observe several facts. First, the average number of sons per family (i.e., per father) is calculated by using all the sons recorded under each father, including those who were recorded as having died young. With the help of Figure 4.1, we can see clearly that the estimates of the average number of sons per father ranged around about two, with the exception of the 1648–1697 cohort, where wide differences appeared among the lineages, particularly between the Shaoyang Li and Jiangdu Zhu

TABLE 4.3. Numbers of Sons, by Cohorts of Fathers

	1500 Cohorts (b. 1548–1597)					1600 Cohorts (b. 1598–1647)				
	Zhu	Zhao	Xu	Li	Mai	Zhu	Zhao	Xu	Li	Mai
(1) Parity of father										
n = 0	7	24	0	5	5	55	4	0	20	14
n = 1	21	32	1	48	7	71	24	1	45	18
n = 2	29	20	–	23	11	57	16	1	38	20
n = 3	12	9	–	19	8	38	8	0	21	5
n = 4	10	2	–	9	4	22	5	0	12	5
n = 5	5	2	–	1	1	7	2	1	3	3
n = 6	3	3	–	1	–	1	0	–	4	1
n = 7	–	1	–	–	–	–	0	–	3	–
n = 8	–	–	–	–	–	–	0	–	–	–
n = 9	–	–	–	–	–	–	1	–	–	–
n = 10	–	–	–	–	–	–	–	–	–	–
n = 11	–	–	–	–	–	–	–	–	–	–
(2) Total no. of sons	198	142	1	202	74	428	119	8	292	114
(3) No. of sons died young	0	0	0	8	1	15	3	0	2	0
(4) Total no. of fathers	87	93	1	106	36	251	60	3	146	66
(5) Total no. of consorts	118	99	2	114	48	292	73	4	155	86
(6) Average no. of sons per father = (2)/(4)	2.3	1.5	1.0	1.9	2.1	1.7	2.0	2.7	2.0	1.7
(7) Average no. of sons per consort = (2)/(5)	1.7	1.4	0.5	1.8	1.5	1.5	1.6	2.0	1.9	1.3
(8) % of sons died young = (3)/(2) × 100	0	0	0	4.0	1.3	3.5	2.5	0	0.7	0
(9) % of remarried men = [(5) − (4)]/(4) × 100	31.1	6.5	n.a.	7.5	33.3	16.3	21.7	n.a.	6.2	30.3
(10) % of heirless father = (n = 0)/(4) × 100	7.8	25.8	0	4.7	13.8	21.9	6.7	0	13.7	21.2

(*continued*)

TABLE 4.3. (*continued*)

	1650 Cohorts (b. 1648–1697)					1700 Cohorts (b. 1698–1747)				
	Zhu	Zhao	Xu	Li	Mai	Zhu	Zhao	Xu	Li	Mai
(1) Parity of father										
n = 0	55	22	20	28	28	71	63	63	125	96
n = 1	131	52	36	49	39	152	121	89	149	126
n = 2	91	49	36	61	43	129	126	75	172	107
n = 3	38	31	30	65	30	62	87	63	124	66
n = 4	15	24	19	52	18	22	39	34	69	43
n = 5	7	8	4	26	8	8	21	13	30	10
n = 6	4	3	3	9	5	1	7	2	13	5
n = 7	1	1	–	3	1	1	2	1	5	2
n = 8	–	–	–	–	0	–	0	–	–	1
n = 9	–	–	–	–	1	–	1	–	–	1
n = 10	–	–	–	–	–	–	–	–	–	–
n = 11	–	–	–	–	–	–	–	–	–	–
(2) Total no. of sons	553	404	312	779	373	737	960	648	1404	821
(3) No. of sons died young	7	7	0	12	6	14	27	3	43	18
(4) Total no. of fathers	342	190	148	293	173	446	467	340	687	457
(5) Total no. of consorts	396	224	156	311	235	498	514	357	736	596
(6) Average no. of sons per father = (2)/(4)	1.6	2.1	2.1	2.7	2.2	1.6	2.1	1.9	2.0	1.8
(7) Average no. of sons per consort = (2)/(5)	1.4	1.8	2.0	2.5	1.6	1.5	1.9	1.8	1.9	1.4
(8) % of sons died young = (3)/(2) × 100	1.3	1.7	0	1.5	1.6	1.9	2.8	0.5	3.1	2.2
(9) % of remarried men = [(7) − (4)]/(4) × 100	15.8	17.9	5.4	6.1	35.8	11.7	10.1	5.0	7.1	30.4
(10) % of heirless father = (n = 0)/(4) × 100	16.1	11.6	13.5	9.6	16.2	15.9	13.5	18.5	18.2	21.0

(*continued*)

TABLE 4.3. (*continued*)

	1750 Cohorts (b. 1748–1797)					1800 Cohorts (b. 1798–1847)				
	Zhu	Zhao	Xu	Li	Mai	Zhu	Zhao	Xu	Li	Mai
(1) Parity of father										
n = 0	112	163	134	169	157	187	214	186	224	299
n = 1	223	216	152	220	209	336	243	197	243	268
n = 2	163	179	148	118	185	198	193	157	173	199
n = 3	112	125	83	122	129	110	156	90	145	109
n = 4	35	75	40	81	60	45	88	52	90	45
n = 5	3	48	26	28	24	11	46	17	34	27
n = 6	0	20	2	11	10	4	19	4	10	13
n = 7	1	7	1	7	3	–	10	2	5	2
n = 8	–	–	1	–	3	–	8	4	0	1
n = 9	–	–	0	–	0	–	1	–	1	–
n = 10	–	–	1	–	0	–	–	–	–	–
n = 11	–	–	–	–	1	–	–	–	–	–
(2) Total no. of sons	1647	1658	1024	1401	1442	1321	1936	1144	1658	1408
(3) No. of sons died young	21	200	7	41	97	21	393	51	92	127
(4) Total no. of fathers	664	841	588	807	781	891	978	709	925	963
(5) Total no. of consorts	740	961	630	888	973	991	1142	792	1057	1180
(6) Average no. of sons per father = (2)/(4)	1.7	2.0	1.7	1.9	1.8	1.5	2.0	1.6	1.8	1.5
(7) Average no. of sons per consort = (2)/(5)	1.5	1.7	1.6	1.7	1.5	1.3	1.7	1.4	1.6	1.2
(8) % of sons died young = (3)/(2) × 100	1.9	12.1	0.7	2.7	6.7	1.6	20.3	4.5	5.5	9.0
(9) % of remarried men = [(7) − (4)]/(4) × 100	11.4	14.3	7.1	10.0	24.6	11.2	16.8	11.7	14.3	22.5
(10) % of heirless father = (n = 0)/(4) × 100	16.9	19.4	22.8	20.9	20.1	21.0	21.9	26.2	24.2	31.0

(*continued*)

TABLE 4.3. (continued)

	Total				
	Zhu	Zhao	Xu	Li	Mai
(1) Parity of father					
n = 0	487	490	403	571	597
n = 1	937	688	475	1129	667
n = 2	667	583	417	636	565
n = 3	372	416	266	496	347
n = 4	149	233	145	313	175
n = 5	41	127	61	122	73
n = 6	13	52	13	48	34
n = 7	3	21	4	23	8
n = 8	–	8	5	0	4
n = 9	–	3	0	1	2
n = 10	–	–	1	–	0
n = 11	–	–	–	–	1
(2) Total no. of sons	4287	5219	3148	6209	4224
(3) No. of sons died young	78	630	61	198	249
(4) Total no. of fathers	2669	2621	1790	2964	2473
(5) Total no. of consorts	3035	3013	1941	3261	3118
(6) Average no. of sons per father $= (2)/(4)$	1.6	2.0	1.8	2.0	1.7
(7) Average no. of sons per consort $= (2)/(5)$	1.4	1.7	1.6	1.8	1.3
(8) % of sons died young $= (3)/(2) \times 100$	1.8	12.1	1.9	3.2	5.9
(9) % of remarried men $= [(7) - (4)]/(4) \times 100$	13.7	15.0	8.4	10.0	26.1
(10) % of heirless father $= (n = 0)/(4) \times 100$	18.2	18.7	22.5	17.1	24.1

lineages. These variations can be explained in terms of the different situations that these two areas encountered after the crisis of the Ming-Qing dynastic transition (Perkins 1969:24). The sparsely populated river basins in Hunan, such as the Zi River basin, where Shaoyang is located, had more favorable conditions for population recovery than the already densely populated Lower Yangzi River area where Jiangdu is located. Although the official population registers should not be taken as accurate (see Ho 1959, 3:97; Skinner 1987), we can still use the available statistics to give a general idea of relative population density in these two areas. According to these figures, the population density in Jiangsu in 1685 was 26.89 persons per square kilometer; in Hunan it was 1.36. In 1820, Yangzhou prefecture, of which Jiangdu is a constituent county, had 201.69 persons per square kilometer, while Baoqing prefecture, the site of Shaoyang, had only 78.46 (Liang Fanzhong 1980:272–76). This comparison at least indicates that Shaoyang was much more sparsely populated than Jiangdu. Moreover, in Shaoyang, "where the Zi River flows through a broad valley, cultivated land was relatively abundant" (Perdue 1987:46).

Second, we can see variation among the lineages. Except for the 1548–1597 cohort, the Jiangdu Zhu lineage had the lowest average number of sons per father, around 1.5–1.7. Beginning with the 1598–1647 cohort, the estimates of sons per father for the Tongcheng Zhao remained quite stable at 2.0–2.1. The estimates for the Wuchang Xu decline from 2.1 for the 1648–1697 cohort to 1.6 for the 1798–1847 cohort. (The 1548–1597 and 1598–1647 cohorts for this lineage can be ignored, as there were too few families in the population.) The estimates for the Shaoyang Li first increased from 1.9 to 2.7 and then decreased to 1.8; the peak came with the 1648–1697 cohorts. Finally, the Xiangshan Mai followed a zigzag pattern. Their averages were not the lowest and remained stable at 1.8 for the 1698–1747 and 1748–1797 cohorts. In spite of these variations, it is quite clear that the cohorts belonging to the eighteenth century (born 1698–1797) had quite stable total fertility, whereas those born in the nineteenth century (1798–1847) showed a declining average number of sons. This fits with observations about the general trends in fertility found in other articles in this volume.

Third, because some men remarried or took concubines, there were more consorts than husbands. Thus, estimates of the average number of sons per mother were proportionately lower than those of average number of sons per father. The higher the percentage of remarriage, the lower the average number of sons per mother, if the average number of sons per father stays constant. As previously noted, the Xiangshan Mai lineage was particularly noteworthy in this respect, since its members had a larger number of consorts.

Fourth, it is difficult to discern trends in the number and percentage of sons who died young, as well as in percentages of men who remarried. The number of sons who died young were mostly underrecorded in the genealogies, as can be seen from Table 4.3. An exception was the 1798–1847 cohort of the Tongcheng Zhao lineage, in which the sons who died young accounted for about 20%. The percentage of remarriage varied widely among cohorts and lineages. There seems to be no absolute positive correlation between a higher average number of sons per father and a higher rate of remarriage. For example, the 1648–1697 cohort of the Shaoyang Li lineage had the highest estimated number of sons per father, but their remarriage rate was not the highest. However, a regression analysis using the fertility ratio (the number of sons per father divided by the number of sons

TABLE 4.4. Parity Progression Ratios (a_x)

	Zhu	Zhao	Xu	Li	Mai
a0	.818	.813	.775	.829	.759
a1	.571	.677	.658	.592	.644
a2	.464	.596	.543	.621	.533
a3	.356	.516	.463	.505	.461
a4	.277	.475	.367	.383	.411
a5	.281	.398	.274	.371	.402
a6	.188	.381	.435	.333	.306
a7	–	.344	.600	.042	.467
a8	–	.273	.167	1.000	.429
a9	–	–	1.000	–	.333
a10	–	–	–	–	1.000

NOTE: For methods of calculating parity progression ratios and distribution of family size, see Roland Pressat 1972, 219–22. In this table, the calculations are done in terms of male births only.

per mother) as the dependent variable and the average number of consorts per husband as the independent variable for data from fifty different families and lineages confirmed that the remarriage of husbands could explain about 67% of the fertility differences between the husband and the consort (Liu Ts'ui-jung 1992:7).

Fifth, from the estimates of the percentage of heirless fathers (those who had daughters or had unrecorded sons who died young but whose genealogy entries recorded no sons) it is notable that of the men born in the eighteenth and early nineteenth centuries, about one-fifth to one-fourth were heirless, and the percentage of heirless fathers seemed to be increasing. The mean percentage of sonless fathers calculated by Telford for a large number of Tongcheng lineages in 1520–1661 was 17.12% (see Table 3.2). If we look at Table 4.5, we can see that the percentage of sonless fathers (zero sons) ranged from 17.1% to 24.1% among the five lineages investigated. These numbers suggest that the records of sonlessness in the five genealogies studied here are as complete as those used by Telford; the rates are remarkably consistent.

The frequency distribution of the number of sons listed in the first row of Table 4.3 can be used to calculate parity progression ratios and distribution of family size by number of male births, as shown in Tables 4.4 and 4.5, respectively. The calculation of parity progression ratios provides us with an easier way to understand the manner in which different family sizes are distributed (Pressat 1972:219–24). The term parity refers here to the number of sons born to a particular father. This distribution of family size calculated from the parity progression ratios of male births reveals that

TABLE 4.5. Distribution of Family Sizes

Parity	No. of sons per 1000 fathers				
	Zhu	Zhao	Xu	Li	Mai
0	182	187	225	171	241
1	351	263	265	338	270
2	250	222	233	191	228
3	140	159	149	148	141
4	56	89	81	94	71
5	15	48	34	36	29
6	5	20	7	15	14
7	1	8	3	6.7	3
8	–	3	2.4	0	2
9	–	1	0	0.3	0
10	–	–	0.6	–	0
11	–	–	–	–	1

NOTE: See footnote in Table 4.4.

there were only a small number of fathers who had three sons: 140 of every 1000 in the Jiangdu Zhu, 159 in the Tongcheng Zhao, 149 in the Wuchang Xu, 148 in the Shaoyang Li, and 141 in the Xiangshan Mai lineages (see Table 4.5). Those who had four or more sons were even fewer. There was one man who had eleven sons in the Mai lineage, but he was obviously an exceptional case. In general, high-birth-order sons were quite rare. This distribution of family size based on number of sons born also gives us some hints about family structure, which is analyzed in more detail in chapter 5.

MORTALITY

Mortality can be estimated by using data on persons for whom both birth and death dates are recorded in the genealogies. There are, of course, omissions in genealogical records that make it rather difficult to study the mortality of lineage populations in a satisfactory way. The most serious problem here is the aforementioned complete lack of records of infant deaths (but see Lee in chapter 7 for the Imperial lineage, which is a dramatic exception in this regard). Thus it is almost impossible to investigate infant mortality directly from the genealogical records. Moreover, vital dates, especially death dates, are usually not given for those who died young and unmarried. That very few deaths below age fifteen are recorded (although there are some), in turn, makes it somewhat difficult to estimate the mortality below age fifteen or even twenty directly from genealogical data. Even when both birth and death dates are given, we usually have death dates for only about half the males recorded in a relatively complete genealogy. As for the female population, estimates can only be made for consorts, and the available records of their deaths are often less complete than those for men. Despite these shortcomings, however, genealogical data can still tell us something about mortality in lineage populations.

By taking a certain birth cohort with recorded ages at death, distributing it into five-year age groups, and constructing a life table, which shows the mortality chances in a population at different ages, we can investigate the mortality of a lineage population. The first life tables of a Guangdong lineage were constructed about sixty years ago by Yuan I-chin (1931). In the past few years, I have also constructed life tables for lineage populations in Jiangsu, Zhejiang, Anhui, Jiangxi, Hubei, Hunan, and Guangdong Provinces. My findings about the mortality of these southern lineage populations, based on these life tables, can be summarized as follows: (1) women had a higher life expectancy than men, (2) mortality levels differed slightly among lineages, and (3) mortality appeared to be increasing during the late eighteenth and early nineteenth centuries (Liu Ts'ui-jung 1981, 1985, 1986, 1987, 1989b).

In this paper, the five lineages whose fertility patterns are analyzed above will also be examined for their mortality patterns; for this purpose the lineages are divided into their constituent branches (*fang*). The observed numbers of male deaths in each branch are listed in Table 4.6. The frequency distribution of deaths is arranged in five-year age groups from 15–19 to 80+. At the bottom of Table 4.6, mean age at death and median age at death, calculated from each set of grouped data, are also listed. The results demonstrate that even within a lineage, mortality differed slightly among branches, although the order of magnitude was about the same. Moreover, a comparison of the five lineages shows that the Shaoyang Li lineage had a higher age at death than the others.

With the data from Table 4.6, a life table can be constructed for each branch. The values of graduated q_x (the probability of dying at age x) and e_x (the life expectancy at age x) are listed in Tables 4.7 and 4.8, respectively. The graduated values of q_x are reported here because they are derived from the observed values of q_x that are calculated from the observed number of deaths listed in Table 4.6. In addition, the values of R^2 are very high, indicating that the graduated values of q_x are very close to those of observed q_x. In Figure 4.2, the curves of q_x for some branches are depicted against those of Coale and Demeny model life tables[1] for purposes of comparison.

The comparisons with the model life tables in Figure 4.2 reveal several observations about the mortality of these southern lineage populations. First, the Shaoyang Li lineage in Hunan had the lowest mortality among the five lineages. Its mortality level was comparable with Model West Level 8 (life expectancy at birth = 34.89). Above age forty-five, the mortality rates of the

TABLE 4.6. Mortality Patterns of Lineage Males, by Age

Age	Jiangdu Zhu					Tongcheng Zhao		Wuchang Xu			
	I	II	III	IV	V	I	II	I	II	III	IV
15–19	5	3	11	6	3	12	56	11	5	14	19
20–24	10	5	12	8	7	15	56	20	11	22	34
25–29	13	11	16	10	8	31	70	27	15	29	34
30–34	22	8	17	9	12	23	98	24	17	32	48
35–39	22	13	21	23	22	28	105	31	22	42	54
40–44	21	21	38	23	36	41	131	31	19	48	65
45–49	24	21	29	22	30	56	143	41	21	45	68
50–54	25	22	50	18	39	53	157	27	22	59	62
55–59	32	33	45	27	38	56	165	44	19	45	66
60–64	26	16	38	22	38	38	149	38	23	44	70
65–69	25	13	22	12	20	46	111	30	19	47	63
70–74	10	5	20	5	14	39	81	24	19	29	53
75–79	11	9	6	7	9	21	65	13	5	23	25
80+	6	2	5	0	2	18	45	14	9	13	22
Total	252	182	330	192	278	477	1432	375	226	492	683
Mean age at death	50.29	50.41	49.95	48.07	51.45	52.07	50.44	49.86	50.08	50.18	50.67
Median age at death	50.80	51.05	51.10	47.86	51.69	52.07	50.82	49.46	49.68	50.19	50.57

NOTE: Name and span of observed birth years of each branch:
  Zhu I: Xingyi, b. 1563–1847
  II: Xinger, b. 1558–1846
  III: Xingsi, b. 1514–1852
  IV: Xingliu, b. 1582–1850
  V: Xingba, b. 1517–1909
  Zhao I: Dazong, b. 1462–1862
  II: Xiaozong, b. 1465–1849
  Xu I: Yingqi, b. 1673–1871
  II: Yinglin, b. 1663–1872
  III: Yingzhu, b. 1593–1897
  IV: Yingfeng, b. 1639–1907

TABLE 4.6. (continued)

Age	Shaoyang Li						Xiangshan Mai				
	I	II	III	IV	V	VI	I	II	III	IV	V
15–19	2	4	12	5	5	0	30	36	13	15	12
20–24	12	13	32	12	5	5	47	82	22	29	16
25–29	11	11	37	15	7	5	58	81	28	20	33
30–34	14	11	42	22	10	8	32	73	21	26	30
35–39	22	9	54	31	13	7	44	74	22	24	40
40–44	30	11	67	21	20	9	63	103	22	20	29
45–49	39	23	94	32	17	14	61	105	20	22	35
50–54	40	19	91	44	13	14	48	85	22	34	39
55–59	37	20	106	41	31	14	81	84	24	20	35
60–64	51	19	125	69	39	24	43	75	30	35	22
65–69	49	20	100	59	23	25	49	73	19	23	32
70–74	57	19	100	48	25	23	39	47	19	23	17
75–79	29	15	78	31	11	19	39	48	13	13	13
80+	16	12	65	37	9	19	28	36	14	9	12
Total	409	206	1003	467	228	186	662	1002	289	313	365
Mean age at death	56.92	53.73	56.27	57.46	55.43	60.32	49.14	47.73	48.49	48.14	48.02
Median age at death	58.66	54.50	57.42	59.76	57.87	62.54	48.67	46.48	48.13	49.07	47.21

NOTE: Name and span of observed birth years of each branch:
Li I: Tianrong, b. 1537–1880
  II: Tianhua, b. 1566–1879
  III: Tiangui, b. 1516–1885
  IV: Xingren, b. 1519–1871
  V: Xingyi, b. 1503–1882
  VI: Xingzhi, b. 1511–1874
Mai I: Linhui, b. 1428–1875
  II: Yihung, b. 1457–1873
  III: Defu, b. 1463–1846
  IV: Rushi, b. 1466–1876
  V: Nanpu, b. 1435–1870

TABLE 4.7. Graduated q_x of Lineage Males

Age	Jiangdu Zhu					Tongcheng Zhao			Wuchang Xu			
	I	II	III	IV	V	I	II	I	II	III	IV
15–19	.0266	.0188	.0278	.0297	.0122	.0207	.0354	.0384	.0328	.0338	.0339
20–24	.0373	.0289	.0385	.0418	.0206	.0289	.0453	.0486	.0437	.0441	.0438
25–29	.0516	.0433	.0527	.0581	.0337	.0394	.0580	.0616	.0577	.0575	.0564
30–34	.0705	.0634	.0715	.0798	.0533	.0544	.0741	.0778	.0754	.0745	.0726
35–39	.0950	.0906	.0960	.1082	.0816	.0738	.0945	.0981	.0978	.0961	.0931
40–44	.1262	.1265	.1276	.1447	.1210	.0992	.1203	.1235	.1255	.1235	.1191
45–49	.1656	.1725	.1678	.1912	.1735	.1323	.1530	.1553	.1597	.1580	.1519
50–54	.2142	.2296	.2185	.2493	.2408	.1750	.1941	.1948	.2013	.2012	.1932
55–59	.2735	.2986	.2816	.3209	.3235	.2294	.2460	.2441	.2515	.2552	.2451
60–64	.3444	.3792	.3593	.4078	.4205	.2984	.3112	.3053	.3112	.3222	.3101
65–69	.4279	.4703	.4538	.5116	.5291	.3847	.3930	.3812	.3816	.4050	.3912
70–74	.5245	.5696	.5673	.6335	.6444	.4920	.4956	.4751	.4635	.5070	.4922
75–79	.6343	.6738	.7020	.7745	.7595	.6238	.6239	.5912	.5580	.6318	.6177
80+	1.0000	1.0000	1.0000	1.0000	1.0000	1.0000	1.0000	1.0000	1.0000	1.0000	1.0000
R^2	.9728	.9594	.9772	.9567	.9900	.9686	.9931	.9712	.9479	.9895	.9883

NOTE: For graduation the formula $\log q_x = a + bx + cx^2$ is used. See Yuan I-chin 1931:161.

TABLE 4.7. (continued)

| | Shaoyang Li | | | | | | Xiangshan Mai | | | | |
Age	I	II	III	IV	V	VI	I	II	III	IV	V
15–19	.0099	.0315	.0174	.0155	.0193	—	.0561	.0532	.0643	.0632	.0419
20–24	.0155	.0383	.0240	.0214	.0258	.0256	.0633	.0636	.0700	.0695	.0539
25–29	.0239	.0469	.0330	.0294	.0345	.0309	.0723	.0763	.0784	.0778	.0689
30–34	.0361	.0580	.0450	.0403	.0461	.0380	.0837	.0918	.0890	.0885	.0875
35–39	.0535	.0721	.0610	.0548	.0617	.0476	.0982	.1109	.1027	.1025	.1106
40–44	.0779	.0907	.0823	.0743	.0825	.0606	.1167	.1345	.1202	.1207	.1388
45–49	.1100	.1149	.1105	.1004	.1104	.0786	.1406	.1635	.1428	.1447	.1732
50–54	.1554	.1468	.1473	.1349	.1478	.1036	.1716	.1996	.1722	.1765	.2149
55–59	.2133	.1892	.1954	.1805	.1979	.1391	.2122	.2444	.2107	.2189	.2651
60–64	.2875	.2459	.2576	.2404	.2651	.1900	.2659	.3004	.2617	.2762	.3251
65–69	.3800	.3223	.3378	.3188	.3551	.2641	.3377	.3704	.3299	.3547	.3962
70–74	.4928	.4260	.4405	.4209	.4759	.3735	.4346	.4584	.4221	.4632	.4801
75–79	.6270	.5678	.5710	.5532	.6380	.5377	.5667	.5692	.5480	.6156	.5784
80+	1.0000	1.0000	1.0000	1.0000	1.0000	1.0000	1.0000	1.0000	1.0000	1.0000	1.0000
R^2	.9587	.9453	.9834	.9719	.9721	.9817	.9473	.9544	.9582	.9542	.9511

TABLE 4.8. Life Expectancies (e_x) of Lineage Adult Males

Age	Jiangdu Zhu					Tongcheng Zhao		Wuchang Xu			
	I	II	III	IV	V	I	II	I	II	III	IV
20–24	31.98	32.15	31.62	29.95	32.63	35.01	32.32	31.89	32.04	31.95	32.42
25–29	28.12	28.03	27.78	26.14	28.27	30.97	28.63	28.39	28.39	28.31	28.79
30–34	24.51	24.19	24.19	22.60	24.17	27.14	25.24	25.09	24.98	24.88	25.36
35–39	21.18	20.65	20.86	19.35	20.39	23.56	22.06	22.00	21.81	21.69	22.15
40–44	18.15	17.46	17.81	16.39	16.98	20.24	19.10	19.12	18.91	18.73	19.17
45–49	15.41	14.63	15.05	13.74	13.97	17.19	16.37	16.46	16.26	16.01	16.42
50–54	12.97	12.16	12.58	11.40	11.38	14.43	13.87	14.03	13.88	13.55	13.92
55–59	10.82	10.04	10.40	9.35	9.19	11.96	11.61	11.82	11.74	11.33	11.65
60–64	8.95	8.24	8.49	7.59	7.39	9.78	9.58	9.83	9.85	9.36	9.62
65–69	7.34	6.75	6.85	6.09	5.94	7.87	7.78	8.05	8.17	7.62	7.83
70–74	5.96	5.53	5.47	4.85	4.81	6.23	6.21	6.46	6.66	6.10	6.25
75–79	4.78	4.53	4.36	3.90	4.00	4.85	4.85	5.05	5.26	4.80	4.89
80+	3.74	3.73	3.73	3.73	3.73	3.75	3.74	3.74	3.75	3.74	3.74

NOTE: Life tables are constructed by using q_x of Table 4.7 with $l_x = 10000$ for age 20–24.

TABLE 4.8. (continued)

Age	Shaoyang Li						Xiangshan Mai				
	I	II	III	IV	V	VI	I	II	III	IV	V
20-24	37.86	35.89	37.42	38.67	37.03	40.78	31.96	30.00	31.38	31.11	30.38
25-29	33.41	32.22	33.28	34.46	32.94	36.79	28.95	27.22	28.55	28.25	26.97
30-34	29.17	28.68	29.33	30.43	29.03	32.88	26.01	24.27	25.77	25.42	23.78
35-39	25.17	25.30	25.59	26.60	25.31	29.08	23.16	21.47	23.04	22.65	20.82
40-44	21.45	22.07	22.09	23.00	21.81	25.41	20.41	18.83	20.40	19.95	18.10
45-49	18.05	19.02	18.85	19.64	18.55	21.89	17.77	16.37	17.84	17.35	15.62
50-54	14.97	16.16	15.88	16.55	15.54	18.54	15.27	14.08	15.40	14.86	13.37
55-59	12.27	13.52	13.19	13.75	12.81	15.40	12.92	11.97	13.08	12.51	11.34
60-64	9.91	11.09	10.78	11.22	10.35	12.48	10.72	10.03	10.90	10.31	9.53
65-69	7.91	8.89	8.66	8.98	8.18	9.82	8.70	8.27	8.88	8.29	7.91
70-74	6.22	6.92	6.80	7.02	6.31	7.45	6.86	6.67	7.02	6.47	6.47
75-79	4.83	5.21	5.19	5.30	4.76	5.41	5.21	5.19	5.33	4.90	5.13
80+	3.75	3.76	3.76	3.77	3.75	3.79	3.75	3.74	3.75	3.75	3.74

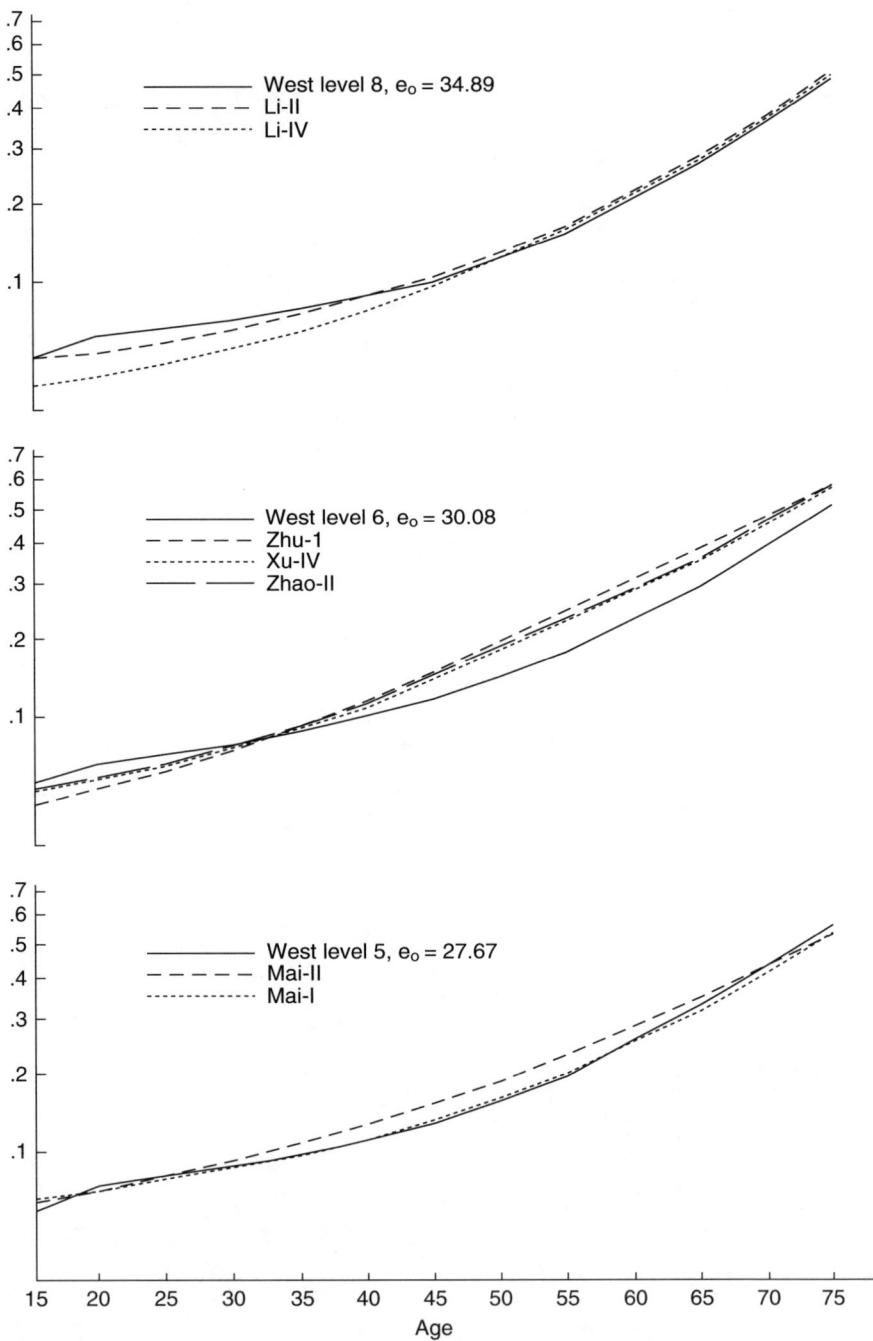

Figure 4.2. Mortality Levels of Lineage Males

model population and the Li lineage appear to be very close to each other; at younger ages, between fifteen and forty-five, the mortality of the Li lineage is somewhat lower than that of the model population. Second, the Xiangshan Mai lineage in Guangdong had the highest mortality of the five lineages. Its mortality level was comparable to the Model West Level 5 (life expectancy at birth = 27.67). In fact, the curve of the Mai-I branch fits perfectly with that of the model population. The Mai-II, however, appears to deviate from the model population between the ages of twenty-five and sixty-five. Third, the Jiangdu Zhu lineage in Jiangsu, the Tongcheng Zhao lineage in Anhui, and the Wuchang Xu lineage in Hubei all appear to have had the same level of mortality. As shown in Figure 4.2, the curves of Zhu-I, Zhao-II, and Xu-IV lay above Model West Level 6 (life expectancy at birth = 30.08) at ages thirty-five and above, whereas below that age the opposite is true. The mortality level of these lineages may also be compared with the Model West Level 5, as we can see from the nearly parallel curves in Figure 4.2.

In short, the above comparisons suggest that the mortality level of the southern lineages presented here was between levels 5 and 8 of the Model West populations. A peculiar difference between the southern lineages and the Model West populations was that the former had lower mortality rates at younger ages, between fifteen and forty-five. This peculiarity, which I also found in two Zhejiang lineages (Liu Ts'ui-jung 1985:49), is not easy to explain, but it could be due to omissions of those whose ages at death were unknown. Alternatively, the actual mortality of the Chinese populations may have been different, since Model West life tables are derived mostly from Western populations, although a few tables from Japan and Taiwan are also included. In any case, it is interesting to note that a Far-Eastern pattern of mortality, characterized by excess mortality of older men, has been found by some demographers (Goldman 1980:5–6). The statistics derived from these genealogies seem to conform with this pattern; this Far-Eastern pattern is a topic that requires further research.

It should be noted that the life expectancy of the lineage males listed in Table 4.8 demonstrates the same variation as that shown by the mean and median ages at death listed in Table 4.6. The branches of the Shaoyang Li lineage had a higher life expectancy above age twenty than did the branches of the other lineages. This difference could be due to the fact that the environment in which the Li lineage resided was more favorable, as discussed above with regard to fertility.

In addition to the above examples showing branches of the five lineages, an investigation of mortality by cohorts can also be performed in order to discern changes through time. Here, data from the Shaoyang Li lineage will serve as an example. Table 4.9 shows the observed numbers of male deaths, arranged by five-year age groups and by fifty-year birth cohorts (the 1300

TABLE 4.9. Distribution of Deaths of Shaoyang Li Males, by Cohort

Age	Mid-point	1300 (b. 1298–1397)	1400 (b. 1398–1447)	1450 (b. 1448–1497)	1500 (b. 1498–1547)	1550 (b. 1548–1597)	1600 (b. 1598–1647)	1650 (b. 1648–1697)	1700 (b. 1698–1747)	1750 (b. 1748–1797)	1800 (b. 1798–1822)
15–19	17	0	0	0	1	0	0	1	2	3	2
20–24	22	0	0	0	0	0	0	1	7	13	14
25–29	27	0	0	1	0	1	3	4	9	20	14
30–34	32	0	1	1	1	1	7	5	12	19	22
35–39	37	0	0	1	0	4	3	8	18	29	19
40–44	42	0	0	0	3	2	5	9	16	32	31
45–49	47	0	0	0	4	4	10	15	42	45	42
50–54	52	0	2	3	7	11	14	18	33	48	48
55–59	57	0	2	2	7	10	14	14	37	71	32
60–64	62	1	2	9	16	30	20	38	42	89	44
65–69	67	3	6	7	9	19	15	30	40	77	57
70–74	72	3	11	7	11	8	16	35	55	88	43
75–79	77	6	0	4	6	6	11	29	45	52	29
80+	85	3	3	6	4	3	15	26	45	36	26
Total		16	27	41	69	99	133	233	403	622	423
Mean age at death		74.75	67.52	66.22	62.54	61.08	61.21	63.30	60.76	58.90	56.29
Median age at death		74.83	69.23	66.50	62.59	61.75	61.63	64.58	62.04	60.74	57.05

TABLE 4.10. Life Expectancies (e_x) of Shaoyang Li Adult Males, by Cohort

Age	1650 (b. 1648–1697)	1700 (b. 1698–1747)	1750 (b. 1748–1797)	1800 (b. 1798–1822)
20–24	44.04	41.44	39.73	37.09
25–29	39.35	37.15	35.54	33.20
30–34	34.79	33.00	31.49	29.45
35–39	30.39	29.01	27.61	25.87
40–44	26.21	25.20	23.91	22.48
45–49	22.28	21.60	20.42	19.28
50–54	18.65	18.23	17.16	16.31
55–59	15.35	15.11	14.16	13.56
60–64	12.39	12.26	11.43	11.06
65–69	9.79	9.71	8.99	8.81
70–74	7.54	7.44	6.86	6.82
75–79	5.59	5.47	5.07	5.12
80+	3.80	3.79	3.77	3.76

NOTE: Life tables are constructed based on the q_x values derived from number of deaths listed in Table 4.8 beginning with age twenty.

cohort lumps two fifty-year cohorts in order to put together enough cases, and the 1800 cohort is limited to twenty-five years because of right-censoring in the genealogy, which was compiled in 1904). From the distribution of deaths listed in Table 4.9, it is quite clear that in the early years of a lineage those deaths that were recorded tended to be at high ages. This phenomenon was also found in other lineages (Liu Ts'ui-jung 1989a:254–55). The low mortality rate reflected in these data recorded from the early years of a lineage should not be considered as representing the real situation of the time when these cohorts were active, for the data were apparently biased by a tendency for those men who lived longer to become founders of lineages or lineage branches. In other words, a lineage would not have formed if its ancestors were all very short-lived. From the 1498–1557 cohorts on, as the number of observations became large enough and the distribution of deaths covered almost every age group, the bias toward high age at death seems to have diminished.

As for changes in mortality through time, Table 4.9 shows that the mean and median ages at death of the 1498–1547, 1548–1597, and 1598–1647 cohorts were at about the same level, the ages at death were somewhat older in the 1648–1697 cohort, the ages returned to previous levels in the 1698–1747 cohorts, and decreased in the eighteenth century. The life tables constructed for the last four cohort groups as shown by the life expectancies listed in Table 4.10 also demonstrate the trend of increasing mortality in the eighteenth and nineteenth centuries, a trend that is corroborated by figures in other chapters in this volume.

From the data on these five lineages, we can thus begin to paint a provisional picture of general trends in demographic rates in late Ming and Qing China, at least for lineage populations in the southern provinces. Fertility was moderate and mortality high in the latter half of the Ming dynasty and at the time of the dynastic transition. In the first hundred years of the Qing, until 1750 or so, there was a marked increase in fertility and a concomitant decrease in mortality. Since this was a period of prosperity in most of the empire, it is not surprising that we find a high rate of population increase.

Toward the end of the eighteenth century and on into the nineteenth, however, both fertility and mortality began to turn the other way. Fertility showed a decline with the early-nineteenth-century cohorts, and mortality began to rise with the eighteenth-century birth cohorts, who were dying in the latter half of the eighteenth and first half of the nineteenth centuries. Many social and economic historians see a general downturn in economic conditions and in social stability during this period (Ho 1959:196–253; Perkins 1969:26–29), so it is not surprising to see this reflected in the demographic rates of so many lineages in so many parts of the empire.

NOTE

1. The tables used here are the Model West life tables provided by Coale and Demeny. Their work consists of a series of mortality tables with different levels of mortality in four regional patterns derived primarily from European demographic rates. The North, South, and East patterns all show distinct deviations from the general world experience, but the West pattern includes a large residual group of tables, mostly from Western populations but also from Taiwan and Japan, and is not characterized by any specific form of deviation from general experience (Coale and Demeny 1966, pt. 1:11–14). This is the reason for using Model West as the comparison case here.

FIVE

Demographic Constraint and Family Structure in Traditional Chinese Lineages, ca. 1200–1900

Liu Ts'ui-jung

INTRODUCTION

This chapter attempts to deal with the question of the relationship between family structure and demographic rates in traditional Chinese lineages. Four lineage genealogies were chosen to provide data for discussion in this paper: the Wujin Zhou of Jiangsu, the Yihuang Huang in Jiangxi, the Wuchang Xu in Hubei, and the Shaoyang Li in Hunan. (The last two are also analyzed in chapter 4). Here as elsewhere, the most important criterion for choosing a genealogy for historical demographic analysis is the completeness of its recorded vital dates, and these four genealogies all fulfill this basic requirement. The data used for this paper are not the records of the entire population enumerated in the genealogy but are only a portion containing ten generations in a single patriline, including all patrilineal male descendants of an ancestor who stands at the genealogical apex of this particular segment. Five such patrilines were selected from these four genealogies—two from the Yihuang Huang, one from the first through tenth generations and another from the fourteenth to the twenty-third, and one line each from each of the other three lineages. These five lines were selected because they contained the most complete records of the vital dates of their members.

As mentioned by Harrell and Pullum in chapter 6, there is no way to discover from the genealogical data whether the families in question actually formed any particular type of households. But because the record of vital dates is reasonably complete, we can investigate the problem of family structure by carefully scrutinizing all vital dates in order to find out whether some complex form of family would have existed if the family did not divide before the death of the eldest generation male. Although this assumption about family division may not have actually held in all cases, ethnographic studies have pointed out that family division often "occurred when one or both parents were still alive but well-advanced in years" (Cohen 1976:74). Genealogies occasionally mention the event of family partition. For example, in a biography of the wife (née Li, 1789–1857) of Huang Juezi (1793–1853), the most eminent member of the Yihuang Huang lineage and an important official involved in the Opium War, it was mentioned that she took charge of dividing the family property among five sons in 1855 (biography in the Huang genealogy, pt. 2, p. 40). The timing of this family division fits the description cited above from Cohen's ethnographic analysis. Thus the assumption of no partition until the death of the eldest generation male, along with actual vital dates as recorded in the genealogies, allows us to investigate the issue of family structure with Chinese genealogies.

For different forms of the Chinese family, scholars sometimes use different terms. According to Wolf, a stem family is "a family that contains two or more basic [conjugal] units linked by filial ties," and a grand family is "a family that contains a minimum of three units, two of which are in the same generation and descended from a third" (Wolf 1985a:22). In usage, Wolf's "stem family" is identical with other scholars' usage of that term, and his "grand/frèrèches" family is equivalent to what others have called a "joint family" (Cohen 1976:61). In this paper, stem family is used consistently, while joint and grand are used interchangeably.

In this chapter, my aim is to discover whether the demographic regime of the lineages in question would have supported various forms of extended families, particularly three- and four-generation stem and joint families. As the genealogies do not provide this sort of information directly, the best we can do is to examine whether it would have been possible to form or maintain households of these types, had the people chosen to do so. Nevertheless, this examination is a potentially valuable contribution to the debate about the prevalence of extended families in traditional Chinese communities (see Wolf 1985a).

FAMILY STRUCTURE

Statistics related to the family structure of the five patrilines under study here are presented in Table 5.1. There are altogether 808 men recorded in the five lineages; among them 104 belonged to the Zhou, 119 to the Huang (1), 277 to the Huang (2), 192 to the Xu, and 116 to the Li. If every married man formed a conjugal family (2-G F), then the number of conjugal families formed by the first nine generations of men in the five cases can be tabulated as shown in Table 5.1.[1] Starting with one family in each case, the total number of 2-G F formed was 63 in the Zhou patriline, 77 in the Huang (1), 107 in the Huang (2), 116 in the Xu, and 52 in the Li.

TABLE 5.1 Summary of Family Possibilities in the Five Lineages

Gen. No.	No. Males[a]	Died Young	Unmarried[b]	Moved Away	Remarried	Married No Heir	No. Family Type			No. Males	
							2-G F	3-G F	4-G F	3-G F	4-G F
Zhou											
51–60	104[15]										
51–59	83[15]	12	4	4	7	15	63			48	7
% of Total[c]		(14.5)	(4.8)	(4.8)	(8.4)	(18.1)	(75.9)			(57.8)	(8.4)
% of 2-G F[d]					(11.1)	(23.8)					
51–58	59[11]						45	17			
% of Total								(28.8)			
% of 2-G F								(37.8)			
51–57	40(6)						30		2		
% of Total									(5.0)		
% of 2-G F									(6.7)		
Huang (1)											
1–10	119[14]										
1–9	79(10)	0	2	0	8	17	77			55	42
% of Total[c]		(0)	(2.5)	(0)	(10.1)	(21.5)	(97.5)			(69.6)	(53.2)
% of 2-G F[d]					(10.4)	(22.1)					
1–8	52[3]						50	20	7		
% of Total								(38.5)	(23.3)		
% of 2-G F								(40.0)	(24.1)		
1–7	30[1]						29				

(*continued on next page*)

TABLE 5.1 (continued)

Gen. No.	No. Males[a]	No. Males					No. Family Type			No. Males	
		Died Young	Unmarried[b]	Moved Away	Remarried	Married No Heir	2-G F	3-G F	4-G F	3-G F	4-G F

Huang (2)

Gen. No.	No. Males[a]	Died Young	Unmarried[b]	Moved Away	Remarried	Married No Heir	2-G F	3-G F	4-G F	3-G F	4-G F
14–23	277[104]										
14–22	237[64]	75	37	5	26	26	107			113	32
% of Total[c]		(31.6)	(15.6)	(2.1)	(11.0)	(11.0)	(46.8)				
% of 2-G F[d]					(24.3)	(24.3)					
14–20	142[39]						65	22			
% of Total								(15.5)		(47.7)	
% of 2-G F								(33.8)			
14–19	98[25]						46		3		13.5
% of Total									(3.1)		
% of 2-G F									(6.5)		

Xu

Gen. No.	No. Males[a]	Died Young	Unmarried[b]	Moved Away	Remarried	Married No Heir	2-G F	3-G F	4-G F	3-G F	4-G F
10–19	192[6]										
10–18	153[3]	4	33	0	18	28	116			114	32
% of Total		(1.8)	(21.6)	(0)	(11.8)	(18.3)	(75.8)				
% of 2-G F					(15.5)	(24.1)					
10–17	108[3]						87	25			
% of Total								(23.1)		(74.5)	
% of 2-G F								(28.7)			
10–16	75						59		4		(20.9)
% of Total									(5.3)		
% of 2-G F									(6.8)		

	Total													
													Li	
10–19	116[13]													
10–18	110[13]	2		41		10		0		9		52		59	24
% of Total[c]		(1.8)		(37.3)		(9.1)		(0)		(8.2)		(51.8)		
% of 2-G F[d]										(17.3)				
10–17	88[9]											50	15	
% of Total													(17)	(53.6)
% of 2-G F													(30)	
10–16	63[7]											36	3	
% of Total													(4.8)	
% of 2-G F													(8.3)	

Total

	All													
All	808[142]													
9 gens	662[105]	93		117		19		59		95		415		389	137
% of Total[c]		(14)		(17.7)		(2.9)		(8.9)		(14.4)		(62.7)		
% of 2-G F[d]								(14.2)		(22.9)				
7–8 gens	449[65]											297	99	
% of Total													(22.0)	(58.8)
% of 2-G F													(33.3)	
6–7 gens	306[39]											200		19
% of Total														(6.2)	(20.7)
% of 2-G F														(9.5)

[a] Numbers in brackets are number of males with birth years unknown.
[b] In Xu and Li lineages, this figure includes some men whose marital status is uncertain in the records.
[c] Percentage of number of males in generations concerned.
[d] Percent calculated using number of males with two-generation families as the denominator.

Altogether, then, there were 415 married men who, according to the assumption of this model, formed conjugal families. They accounted for 62.7% of the 662 recorded males in the first nine generations.

In each lineage, there were some men who died young or unmarried or moved out of the lineage. These men did not form conjugal families as part of the local lineage. Sons who died young were apparently not recorded systematically in all the genealogies, as the number and percentage varied greatly among the five cases. It is notable that the Huang (2) genealogy recorded seventy-five sons who died young in the nine generations, accounting for 31.6% of the total number of males. The number of unmarried men also varied among the five cases, with the percentage ranging from 2.5 to 37.3%. Except for the cases of the Zhou and the Huang (1), in which the numbers of unmarried men recorded were small, the numbers recorded were quite large, most of the men having died unmarried simply because they died young. As for emigrants, there were not many recorded. But it is noteworthy that in the case of the Shaoyang Li, there were ten men who moved, and of these eight belonged to the same generation (G15) and comprised one-third of all males in that generation.[2] With a total of nine generations in each case, there were altogether ninety-three men who died young (14.0%), ninety-seven who died unmarried (14.7%), and nineteen who emigrated (2.9%). As these events occurred, mainly in later generations, they obviously checked the pace of population growth to some extent.

Table 5.1 also lists the numbers of married men who were heirless and the numbers who remarried. These numbers are again varied. When the percentages are calculated against the total numbers of married men (i.e., the number of 2-G F in Table 5.1), the remarried men accounted for 0 to 24.3%,[3] and the heirless for 17.3 to 24.3%. Altogether, there were fifty-nine men (or 14.2%) who remarried at least once and ninety-five men (or 22.9%) who had sons but eventually became heirless. It should be noted that when the percentages are calculated against all males in the generations concerned, then the percentages of both remarried and heirless are reduced. Altogether, the remarried men counted for 8.9% and the heirless for 14.4%.

Here it may be mentioned in passing that a family might overcome its fate of heirlessness by means of adoption. In the five genealogies, incidents of adoption are identified, but in counting the number of males in a family, adoptive relations are not taken into consideration, in order to simplify the analysis. This simplification, of course, is not at all satisfactory, for in reality an heir can be adopted. However, since the timing of adoption in these cases was not at all clear, to take it into consideration would make the counting more difficult. Moreover, some adoptive relations might have been arranged just for the sake of ancestor worship, so a son could be adopted in this way by a number of families while remaining a member of his natural father's descent line (examples of such relationships exist in the Xu patriline).[4]

Furthermore, if the family did not divide before the death of the eldest generation male, then some of the conjugal families could become three- or four-generation families. In seeking three-generation families, observation of family units ended with the seventh generation in the Huang (2) because there were no records of birth dates in this lineage's tenth generation, and observation ended with the eighth generation in the other four cases. In this way, it was found that there were altogether 99 three-generation families, 33.3% of the 297 conjugal families in the generations tabulated. The 99 men who lived to be grandfathers comprised 22% of the 449 males in the generations concerned.

As for four-generation families, observations ended one generation earlier than for three-generation families. There were altogether 19 four-generation families in the five patrilines, or 9.5% of the 200 conjugal families in the generations concerned. In other words, 19 (9.5%) of the men who became fathers eventually became great-grandfathers of at least one great-grandson. These 19 great-grandfathers comprised 6.2% of the 306 males of the generations observed.

In terms of individual members, the number who would have lived in three-generation families before the deaths of their grandfathers was 48 (57.8%) of the Zhou, 55 (69.6%) of the Huang (1), 113 (47.7%) of the Huang (2), 114 (74.5%) of the Xu, and 59 (53.6%) of the Li, for a total of 389 men (58.8%) in the five patrilines studied. As for those who would have lived in four-generation families, there were altogether 137 men (20.7%). These calculations are performed by counting each man only once, regardless of his position in individual families. It should be noted here that the percentage of men who would have lived in three-generation families is somewhat smaller than that calculated for three Xiaoshan lineages by Harrell and Pullum in chapter 6 and also smaller than the 70–80% Wolf found lived in grand and frèrèches families in Taiwan between 1906 and 1946 (1985a:35). However, the percentages in the Huang (1) and Xu cases were rather close to the proportions found for the Xiaoshan and Taiwan cases. It should be added, of course, that this comparison is only approximate, since the data bases and methods of calculation are different.

In short, Table 5.1 demonstrates the fact of variation in family structure among lineages. The next task is to find out how demographic characteristics relate to this variation.

DEMOGRAPHIC CHARACTERISTICS AND FAMILY STRUCTURE

Demographic characteristics of fertility and mortality will affect family structure through family size and through the longevity of family members. From genealogies, the size of a family can only be estimated from the number of male family members, since daughters are everywhere unrecorded or underrecorded. Within these limitations, the simple method of calculating an average number of sons per family will serve our purpose. As for the longevity of family members, only those males whose age at death was known will be taken into consideration in calculating an average age at death. Let us first look at the size of the family.

If the size of family is defined as the number of males in a two-generation conjugal family, the averages for our five cases are as follows: 2.63 for the Zhou lineage, 2.53 for the Huang (1), 3.58 for the Huang (2), 2.65 for the Xu, and 3.21 for the Li. It is notable that in all the lineages except for the Huang (1), there are some second-generation males who died young, and when they are excluded, the average size of the conjugal family shrinks. The average number of males in a conjugal family for all five cases is 2.93 when those who died young are included and 2.68 when they are excluded.

The differences in family size are due primarily to fertility. The fertility of fathers in the five cases is set out in Table 5.2. In row 1 of this table, the parities of fathers of the conjugal families are displayed under two conditions: in columns I, sons who died young are included, and in columns II, they are excluded. Parities ranged from 0 to 9. It should be noted that the parity figures obtained under the two conditions differed for all the lineages except the Huang (1), which did not record sons who died young. The largest difference was observed for the Huang (2), which had the largest recorded proportion of sons who died young, some even with precise vital dates.

Row 2 of Table 5.2 lists the total number of sons, and row 3 lists the total number of fathers, which is the same as the total number of conjugal families. The average number of sons per father, listed in row 4, shows the variation in fertility among these five cases. Fertility can also be estimated using only the men who had at least one son (i.e., excluding those listed as n=0 in row 1). The results are listed in row 5. Both sets of estimates for the Huang (2) show that the figures obtained excluding sons who died young are only about 68% of those including them (1.75/2.58). As the record of sons who died young seems rather complete in the case of the Huang (2), this example gives us some idea about underrecording of male births in the genealogies that did not record early deaths as completely as this one. In terms of family members, however, those sons who died young did not exist for very long and were probably neglected by most compilers of genealogies.

Table 5.2 also lists the percentage of heirless fathers in row 7. It can be seen that for the Huang (1) and Xu, estimates of the two sets are the same, whereas in the other cases, estimates are quite different. Again, in the case of Huang (2), the percentages calculated including sons who died young

TABLE 5.2. Summary of Conjugal Families, by Lineage

	Zhou		Huang (1)		Huang (2)		Xu		Li	
	I[a]	II[b]	I	II	I	II	I	II	I	II
(1) Parity										
n = 0	11	15	17	17	16	26	28	28	8	9
n = 1	21	21	28	28	21	25	31	33	8	8
n = 2	16	15	14	14	17	28	31	30	19	18
n = 3	11	9	10	10	23	15	15	14	7	7
n = 4	3	2	8	8	15	6	6	6	7	7
n = 5	1	1	–	–	6	5	3	3	1	1
n = 6	–	–	–	–	5	2	1	1	1	1
n = 7	–	–	–	–	1	0	0	1	0	0
n = 8	–	–	–	–	2	0	1	0	0	0
n = 9	–	–	–	–	1	0	–	–	1	1
(2) Total No. of sons	103	91	118	118	276	187	191	187	115	113
(3) Total No. of fathers	63	63	77	77	107	107	116	116	52	52
(4) Average No. of sons per father = (2)/(3)	1.63	1.44	1.53	1.53	2.58	1.75	1.65	1.61	2.21	2.17
(5) No. of reproductive fathers = (3) − (n = 0)	52	48	60	60	91	81	88	88	44	43
(6) Average No. of sons per reproductive father = (2)/(5)	1.98	1.75	1.97	1.97	3.03	2.05	2.17	2.13	2.61	2.57
(7) % heirless = (n = 0)/(3) × 100	17.46	23.81	22.08	22.08	14.95	24.30	24.14	24.14	15.38	17.31
(8) Total No. of wives	86		86		144		138		52	
(9) Average No. of wives per husband	1.37		1.11		1.35		1.19		1.00	
(10) No. of concubines	0		0		4		2		0	

[a] Sons who died young included.
[b] Sons who died young excluded.

and those calculated excluding them are much different from each other, 14.95% and 24.30%, respectively. In reality, the second, larger percentage of heirless seems closer to the actual situation, as fathers who had only one or two sons, both of whom died young, would eventually become heirless. At any rate, the percentages of heirless fathers were quite high in all five cases, ranging from 15 to 24%. These percentages are quite similar to those presented in Telford's chapter 3 and my chapter 4 in this volume.

Moreover, from the total number of wives, shown in row 8, and the average number of wives per husband, shown in row 9, it seems that remarriage itself did not affect the complexity of family structure to any drastic extent, for most remarriages involved only successive wives not concubines. As a matter of fact, the number of concubines, listed in row 10, demonstrated that the chance of two consorts coexisting at the same time was not great. In the five cases concerned, remarriage and concubinage did not affect the number of female family members to a significant extent. Families with a large number of concubines must have been quite exceptional. A preliminary investigation of over twenty-three southern genealogies found that the percentages of concubines ranged from 0 to 17.8%, with an average of 3.7% (Liu Ts'ui-jung 1983:288). Another study of three lineages in north China found that a Wang lineage in Wanping, Hebei, had an exceptionally high percentage of concubines, accounting for 35% of all consorts, whereas the other two lineages had only 4.3% and 5.5% (Liu Ts'ui-jung 1989b:78). This information suggests that for most of the families, remarriage and concubinage did not add to the complexity of family structure to any great extent. It was not possible to address the question of the effect of the longevity of mothers on family structure and division in this paper.

If the five cases are taken together, the parity progression ratios and distribution of family sizes in terms of male births can be calculated based on the distribution of fathers with different parities, as shown in Table 5.3. Again, two sets of estimates are calculated here, including and excluding sons who died young. These two sets of estimates show that for every 1,000 fathers, there were 193–229 who had no sons, 262–277 who had one son, 234–253 who had two sons, and so on. From parity 0 to parity 2, the second set of estimates was larger than the first one, whereas from parity 3 upward, the first set of estimates was larger. This change can be explained easily, as parities go down when sons who died young are excluded. At any rate, these two sets of estimates may be compared with those listed in Tables 4.4 and 4.5 (in chapter 4), to which they are rather similar in order of magnitude.

Since only those fathers who had at least two sons would have a chance to become head of a grand or joint family, about 50% of the conjugal families under investigation would have a chance to become grand families if the fathers of these families lived long enough to see their sons marry and have at least one descendant. In other words, assuming that fertility remains

TABLE 5.3. Summary of Conjugal Families, All Lineages

Parity	No. of Fathers		Parity Progression Ratios (a_x)		Distribution of Family Size (No. sons per 1000 fathers)	
	I[a]	II[b]	I	II	I	II
n = 0	80	95	.807	.771	193	229
n = 1	109	115	.675	.641	262	277
n = 2	97	105	.571	.488	234	253
n = 3	66	55	.488	.450	159	132
n = 4	39	29	.381	.356	94	70
n = 5	11	10	.542	.375	27	25
n = 6	7	4	.462	.333	17	9
n = 7	1	1	.833	.500	2	3
n = 8	3	0	.400	1.000	7	0
n = 9	2	1	.000	.000	5	2
Total No. of Sons	803	696				
Total No. of Fathers	415	415				
Total No. of Wives	506					

[a] Sons who died young included.
[b] Sons who died young excluded.

the same, a 50% chance for conjugal families to become grand families would seem the theoretical maximum, since mortality has not yet been taken into consideration.

If we assume that the families did not divide before the death of grandfathers, it is possible to find three-generation families in the records. The statistics for these families are summarized in Table 5.4. Counted by generation, the Zhou had eight generations in which three-generation families were formed, both the Huang (1) and Huang (2) had seven such generations, the Xu had five, and the Li had six. In other words, not every generation contained males who could have become grandfathers and formed three-generation families. In total, the Zhou formed seventeen three-generation families, the Huang (1) twenty, the Huang (2) twenty-two, the Xu twenty-five, and the Li fifteen. These numbers comprised 37.8%, 40.0%, 33.8%, 28.7%, and 30.0%, respectively, of the conjugal families in the five cases listed in Table 5.1. Altogether, there were ninety-nine possible three-generation families, of which thirty-three were stem families and sixty-six were grand families.

The total number of male members in these three-generation families ranged from three to eighteen. The average was 5.24 for the Zhou, 5.90 for the Huang (1), 7.14 for the Huang (2), 6.88 for the Xu, and 6.80 for the Li; the average number of male family members for all five cases was 6.44.

TABLE 5.4. Three-Generation Families

Lineage	Time	No. Family Type[a]		No. of Males in Families					Average Overlap Years	Age at Death of G1	Age at Birth of G3
		S	G	G1	G2	G3	Total	Average			
Zhou	1588–1786	6	11	17	34	38	89	5.24	12.41	67.47	27.65
Huang (1)	1299–1510	10	10	20	40	58	118	5.90	22.55	76.95	25.00
Huang (2)	1677–1887	6[b]	16[c]	22	58	77	157	7.14	15.86	67.86	23.27
Xu	1757–1915	6[d]	19[e]	25	63	84	172	6.88	13.92	67.88	25.72
Li	1771–1902	5[f]	10	15	32	55	102	6.80	15.07	67.40	21.60
Total		33	66	99	227	312	638	6.44	16.01	67.70	24.74

[a] S stands for stem family and G for grand family.
[b] One family observed in 1842 was counted fifteen years before the death of G1, when the only member of G2 was still alive.
[c] One family observed in 1852 was counted three years before the death of G1, when one member of G2 was still alive.
[d] One family observed in 1888 was counted one year before the death of G1; in the next year, neither G1 nor G2 was still alive.
[e] One family observed in 1810, another in 1897, and another in 1912 were counted, respectively, five, ten, and seven years before the death of G1.
[f] One family observed in 1893 was counted two years before the death of G1, when the only member of G3 was still alive.

These numbers were taken from the time period starting a few years before the death of G1 and ending with the death of G1, when the three generations were all alive at the same time.

Table 5.4 also lists the maximum number of years that three-generation families could have existed, i.e., the maximum overlap in the lifetimes of the first and third generations. As calculated from the charts, the years of overlap varied greatly, ranging from only one to as many as forty-two years. The averages for the five cases were 12.41 for the Zhou, 22.55 for the Huang (1), 15.86 for the Huang (2), 13.92 for the Xu, and 15.07 for the Li. The average overlap for all five cases was 16.01 years, the average numbers of years that grandfathers in these lineage populations could enjoy having at least one grandson in their families.

The chance of being born as a grandson may be calculated from the numbers of sons (G2 in Table 5.4) and grandsons (G3 in the table). Since our observation started with a certain generation in each case, sons in the second generation had no chance of being grandsons and should be excluded. Moreover, in the case of Huang (2), forty sons belonging to the twenty-third and last generation should also be excluded, since they had no birth years recorded and were not included in the tabulations of three-generation families. These exclusions leave 755 sons, of whom 312 (41%) were born as grandsons. In other words, the chance of being born as a grandson was about two in five.

TABLE 5.5. Fathers' Ages at Birth of the First Son in Conjugal Families

	Midpoint	Zhou	Huang (1)	Huang (2)	Xu	Li	Total
15–19	17	1	10	2	6	4	23
20–24	22	10	10	28	23	12	83
25–29	27	10	13	13	28	8	72
30–34	32	11	4	12	19	9	55
35–39	37	6	1	5	5	3	20
40–44	42	3	4	2	4	1	14
45–49	47	1	4	1	1	2	9
50–54	52	0	2	4	0	0	6
55–59	57	1	1	1	0	0	3
60–64	62	0	2	0	0	0	2
Total		43	51	68	86	39	287
Mean age		30.49	30.33	28.91	27.58	27.77	28.85
Median age		29.25	26.12	25.54	26.50	26.19	26.60

A related question concerns how early a man had to become the father of a son in order to expect to enjoy the privilege of being a grandfather in a three-generation family. This age may be investigated through a calculation of age at birth of the first son. Listed in Table 5.5 are the results of calculations for the conjugal families in the five cases. The frequency distribution is arranged by five-year age groups. The estimates show that the mean age at birth of a first son in the five cases was 30.49 for the Zhou, 30.33 for the Huang (1), 28.91 for the Huang (2), 27.58 for the Xu, and 27.77 for the Li. The overall average was 28.85. The overall median age at birth of first son was somewhat lower than the mean; for the five cases together, the median was 26.60.

As for those men who formed three-generation families, their ages at the births of their first male descendants are shown in Table 5.6. The results show that the mean age of G1 at the birth of G2 was 26.71 for the Zhou, 29.25 for the Huang (1), 24.95 for the Huang (2), 27.80 for the Xu, and 28.00 for the Li. These estimates reveal that the Zhou and Huang (2) males who formed three-generation families had sons at a slightly lower age than the average man, whereas the Huang (1), Xu, and Li males were very close to the average. Between the second and the third generations, however, it is quite clear that those who formed three-generation families had a much lower age at birth of the first male in G3 than did the average man in the whole population. The average of the five cases shows that the mean interval between the first and second generations was 27.34, and that between the second and third generations was 25.34; the median age difference between first and second generations was 25.62, and that between the second and third generations was 23.64. This contrasts with an average age of fathers

TABLE 5.6. Fathers' Ages at Birth of the First Son in Three-Generation Families

	Mid-point	G1 Fathers					G2 Fathers				
		Zhou	Huang (1)	Huang (2)	Xu	Li	Zhou	Huang (1)	Huang (2)	Xu	Li
15–19	17	1	3	2	1	1	1	7	2	2	2
20–24	22	6	5	10	7	5	7	2	11	9	7
25–29	27	4	5	6	7	4	4	8	7	8	4
30–34	32	5	2	3[a]	8	3	2	1	2[a]	5	1
35–39	37	1	0	1	1	0	2	0	0	1	1
40–44	42	0	3	0	1	1	1	0	0	0	0
45–49	47	0	1	0	0	1	0	1	0	0	0
50–54	52	0	1	0	0	0	0	1	0	0	0
Total		17	20	22	25	15	17	20	22	25	15
Mean age		26.71	29.25	24.95	27.80	28.00	27.00	25.50	24.05	25.80	24.33
Median age		25.88	26.00	23.50	26.86	25.88	24.63	24.63	23.09	22.94	22.93
Overall Mean Age				27.34					25.34		
Overall Median Age				25.62					23.64		

[a] One in each case was the second son, as the first son died young with birth year unknown.

TABLE 5.7. Ages at Death, All Men

	Mid-point	Zhou	Huang (1)	Huang (2)	Xu	Li	Total Including Huang (1)	Total Excluding Huang (1)
0–4	2	0	0	5	1	0	6	6
5–9	7	0	0	4	2	2	8	8
10–14	12	0	0	2	1	0	3	3
15–19	17	0	0	4	1	0	5	5
20–24	22	3	0	2	6	0	11	11
25–29	27	2	0	8	7	2	19	19
30–34	32	3	3	7	11	1	25	22
35–39	37	4	0	8	8	2	22	22
40–44	42	9	1	5	11	3	29	28
45–49	47	5	1	12	6	1	25	24
50–54	52	7	4	10	14	9	44	40
55–59	57	10	1	12	8	4	35	34
60–64	62	12	7	6	7	7	39	32
65–69	67	6	16	8	6	5	41	25
70–74	72	7	14	9	6	8	44	30
75–79	77	4	3	3	3	3	16	13
80+	85	1	17	4	4	6	32	15
No. of age known		73	67	109	102	53	404	336
No. of age unknown		25	48	61	90	64	288	240
Total		98	115	170	192	117	692	576
% age known		75	58	64	53	45	58	58
No. of age known from 15 to 80+		73	67	98	98	51	387	320
Mean age at death		54.16	69.25	50.60	48.60	61.08	55.33	52.42

at the birth of their sons in the whole population of 28.85. In other words, those who became grandfathers were those who had at least one son who, in turn, was able to have a son at a younger-than-average age.

The inverse of the previous question is also important: how long did a man need to live in order to become a grandfather in a three-generation family? In answer to this question, the average age at death was calculated for all men and for those who became grandfathers. Listed in Table 5.7 are the distributions of ages at death for all men recorded in the five cases. The numbers of men with known age at death are first distributed by five-year

TABLE 5.8. Ages at Death, Grandfathers in Three-Generation Families

	Midpoint	Zhou	Huang (1)	Huang (2)	Xu	Li	Total[a]
45–49	47	0	0	1	1	0	2
50–54	52	0	0	3	1	3	7
55–59	57	3	0	2	4	1	10
60–64	62	5	1	1	4	2	12
65–69	67	2	2	4	4	2	12
70–74	72	3	6	5	5	3	16
75–79	77	3	3	3	2	2	10
80+	85	1	8	3	4	2	10
Total		17	20	22	25	15	79
Mean age at death		67.47	76.95	67.86	67.88	67.40	67.70

[a] Not including Huang (1); for an average including all observations, see Table 5.4.

age groups. It should be noted that there are quite a number of men whose ages at death are not known and that the proportions vary among the five cases. Although it is possible to estimate ages at death for men whose death dates are not actually given (Harrell 1985:84–85), it should suffice here to compute the age at which a man became a grandfather using only those cases where the age at death is known.

From Table 5.7 we can thus see that the mean age at death varied among the five cases. These estimates are derived using only the distribution of deaths from ages fifteen to eighty and above. The estimates for the Xu and Li males are comparable to those listed in Table 4.6 in chapter 4, as they belong to the same lineages. The estimates for the Zhou males are somewhat higher than those listed for the Jiangdu Zhu in chapter 4. The estimate for the Huang (1) is exceptionally high compared with those for the Huang (2) and the other cases. It should be noted that the Huang (1) males belonged to the first ten generations of this lineage and that their active period was around 1200–1500. As mentioned in chapter 4, the observed deaths for the early years of a lineage tended to be at higher ages, and the difference between the Huang (1) and Huang (2) provides a good example to support this argument. Excluding the Huang (1), the mean age at death of adult males was 50.65.

Listed in Table 5.8 are the distributions and estimates of mean ages at death for those men who became grandfathers in three-generation families. Except for the Huang (1), all the lineages had mean ages at death of about sixty-seven or sixty-eight. With all observations of the five cases combined, the average age at death for these grandfathers was 69.55. These findings suggest that for an average man, who died around age fifty, the chances of becoming a grandfather were not very great.

TABLE 5.9. Four-Generation Families

Lineage	Gen. No.	Time	Type[a]	G1	G2	G3	G4	Total	No. of Overlap Years	Age at Death of G1	G3's Age at Birth of G4
Zhou	51	1588	S	1	1	2	1	5	2	79	19
	52	1617	G	1	1	2	1	5	2	84	29
Huang (1)	2	1305	G	1	2	3	3	9	13	91	18
	2	1299	S	1	1	1	1	4	6	81	16
	5	1392	G	1	3	8	1	13	8	69	16
	6	1425	G	1	4	7	3	15	9	83	32
	6	1432	G	1	3	4	1	9	14	87	23
	7	1455	G	1	2	1	2	6	8	71	26
	7	1447	G	1	3	3	3	10	10	79	21
Huang (2)	14	1677	G	1	3	4	2	10	5	77	23
	15	1703	G	1	1	6	1	9	9	82	22
	19[b]	1852	G	1	1	4	7	13	9	87	21
Xu	15[c]	1888	G	1	1	6	5	13	18	84	19
	16	1858	S	1	1	1	1	4	3	83	20
	16	1907	G	1	1	2	1	5	7	84	19
	16	1907	G	1	1	8	2	12	4	86	19
Li	12	1777	G	1	1	9	2	13	4	82	23
	13	1797	G	1	5	12	1	19	8	75	22
	13	1801	G	1	3	9	2	15	3	69	19
Total			3S 16G	19	38	92	40	189	142	1538	412
Average								9.95	7.47	80.95	21.68

[a] S stands for stem family and G for grand family.
[b] This family was counted three years before the death of G1, when one of G2 was still alive; at the death of G1 the family contained only three generations without G2.
[c] This family was counted one year before the death of G1.

In addition to three-generation families, it is also feasible to find some possible four-generation families, again assuming that the families did not divide before the fourth generation was born. Listed in Table 5.9 are the nineteen four-generation families. Of these nineteen, two belonged to the Zhou, seven to the Huang (1), three to the Huang (2), four to the Xu, and three to the Li. It is reasonable that we find more four-generation families in the Huang (1) lineage, since its mean age at death was much higher than the other cases. Of these nineteen families, three were stem only, and the other sixteen were possibly grand.

The results of simple calculations show that four-generation families had a larger average number of male family members than did three-generation families (9.95 vs. 6.44), that they existed for a shorter period (7.47 vs. 16.01

years), that they had a higher average age at death for the first generation (80.95 vs. 69.55), and that they had a lower father's age at birth for the last generation (21.68 vs. 25.34). The chance of being born as a great-grandson in a four-generation family was much smaller than the chance of being born as a grandson (one in twenty vs. two in five). In short, the chance for an average man in these traditional Chinese lineages to become a great-grandfather was indeed very small. And we should add that there were no five-generation families formed in the five cases investigated. Although the possibility of the formation of such a family cannot be ruled out, these families must have been very rare indeed and have remained nothing but an ideal in Ming-Qing China.

In sum, the above investigation demonstrates that the predominant family type in these lineages was the simple two-generation conjugal family, for even when the family was not divided, sheer demographic conditions would not allow three- or four-generation families to become prevalent. It should also be noted, however, that most of the possible three- and four-generation families were potentially of the grand type, indicating the complexity of family structure.

CONCLUDING REMARKS

In the five cases investigated here, there were 808 males, among whom 662 belonged to the first nine generations of these patrilines. Among these 662 males, 93 (14%) died young; another 97 (14.7%) died unmarried and 20 (3.0%) had uncertain marital status; and 19 (2.9%) moved out of their lineages. These 238 males (36%) did not form conjugal families. There were 415 men (62.7%) who married and became fathers. Furthermore, of the 662 males in the first nine generations, 389 (58.9%) could have lived in three-generation families, and 137 (20.7%) in four-generation families.

There were altogether 99 men who may have become grandfathers in three-generation families. In terms of family units, the 99 three-generation families counted for one-third of the 297 conjugal families in the first seven or eight generations of those patrilines. In other words, 99 men (one-third) who were heads of conjugal families also became heads of three-generation families. As individuals, these 99 grandfathers were 22% of the 449 males in the generations concerned. In addition, there were 19 men who became great-grandfathers and thus may have formed four-generation families. As individuals, these 19 great-grandfathers counted for 6.2% of the 306 males in the generations concerned. This calculation may also be done the other way around. From the standpoint of sons under observation, 312 (41%) of 755 in the generations concerned were born while their grandfathers were still alive and thus may have lived in three-generation families; 40 (5%) of 741 were born while their great-grandfathers were still alive and thus may have been great-grandsons in four-generation families.

No matter how the calculations are done, these results seem to suggest that for a traditional Chinese male, the chance of becoming a grandfather was about one in five, of being born as a grandson, about two in five, and of becoming a great-grandfather or being born as a great-grandson both very small, about one in twenty.

The average size of a conjugal family was 2.93 males, of a three-generation family 6.44 males, and of a four-generation family 9.95 males. An average man became father of a son when he was 28.95 years old. In those families that had the possibility of forming a three-generation family, the first descendant in the third generation was born, on the average, 3.51 years earlier than the average first son in the entire population, and in those that may have formed a four-generation family, a fourth-generation descendant was born an average of 7.17 years earlier. The average age at death of an adult male was 52.42, that of a man who became a grandfather was 69.55, and that of a man who became a great-grandfather was 80.95. Five-generation families were very rare and, even if formed, would not have lasted very long, for the overlap of generations in even a four-generation family was on the average less than eight years.

Although a stem family with a depth of three or four generations is quite complex, the structural form of the three- and four-generation families in this study was very likely dominated by the grand type, indicating complex intrafamilial relations between quite a large number of individual members. It is perhaps in this respect that the traditional Chinese family could be described as being complex. However, the findings in this paper seem to suggest that because of demographic constraints, a synchronic sample of traditional Chinese families would not have been dominated by three- and four-generation households, and certainly not by five-generation ones. The ideal type of five generations living together (*wushi tongtang*) remained just an ideal for the Chinese people, and demographic constraints made it difficult for them to realize that ideal.

NOTES

1. Numbers in the tenth generation of each case are not included, as the records of this generation are not as complete as those of the first nine.

2. For details of migration in the Shaoyang Li lineage, see Liu Ts'ui-jung 1983: 311–13; for a detailed study of migration in Fujian lineages, see Wang in chapter 8 of this volume.

3. It just happened that this particular patriline of the Li lineage did not have any remarried men. The Li lineage, as recorded in its genealogy, did not have a very

high percentage of remarried men altogether (7.3% remarried once, 6.8% remarried twice). See Liu Ts'ui-jung 1983:288.

4. The adoption of a son by one or more families while he remained a member of his own father's line was known as *jiantiao*. For other examples of this practice, see Liu Ts'ui-jung 1987:411–12. For legal regulations and customs regarding this practice, see Shiga 1981.

SIX

Marriage, Mortality, and the Developmental Cycle in Three Xiaoshan Lineages

Stevan Harrell and Thomas W. Pullum

Were complex families part of the typical Chinese developmental cycle? In two recent articles (1984, 1985a), Arthur Wolf has argued that the large, complex Chinese family of legend, once generally believed to be a myth (Hsu 1943), a demographic improbability (Levy 1949:46–52), or at most a phenomenon to be found only among the elite (Freedman 1958:19; Fei 1939), was in fact quite common in twentieth-century China, not only in the area of North Taiwan where Wolf did his own research but also in several North China areas where surveys were conducted in the 1920s and '30s. In Wolf's own sample, stem and joint families (the latter category including what he calls grand and *frèrèches* families)[1] typically accounted for about 50 to 65% of the families in a synchronic sample and usually contained around 70 to 75% of the population at any one time (Wolf 1985a: 35). Furthermore, in this North Taiwan population it appears that almost everybody experienced life in a complex (stem or joint) family at some point in the life cycle; about 90% of the men who remained in the sample for over thirty-five years experienced life in a joint family, and almost all the remainder at least experienced life in a stem family at one time or another (Wolf 1985a:44).

Such diachronic data are not available in the reports Wolf examines concerning North China communities, but the situation seems generally similar. The configuration of family types in the North Taiwan sample yields a mean family size of 6.5 to 8.5 members, and the data for Ding *xian* in the 1920s indicate an average size of 6.93, well within this range; a study by Feng Zigang done in Lanji *xian* indicates family sizes of over seven for resident landlords and owner-cultivators, with smaller family sizes for the very poor tenants and agricultural laborers, who form a minority of the population (Feng 1935). From these data Wolf draws the conclusion that although the very poor, the people who could not adequately feed and clothe themselves, may have had somewhat simpler and smaller families, the great majority of the population in fact lived in a world where stem and joint family life was a part of nearly everyone's experience (Wolf 1985a).

These conclusions are rather impressive, but they apply only to twentieth-century China. So far, the only similar data for pre-twentieth-century communities come from James Lee's study of the village of Daoyi in Liaoning, a village inhabited by Qing banner families. He reports, for example, that multiple-family (stem and joint) households constituted 44% of households in the 1801 household registers for that village (Lee and Gjerde 1986). Furthermore, in that village, between 60 and 80% of the population in 1801 was living in stem or joint families.

Lee's data, however, seem destined to be challenged, at least in their capacity to represent what was typical of China in the middle and late Qing. A considerable amount of discussion at a Qing population workshop held in 1985, for example, was focused on just this question. Some participants argued that the data were representative of a Manchu rather than Chinese cultural pattern or that the customs of landholding among the banner population, or perhaps the taxation system or the household registration system itself, influenced these people to retard family division to the point where complex families would be formed as part of the developmental cycle of most families in each generation. More recent work by Lee (see chap. 7) seems to eliminate the question of ethnicity, but there is still the effect of the banner land-registration system to account for.

The purpose of this paper is to try out another case, to use genealogical data to determine the nature of the developmental cycle in a population of indisputably Han people in the late Ming and early and middle Qing dynasties, with particular reference to the frequency and nature of stem and joint families.

METHODOLOGICAL CONSIDERATIONS

To study the developmental cycle on the basis of genealogical data is a bit of a challenge. Genealogies are constructed to keep track of lineage relationships, not family structure or the developmental cycle. We must thus extrapolate from what is recorded in the genealogies to what is not—from the life cycles of individual men to the nature of the families these men were living in at particular stages of their life cycles. In other words, we must convert indirect indications of family composition, available from the genealogies, into probable reconstructions of what the families looked like.

There are three factors that contribute to the frequency of stem and joint families in a patrilocally marrying population—the overlap of generations, the size of the sibling set (or, more precisely, the brother set), and the timing of family division. We can calculate the magnitude and effect of the first two factors from the genealogies, but unfortunately we can say nothing about timing of family division. We can thus determine the potential for the formation of stem and joint families in these lineages, but we cannot calculate the actual rates, since we do not know when the families divided. We can thus test fairly conclusively the argument made by Levy, who argues against the prevalence of large families on demographic grounds, whereas we cannot conclusively test the hypotheses of Fei and Hsu that large families were rare because even people who could have stayed together probably did not for economic reasons. Since stem families can only be broken up by the migration of all of a couple's sons, the presence of three generations in a genealogy with no indication of migration is conclusive evidence that the family grew to the stem form. We cannot say conclusively, however, whether or not joint families existed unless we have records of family division, which are not present in any genealogies. In light of more recent work by Wolf (1985a) and Cohen (1976), however, we might be bold enough to make some educated guesses about the timing of family division and to calculate percentages of possible family types based on these guesses. Our analysis here is thus similar to that of Liu Ts'ui-jung (chapter 5), who calculates the demographic possibility, rather than the economic actuality, of joint families. Of the three factors that together account for the frequency of various types of families, the two that we can study from genealogies are, of course, types of demographic rates. Generational overlap is a function of three demographic rates—age at marriage, birth interval, and age at death; the size of the sibling set is a type of fertility variable. In other words, in order to answer questions about family composition from genealogies, which do not give family composition directly, one must be able to calculate demographic rates of various sorts. This paper is thus offered, first, as an attempt to suggest the probable frequency of certain family types, and, second, in the service of this first goal, as a preliminary attempt to evaluate and improve on earlier analyses by Liu Ts'ui-jung (1985) and others of real demographic rates as derived from Chinese genealogies. Bearing in mind that certain assumptions are just that but at the same time believing that certain assumptions are better than others, we will examine the demographic rates contributing to the possibility of the formation of certain family types in the Lin, Shi, and Wu lineages of Xiaoshan.

THE LINEAGES AND THEIR GENEALOGIES

The lineages selected for analysis here are the Lin, Wu, and Shi lineages of Xiaoshan County, Shaoxing Prefecture, Zhejiang Province.[2] Xiaoshan is a wealthy county in the regional core of the Lower Yangzi macroregion (Skinner 1977:214) and is right across the river from the provincial capital at Hangzhou.[3] The county was home to many strong and powerful lineages from Ming times on; they produced a considerable number of degree holders, as did the neighboring counties of Shaoxing Prefecture (Schoppa 1989; Cole 1980). The lineages examined in this paper, though not among the most prominent in the county, still produced the occasional degree holder and even turned out a few prominent officials.

The first member of the Lin lineage to settle in Xiaoshan was Lin Yongbian (1353–1433), who went there temporarily with his son Zhixiu. Both of them later returned to their ancestral home in Fuqing, Fujian, but Zhixiu's youngest son, named Meiju, changed his home registration to Xiaoshan and earned a *jinshi* degree in 1462. All members of the Qing dynasty lineage were descended from Meiju's sixth-generation descendant Kuanlou; the descendants of each of this man's three sons formed one of the *fang* (segments) into which the lineage was divided. Judging from their name, the East Gate Lins, they lived right outside the eastern gate of the county town. The Lin genealogy, compiled in 1897, is the smallest of the three, containing 452 full entries.

The Wu lineage was founded as a corporate body in Xiaoshan by Wu Shouyu, who lived in the late sixteenth century and had five sons, Hua, Shican, Xun, Si, and Qun. There were Wus in the area earlier, living along the east shores of Xiang Lake to the west of the county town (Schoppa 1989:46–47), but the Wus who wrote the genealogy published in 1904 consist entirely of the descendants of Shouyu. The descendants of each of his five sons formed the five *zhi*, or branches, into which the lineage was divided. By the nineteenth century, these *zhi* had been divided into *fang*, each descended from a grandson of the founder. The Wu genealogy was compiled in 1904 and contains full entries for 1078 men.

The Shi lineage was of earlier provenance, having been founded in Xiaoshan in the thirteenth century by Shi Wanyi, who came from a place called Jishan and settled on the north side of Hangwu Mountain, which lies about eighteen kilometers to the east of the county seat (Xiaoshan 1987, map 1). Ever since then the lineage has been known as the "Shi to the north of the mountain." At the time of the compilation of the genealogy, in 1888, the lineage was divided into two great *fang*, descended from the two sons of the founder. The Shi genealogy contains 1994 full entries.

DEMOGRAPHIC RATES BEARING ON GENERATIONAL OVERLAP

To calculate a man's chances of experiencing life in a stem family, one needs to know the probability that he will live in the same family with his grandparents at the beginning of his life cycle, with his parents and his children in the middle of his life cycle, or with his married son at the end of his life cycle. To calculate the chances of living in a joint family, one must calculate a man's chances of living with his grandparents and his patrilateral parallel cousins at the beginning of the life cycle, with his father and his brother and his children in the middle of his life cycle, or with his married sons and their children at the end of the life cycle. All these probabilities are determined, in turn, by three sets of factors. One includes age at marriage and generational depth, a second includes life expectancy, and a third includes the average number of sons a man can expect to see grow to adulthood.

Age at Marriage and Generational Span

One can, using the material in the genealogies, calculate directly the number of cases in which grandfathers' life-spans overlap with grandsons'. But since the existence of this overlap is directly dependent on age at marriage, our analysis is more realistic if we examine the probable ages at marriage that partially determine this degree of generational overlap.

Calculating age at marriage from Chinese genealogies is difficult. They contain no explicit data on age at marriage whatsoever, so that age at marriage has to be inferred from other kinds of information. One method, used by Liu (1985), involves the procedure developed by Hajnal, which bases estimates of marriage age on percentages unmarried at particular ages. Liu uses this kind of estimate to derive a range of figures for two Xiaoshan lineages: in the Xu lineage, for example, an estimate based on the assumption that all men who do not have sons are single gives a mean age of first marriage of 25.02. Another estimate is derived from a very different assumption: that only those who died unmarried were unmarried at a particular age. This gives an estimated mean male age at marriage of 17.58 years. Neither of these assumptions seems to us to yield estimates remotely related to actual age at marriage. Liu recognizes this and takes the happy expedient of averaging them, since one is obviously way too high and the other way too low. This procedure gives a final estimate of 21.3 years, which turns out to be close to the Princeton reanalysis of the Buck survey data for South China in the 1930s, so Liu accepts it as correct. It strikes us that this whole exercise is based on a faulty assumption. What is in fact assumed is that approximately half of those men who are still alive but do not have a son at a particular age are not married. We see no reason to accept this assumption.

Another, and perhaps somewhat more satisfactory, way of estimating age at marriage is to work backward from age at the birth of the first son, subtracting from this latter figure an amount equal to an estimate of the average time from the marriage until the first son's birth. This latter must be calculated semiempirically from the data contained in the genealogies. First, we find the mean birth interval. For the Xiaoshan lineages we have not intervals between births but simply intervals between births of sons who survived to maturity and are thus included in the genealogies. The mean interval between births of first and second surviving sons is 6.7 years in the Shi lineage and 7.1 years in the Wu lineage. If we assume, for simplicity's sake, that half the births are female and that females have the same mortality as males at young ages,[4] then the mean birth interval for those who survived to adulthood is 4.6 years for the Shi and 4.7 for the Wu.[5]

Now we have to come up with a figure for the interval between marriage and birth of the first surviving child. There is no indication at all what figure we should use for this, but two years cannot be far off. Then approximately half the couples will have their first son at a mean of two years after their marriage. Another quarter of the couples will have first a daughter, then a son. Adding the 2 years from the marriage to the daughter's birth to the 4.6 years (for the Shi lineage) until the son's birth, we have 25% of the couples with a son born a mean of 6.6 years after marriage. Similarly, 12.5% of the couples will have first two daughters, then a son; their son will be born a mean of 2+2 (4.6), or 11.2, years after their marriage. And so on until we reach insignificant quantities of people who will have a lot of daughters and finally a son. This procedure yields an average interval from marriage to birth of first surviving son of 6.5 years for the Shi lineage and 6.7 years for the Wu lineage.

But we cannot simply calculate backward from age at birth of first son to age at marriage, at least not for males. If we do, we find that for the Shi lineage, for example, the average age at marriage for women is 17.6, and the mean age for men is 24.1. These averages sound reasonable enough for a human population, if suspiciously late for a Chinese one. But when we calculate the mean age difference between husband and wife, we come up with a figure of only 3.32 years. Clearly our figures contradict each other.

Fortunately, there is a way out. In both lineages, considerable numbers of men had second wives and concubines. Some of the first sons from whose births we calculated age at marriage were sons of second wives. Since almost no men married women who were previously married, reckoning back from the age at first son's birth turns out to be a legitimate procedure for women, and we can take the calculated ages of 17.6 for the Shi and 19.1 for the Wu as being reasonably accurate. To obtain the male ages, we simply add the mean age difference between husbands and wives to the wives' estimated ages at marriage and thus obtain more realistic figures of 20.9 for the Shi lineage and 22.4 for the Wu.

Mortality

As with age at marriage, we could skip over explicit calculations of mortality entirely and proceed directly to analysis of generational overlap. But again it seems that our analyses gain credibility if we attempt to connect the rates

TABLE 6.1. Age- and Period-Specific Death Rates from the Genealogies (× 1000 Person-Years)

	Age at Death				
	20–29	30–39	40–49	50–59	60–69
Lin					
1600–1699	12	5	5	25	16
1700–1799	9	8	28	33	81
1800–1874	19	15	35	57	56
Wu					
1600–1699	9	6	8	13	87
1700–1799	11	14	29	48	62
1800–1874	15	15	27	56	86
Shi					
1600–1699	2	5	29	43	92
1700–1799	6	11	24	36	75
1800–1874	10	21	32	42	95

NOTE: Restricted to males for whom both a birth year and a death year are stated.

of generational overlap to the mortality rates that are partially responsible for determining them.

Efforts to describe the mortality of the populations in the genealogies have proceeded in two steps. The first step was the construction of standard age- and period-specific death rates, exactly as in normal demographic practice. Each population was reduced to those individuals for whom both a year of death and a year of birth were available, since birth year is necessary for the calculation of age at death. The numerator used to calculate each death rate is the number of deaths in an interval of age and time. It is divided by the population's exposure to the risk of death, which is measured by the total number of person-years lived in that interval of age and time. Table 6.1 presents the rates calculated in this way, aggregated into ten-year intervals of age between twenty and sixty-nine and into three intervals of time: 1600–1699, 1700–1799, and 1800–1874. Outside of this range, there were generally too few cases for the rates to be statistically stable. Also, rates for the last part of the nineteenth century are biased because long-lived individuals tended not to have a death date in the records and, therefore, had to be omitted. The rates include a factor of one thousand and are to be interpreted as the number of deaths per thousand person-years of exposure to risk.

Although these death rates show some obvious inconsistencies (for example, the rates do not always increase monotonically with age, which they should do in the range from twenty to sixty-nine years), they generally are

TABLE 6.2. Estimated Life Expectancies at Birth, by Time Period, Lin, Wu, and Shi Lineages

	Lin	Wu	Shi
1600–1699	54	50	54
1700–1799	38	31	41
1800–1874	25	27	28

plausible, so we have proceeded to summarize them with estimates of the corresponding life expectancy for each genealogy and each time interval, using model life-tables.

Demographers have used empirical data to generate several alternative model life-tables. We have used the series of Model West tables for males developed by Coale and Demeny.[6] Employing the numerators and denominators of the five age-specific rates for ages 20–29 through 60–69 and fitting their ratios to the death rates in the model life-tables with a maximum-likelihood procedure, we estimate the implied life expectancies at birth in Table 6.2.

It must be emphasized that these results are preliminary and would differ somewhat if alternative model life-tables or alternative fitting procedures were used. Note that the proportion of a population who die before age twenty can be substantial. For example, if the life expectancy at birth is forty years, then approximately one-third of all individuals will die before age twenty. If it is twenty-five years, then about half will die before age twenty. Because we lack reliable information on individuals who died before that age, our estimates of life expectancy at birth are very sensitive to the model life-tables' assumed correspondence between mortality before age twenty and mortality after age twenty. Our future analyses will evaluate this sensitivity more carefully. Our reason for using the life expectancy at birth rather than, say, at age twenty, which could be calculated more directly, is simply that it is the most understandable summary measure.

We make the following tentative observations. First, the apparent decline over time in the expectation of life in each genealogy is so great that it must be regarded as spurious. It is likely that in the seventeenth century, the chance that an individual would be included in the genealogy was positively related to that individual's longevity. Alternatively, we may be observing a kind of founder effect here, in which the first few generations of males, because they were successful demographically, managed to found what later became a large lineage. In the nineteenth century, there appears to be a downward bias, despite the omission of the last quarter of the century for the reasons given above (that the omission of individuals without death dates will bias the genealogy toward those individuals who died younger).

TABLE 6.3. Sonlessness and Median Death Age, by Time Period, Wu and Shi Lineages

	Men with No Sons	Men with Sons	Percent Sonless
Wu Lineage			
1600–1699	14	139	9
1700–1799	266	321	45
1800–1869	135	92	59
Median age at death	38	55	
Percent with death dates	35	83	
Shi Lineage			
1600–1699	39	131	23
1700–1799	136	349	28
1800–1849	261	381	41
Median age at death	32	52	
Percent with death dates	15	62	

It may be possible to overcome this latter bias in future analyses, but the rates for twenty-five-year intervals of time (not given here) have suggested that it was only serious toward the end of the century. The figures for the eighteenth century may be the most accurate, but the effects of competing biases, rooted in the relation between inclusion and longevity, are clearly serious.

Second, with the exception of the Wu genealogy in the eighteenth century, there is a remarkable degree of agreement across the three genealogies in any given time interval. This agreement may imply that (a) the true level of mortality, whatever it was, was similar for the three genealogies and, moreover, that (b) whatever the biases regarding inclusion, they were similar for the three genealogies. This consistency may be helpful in our efforts to identify the biases.

Perhaps one way to begin estimating such biases, and the way they change over time, is to look at the types of men for whom death dates are recorded in the genealogies. Table 6.3 gives the pertinent information for the Wu and Shi lineages.

As can be seen from the table, the genealogies in the early years seem heavily biased in favor of men with sons. This is especially true of the Wu lineage, whose rate of only 9% sonlessness in the seventeenth century seems too low to be credible. If we further consider that the genealogies are far more likely to record death dates when a man does have sons (presumably because the sons keep track of their father's death date for purposes of ancestral worship), then we can see that a large number of men who are likely to have died early are probably left out of the genealogy's records for the seventeenth century. Combined with the very low infant mortality figure that would be predicted (from most model life-tables) for a population with life expectancies as high as those recorded for the seventeenth century, we can be nearly sure that the eighteenth-century records are closer to the true mortality figures for these lineages. At this point, we have no way of determining whether the even lower nineteenth-century figures are more or less accurate than the eighteenth-century ones.

With regard to the effects of mortality on the formation stem and joint families, we must return to a simpler and more convenient statistic, the average age at death for a man with sons. This analysis of mortality, however, gives us some confidence that this statistic is not far off of the truth. Because family formation in the older and middle generations involves only men with sons and because the figures in general seem to be fairly accurate for men with sons, we can proceed with some confidence in this regard.

FAMILY COMPOSITION

Stem Families

Mortality, age at marriage, and marital fertility all affect the overlap of generations, which is the most important factor in determining the incidence of stem families. To form stem families, three generations must be alive at once or, in a minimal definition, the second generation must be married while the elder generation is alive, even if the second generation has not produced any children. If we look at an individual's chances of experiencing life in a stem family at some point in the life cycle, we find that he can be part of such a family as a grandson, as a son and father, or as a grandfather. We have examined the data in the three genealogies to show the chances of belonging to a stem family at each of these positions in the generational hierarchy.

A man's first chance to be a member of a stem family is at birth; he will be a member of a stem family if one or the other of his father's parents are alive. We have used a procedure of linking records to calculate the percentages of men whose fathers' fathers were alive at their births for each of eight fifty-year cohorts in each of the three lineages. In each case, the data include only those men whose own birth dates and fathers' fathers' death dates are recorded.

It appears from the data in Table 6.4 that a man in the late Ming had an over 70% chance of being born while his father's father was still alive; the chance slipped to between 22 and 45% during the Qing. The Ming figures are probably unrepresentative of the general population; the early generations of a lineage are almost by definition extraordinarily demographically

TABLE 6.4. Men Who Potentially Belonged to a Stem Family at Birth

Cohort	Father's Father Alive	Father's Father Dead	% Alive
Lin Lineage			
To 1599	11	3	79
1600–1649	12	4	75
1650–1699	18	12	60
1700–1749	20	26	43
1749–1799	14	31	31
1800–1849	38	59	39
1850–1899	19	48	28
Total	132	183	42
Shi Lineage			
To 1599	22	13	63
1600–1649	26	22	54
1650–1699	26	60	30
1700–1749	40	84	32
1749–1799	95	135	41
1800–1849	235	347	40
1850–1899	127	332	28
Total	571	993	37
Wu Lineage			
To 1599	6	0	100
1600–1649	21	6	78
1650–1699	66	53	55
1700–1749	120	172	41
1749–1799	81	195	29
1800–1849	40	131	23
1850–1899	16	42	28
Total	350	599	37

successful, and there is the real possibility of underrecording of men from less successful families. The small number of men belonging to the early cohorts do not, however, weight the overall average, which in all three lineages was around 35 or 40%. A boy in Xiaoshan in the Qing had somewhat better than a one-third chance of having a grandfather when he was born, about the same chance calculated by Liu Ts'ui-jung in chapter 5.

The second juncture at which a man can be a member of a stem family is during the period when he is married and has children and his parents remain alive. We have used a similar linking procedure to determine the percentages of men in the same cohorts in the three lineages who fulfill these conditions. Both men who have no sons and men whose parents die

TABLE 6.5. Men Who Potentially Belonged to Stem Families in Middle Life

Cohort	Stem	No Sons	Father Dead	% Stem
Lin Lineage				
To 1599	7	7	1	47
1600–1649	5	4	2	45
1650–1699	14	1	10	56
1700–1749	12	8	19	31
1749–1799	16	10	10	44
1800–1849	21	42	24	24
Total	75	72	66	35
Shi Lineage				
To 1599	22	5	13	55
1600–1649	14	6	24	32
1650–1699	26	18	32	34
1700–1749	41	36	61	30
1749–1799	65	72	114	26
1800–1849	152	167	177	31
Total	320	304	421	31
Wu Lineage				
To 1599	8	2	0	80
1600–1649	16	1	10	59
1650–1699	52	14	47	46
1700–1749	79	102	117	27
1749–1799	42	143	76	16
1800–1849	13	82	37	10
Total	210	344	287	25

NOTE: The analysis stops with the 1800–1849 cohort, since genealogies compiled in the late 1800s may miss sons of men born after 1850.

before their sons are born fail to meet the conditions. The results are presented in Table 6.5.

About 30% of the men in our sample thus became members of stem families when they were alive at the same time as their father and at least one of their sons. This percentage seems low, but it is also interesting to note that in two of the lineages, the majority of men who failed to become stem family members at this stage did so not because their sons were born after their fathers died but because they had no sons recorded in the genealogy. In the Lin lineage, for example, 65% of the men were not members of stem families at this stage. Of these, 34% of the total lacked sons, and 31% had sons but had them too late to be alive at the same time as the men's own

TABLE 6.6. Men Who Potentially Belonged
to Stem Families as Grandfathers

Cohort	Stem	No Son's Sons	Dead	% Stem
Lin Lineage				
To 1599	5	7	1	38
1600–1649	2	9	4	13
1650–1699	9	7	10	35
1700–1749	7	27	6	18
1749–1799	7	24	19	14
Total	30	74	40	21
Shi Lineage				
To 1599	18	11	15	41
1600–1649	14	6	9	48
1650–1699	14	30	22	21
1700–1749	18	68	48	13
1749–1799	47	89	68	23
Total	111	204	162	23
Wu Lineage				
To 1599	6	3	1	60
1600–1649	17	6	4	63
1650–1699	25	51	41	21
1700–1749	30	156	58	12
1749–1799	10	118	28	6
Total	88	334	132	16

NOTE: This analysis stops with the 1749–1799 cohort because the son's sons of men born in later cohorts might not have been born by the time the genealogies were compiled.

fathers. Corresponding figures for the Wu lineage are 75% who were not members of stem families, of whom 41% of the total lacked sons and 34% had sons who were born too late. Only in the Shi lineage are the proportions reversed, with 69% not forming stem families, of whom 29% of the total lacked sons and 40% of the total had sons who were born too late.

The third and final chance for a man to be part of a stem family is when his sons' children are born. Through a procedure analogous to those used for the first two stages in the life cycle, we have calculated the chances of a man's living to see the birth of his first son's son (see Table 6.6). As in the previous exercise, both men who had no son's son and men whose first son's son was born too late fall into the category of those who did not meet the criterion.

In the Qing dynasty, the period for which the figures are likely to be most complete, we find that on average somewhat less than one-quarter of the

TABLE 6.7. Probability of Being a Member of a Potential Stem Family

Cohort	Lin Lineage	Shi Lineage	Wu Lineage
To 1599	.94	.91	1.00
1600–1649	.88	.84	.97
1650–1699	.85	.64	.77
1700–1749	.64	.59	.56
1749–1799	.61	.67	.44
Overall probability	.77	.67	.64

men lived to be the grandfathers of potential three-generation families. We also find the same pattern we saw with the middle stage of life: in the Lin and Wu lineages, the largest number of those who failed to become grandfathers of stem families failed because they had no grandsons. In the Shi lineage the pattern was reversed; the majority of those who did not form stem families failed because they did not live long enough to see their sons' sons born.

If we sum up all these results, what were a man's overall chances of being alive at the same time as those relatives that would allow him to be part of a stem family? We have not been able to calculate this directly from individual cases but can get a good idea from a product of probabilities: $P = 1 - (q_1 q_2 q_3)$, where P is the probability of being part of a potential three-generation family at some point in one's life, and q_1, q_2, and q_3 are the probabilities of *not* being a member of such a group at the stages of birth, son's birth, and son's son's birth, respectively. The values of P for each lineage in each cohort are presented in Table 6.7.

Our figures thus indicate that in the seventeenth and eighteenth centuries, anywhere from just over 50% to more than 90% of the males in the three lineages lived at the same time as the relatives necessary for them to form families of three or more generations with at least the stem degree of complexity. That such men actually lived in stem family households is highly probable given the almost universal residence of parents with at least one of their married children in all known Chinese communities.

The overall figure of somewhere around 70% is somewhat lower than the figure of over 90% arrived at by Wolf, but we must remember that our methods of calculation are extremely conservative, and in all but the early cohorts, where it is likely that there is a recording bias in favor of men with many descendants, tend to *grossly underestimate* the chances of living in a stem family.

This underestimation stems from two sources. First, the genealogies record only men who lived to age twenty. For this reason men who had, say, a son who died young while the grandfather was still alive and another son after the grandfather died would have experienced life in a stem family but would not show up as such in our figures. Similarly, some grandfathers may have known their grandsons as little tots and would thus have experienced life in stem families, but because their grandsons died in their childhood or teens, these men would not show up in our figures. Since we do not know the extent of mortality before age twenty, we have no way of determining how much underestimation is caused by this figure, but it is probably not great. Second, and more important, is our inability to figure females into our calculations at all. Perhaps the prototypical stem family includes parents, children, and a widowed grandmother. Because women are an average of two to three years younger than their husbands in our sample (see above), it is more likely that the senior generation of an extended family would be a widowed grandmother, and this type of stem family does not show up in our records at all. In addition, there are all the stem families with little granddaughters but no grandsons. Although we again have no means of estimating the effect of this variable, we can posit that it is considerable, and it is very likely that if women were included in our calculations, the percentage of people experiencing life in a three-generation family would approach the 90% or more reported by Wolf for modern Taiwan.

It is also interesting to note that our figure is slightly higher than that calculated by Liu Ts'ui-jung for five lineages in chapter 5. She notes in her paper, however, that two of her five cases show percentages very close to those in our three cases, and that the variation among her cases is within a reasonable range. It should also be noted that her calculations, like ours, are limited to males and thus underestimate the total number of stem families.

Joint Families

The above analysis, of course, tells us nothing yet about the probability of experiencing life in a joint family. A joint family may be of either what Wolf calls the grand form, in which married brothers live together with their parents, or the *frèrèches* form, in which married brothers live in an undivided household after their parents have died. The probability of living in a grand family is of course influenced by the overlap of generations, as just discussed; the possibility of living in *frèrèches* is not, except insofar as brothers may tend to divide their households after their parents die. But, as mentioned, the genealogical records give us no information whatsoever on the timing of family division. We thus need to assume that families divided when the senior male in the eldest generation died. There are exceptions to this principle. In particular, it seems clear that elite families, or those with diversified economies, tended to remain together in the *frèrèches* form after the parents' death, whereas wage-laboring families tended to divide while the grandfather was still alive. But since we have no information, we must perform our calculations based on the original assumption; it would be possible to recalculate the rates if we assumed some other point of division.

We can follow the same kind of procedure in determining the proportion of men who experienced life in joint families that we used for stem families above. As with stem families, there are three points in the life cycle at which a man can be part of a joint family: with his grandparents, parents, father's brother and his wife, and patrilateral parallel cousins; with his parents, wife and children, brother, and brother's wife and children; and with his sons, their wives, and their children. Here we examine in turn the probability of being part of a joint family at each stage.

We can begin with the childhood stage (see Table 6.8). Here we adopt the most rigorous definition of joint family and include as having experienced joint family living only those men who had a father's brother's son born while their grandfather was still alive. Despite the considerable variation from cohort to cohort within each lineage, we get a remarkably consistent figure of about 20% of boys born who might have lived in joint families before their grandfathers died. We have no way, of course, of determining how many boys lived in joint families that either continued beyond their grandfathers' deaths or were formed after the grandfather was dead, that is, how many were born into *frèrèches* or grandmother-headed families. But the 20 to 21% we find here can serve as a minimum figure for this stage.

The next stage at which a man could be a member of a joint family is in early adulthood to middle age, when a man and his brothers, all married, are living in a joint household with their parents, wives, and children. We have calculated the chances of living in a joint family at this stage by counting the percentages of men who had a son and a brother's son, both born while ego's father (the boys' grandfather) was still alive. The results are presented in Table 6.9. Here we find that about 20% of the males in the Lin and Wu lineages and 29% of the males in the Shi lineage might have experienced life in a joint family at the middle stage of life. As with our calculations for the first stage, we have used the most rigorous assumptions and have thus excluded men who lived with their brother and his wife but none of the brother's children; men who lived with their brothers, their wives, and daughters, but no sons; and men who lived with brothers, wives, sons, and a widowed mother but no father. So our figures represent a very conservative minimum figure for membership in joint families at the middle stage of life.

It is also worth pointing out here that it is the size of the sibling set—that is, factors of fertility and early mortality that determine whether men have brothers or not—that seems to be the limiting factor in the formation of

TABLE 6.8. Men Who Potentially Belonged
to a Joint Family in Childhood

Cohort	Joint Families	No Father's Brother's Son	Father's Father Dead	% Joint
Lin Lineage				
To 1599	4	10	0	29
1600–1649	7	6	0	54
1650–1699	4	16	10	13
1700–1749	13	29	4	28
1749–1799	4	30	6	10
1800–1849	5	84	6	5
1850–1899	15	56	0	21
1899–	32	61	3	33
Total	84	292	29	21
Shi Lineage				
To 1599	9	24	2	26
1600–1649	18	25	7	36
1650–1699	14	48	24	16
1700–1749	21	76	27	17
1749–1799	34	144	52	15
1800–1849	123	337	125	21
1850–1899	95	300	66	21
Total	314	954	303	20
Wu Lineage				
To 1599	0	11	0	0
1600–1649	12	11	4	44
1650–1699	36	63	22	30
1700–1749	84	161	52	28
1749–1799	39	199	45	14
1800–1849	20	130	20	12
1850–1899	9	38	11	16
Total	200	613	154	21

joint families. The failure of generations to overlap seems to have been responsible for only 10 to 20% of the cases that did not form joint families.

The third and final life stage in which a man can be a member of a joint family comes when he is the father of married sons with children. We have calculated the likelihood of becoming such a grandfather by looking at the percentage of men who lived to have two sons with sons; the results are presented in Table 6.10.

TABLE 6.9. Men Who Potentially Belonged to a Joint Family in Middle Life

Cohort	Joint	No Son or Brother's Son	Father Dead	% Joint
Lin Lineage				
To 1599	4	10	1	27
1600–1649	4	4	0	50
1650–1699	10	9	6	40
1700–1749	7	23	6	19
1749–1799	8	25	0	24
1800–1849	11	63	9	13
Total	44	134	22	22
Shi Lineage				
To 1599	10	23	7	25
1600–1649	14	22	8	32
1650–1699	24	35	7	36
1700–1749	42	85	11	30
1749–1799	76	148	27	30
1800–1849	131	318	46	26
Total	297	631	106	29
Wu Lineage				
To 1599	3	2	2	43
1600–1649	15	6	5	58
1650–1699	46	43	25	40
1700–1749	71	194	34	24
1749–1799	27	222	14	10
1800–1849	7	118	5	5
Total	169	585	85	20

NOTE: Cohorts born after 1849 are excluded, since many of the sons of this cohort would not yet have been born by the time the genealogy was compiled.

On the whole, even if we allow for the probable underreporting of grandfathers in the Wu lineage in the eighteenth century, we find a lower percentage of men who became grandfathers of joint families than lived in joint families in either the childhood or the middle generation. This finding is not surprising, since mortality eliminates some men before they become grandfathers; though, in fact, we see that in most cases, men failed to become grandfathers because they did not have a grandson through the second son, not because they died before that relative was born. Still, we must point out once again that the definitions of joint family used here are extremely conservative; we did not include men who had grandsons who died before adulthood or men who had only granddaughters before they died.

TABLE 6.10. Men Who Potentially Belonged
to a Joint Family as Grandfathers

Cohort	Joint	No Two Sons with Sons	Dead	% Joint
Lin Lineage				
To 1599	2	9	0	18
1600–1649	1	13	1	7
1650–1699	5	18	3	19
1700–1749	0	37	0	0
1749–1799	3	36	0	8
Total	11	113	4	9
Shi Lineage				
To 1599	5	33	4	12
1600–1649	6	21	2	21
1650–1699	16	47	3	24
1700–1749	23	106	5	17
1749–1799	41	151	11	20
Total	91	358	25	19
Wu Lineage				
To 1599	2	6	2	20
1600–1649	10	12	4	38
1650–1699	21	91	5	18
1700–1749	13	224	7	5[a]
1749–1799	4	149	2	3[a]
Total	50	482	20	9

NOTE: Cohorts born after 1799 are excluded, since it is quite possible that the grandsons of a man born in 1849 would not yet be born by the time of compilation of the genealogy.

[a]As mentioned earlier, record keeping in the Wu lineage seems to have deteriorated in the nineteenth century, or perhaps there was a massive out-migration; we have some evidence of this. In either case, the grandsons of these two cohorts would be lost to the genealogizers, giving us an artificially low percentage of men with grandsons through two different sons.

What does all this tell us about a man's chance of living in a joint family at some time during his life? We can use the same formula that we employed in the case of the stem family, namely, $P = 1 - (q_1 q_2 q_3)$, where P is the probability of being part of a potential joint family at some point in one's life, and q_1, q_2, and q_3 are the probabilities of *not* being a member of such a group in childhood, in middle life, and as a grandfather, respectively. The values of P for each lineage in each cohort are presented in Table 6.11.

Despite obvious problems and inconsistencies in the data, there is a clear pattern visible in all three of the lineages. In each case, the chance of being a member of a joint family at some stage of the life cycle typically remained

TABLE 6.11. Probability of Being a Member of a Potential Joint Family

Cohort	Lin Lineage	Shi Lineage	Wu Lineage
To 1599	.57	.51	.54
1600–1649	.79	.66	.85
1650–1699	.58	.59	.66
1700–1749	.42	.52	.48
1749–1799	.37	.52	.25
Total	.44	.54	.42

around one-half. If we loosen our definition as discussed above, or if we postulate that family division might have occurred a few years after the father's death, permitting the formation of frèrèches, then that chance would probably rise to two-thirds or three-quarters of the total numbers of males. These figures are quite compatible with Wolf's reports for the twentieth century and with Liu Ts'ui-jung's reports in chapter 5. On the other hand, if we postulate that brothers typically divided while their father was still alive, then our percentage obviously drops. We have little to go on here, but division very soon after the father's death is probably the best guess, making our estimates just slightly conservative.

Both the general proportions and the temporal patterns are similar in the three lineages; men were most likely to experience joint family life if they were born in the seventeenth century, particularly the early part, when their children and grandchildren would be born and grow up in the prosperity of the early Qing. And the chances declined in all the lineages for men born toward the end of the seventeenth century and into the eighteenth; the most precipitous declines were in the proportion who became grandfathers, which we would expect to be the first variable to show the effects of deteriorating social conditions, since people became grandfathers several decades after they passed through the other stages. Biases in the data, due either to the founder effect, selective recording in the seventeenth century, or underrecording in the nineteenth, may exaggerate the trends, but it is unlikely, given fertility and mortality figures displayed throughout this volume, that the trends are altogether spurious. And although internal contradictions in the data prevent us from following the trend very far into the nineteenth century, we can postulate that it continued. This downward trend would be a reflection of the downward trends in reproductive rates, and the upward trends in mortality, that this and other papers have documented for the latter part of the Qing.

This whole exercise is, of course, very inexact; it illustrates the difficulties of extracting information about families from a document that is designed to record the history of a lineage, which is a different kind of social group. But it does have the virtue of illustrating that Wolf's contention (1984, 1985a) that a large percentage of Chinese in traditional times had the experience of a stem or joint family is supported by the data from the genealogies of the Xiaoshan lineages. Exactly how large a percentage is impossible for us to know.

CONCLUSIONS

Even though the study of Chinese historical demography, lineage-based and otherwise, may still be in its infancy, we are already beginning to see patterns emerge. We are not only able to begin to calculate and check such figures as fertility and mortality rates but are also beginning to perceive the nature of family formation in the late traditional period. What we find is, surprisingly perhaps, very similar to what has been found in studies of twentieth-century populations. The stem family was a reality at some time or other for almost everyone, and the joint family, not long ago thought to have been an ideal rarely realized, now begins to look like a fact of everyday life for ordinary populations. Of course not everyone experienced life in a joint family, but it is safe to assume now that everyone either lived as part of a joint family or had close relatives or neighbors who did. This means, in turn, that all the study of relationships between mothers-in-law and daughters-in-law, or between the *fang* within a *jia*, that has been carried out in recent ethnographic research probably tells us a lot about the Chinese family of the late Ming and Qing periods.

NOTES

1. A stem family is one that contains at least three generations with no more than one marital unit (couple or remnant of a divorced or widowed couple) in any one generation. A joint family is one that contains at least two marital units in one generation. In Wolf's typology, a grand family is a three-generation joint family, with a single marital unit in the eldest generation and multiple marital units in the second generation. A *frèrèche* is a joint family of two generations, with multiple marital units in the older generation (Wolf 1985a).

2. Previous work has analyzed records of the He, Lin, and Wu lineages, which were in fact three of the four lineages for which data were compiled. The Shi lineage was left out of earlier papers because its genealogy made it very difficult to compute rates by *fang* (the genealogy divided its charts into only two great *fang*, units not particularly interesting for the kind of analysis performed in the earlier paper). Here we have included the Shi because we have managed to get its data into computer-analyzable form, and excluded the He lineage because it was not possible to enter all its data.

3. For a description of the western part of Xiaoshan over the last nine centuries, see Schoppa 1989.

4. Under more realistic conditions (105–106 male births per 100 female births and an undetermined but not necessarily negligible rate of female infanticide), we would find the ratio of the surviving male birth interval to the surviving child birth interval to be a bit smaller than under our simpler assumptions, but the difference will be unlikely to affect age at marriage by more than one or two tenths of a year, which is well inside the accuracy we can expect from genealogies anyway.

5. This figure is counterintuitive; but in fact the average interval between male births is not twice the interval between births. The relationship between the two figures is complex, depending on the average number of births per mother. But if each mother has five total children, the ratio of male-to-male birth interval to child-to-child birth interval is 1.47; it increases as the number of children increases. We will use 1.5 as an estimate.

6. In creating their model life-tables, Coale and Demeny (1966) used a series of historical populations, primarily from Europe. They constructed a typology of mortality patterns, singling out three in particular that were characteristic of northern, southern, and eastern European populations primarily. The residue (which also proves to be very close to a kind of world average) was called the "West" pattern; it is with this model that we compare our empirical data.

SEVEN

A Century of Mortality in Rural Liaoning, 1774–1873

James Lee, Cameron Campbell, and Lawrence Anthony

Between 1700 and 1900 China's population tripled from 150 million to almost 500 million. This dramatic rise in population is probably the most frequently noted achievement of the Qing (1644–1911). Nevertheless, despite considerable research in the population history of this period we still know very little about the demographic characteristics of late imperial China. We have as yet very few precise measures of fertility, mortality, and nuptiality and almost no detailed demographic studies of the family, household, and lineage before 1900 (Ho 1959; Schran 1978). Without these precise measures we cannot fully understand Chinese population history, nor can we place that history within the context of world history.

Detailed population records, however, survive in the historical archives of the Republic of China and the People's Republic of China. Moreover, many methods exist to derive accurate measures of demographic change from these records. In this paper we reconstruct the mortality history of twelve thousand Chinese peasants who lived from 1774 to 1873, for whom we have virtually continuous registration data. First, we discuss these data and their limitations. Second, we adjust the data and present our method of analysis. Third, we calculate summary life tables for sixteen intercensal periods (1792–1795–1798–1801–1804, 1810–1813–1816–1819–1822, 1828–1831, 1837–1840–1843–1846, 1855–1858–1861–1864–1867) for females, as well as for the entire century for males, and assess the changes in mortality over time.

Since this paper was originally written in 1986, numerous other findings on the society and demography of Daoyi have emerged from analysis of the Banner registers described here. Readers interested in learning more about these findings are referred to the forthcoming volume *Fate and Fortune in Rural China* by James Lee and Cameron Campbell.

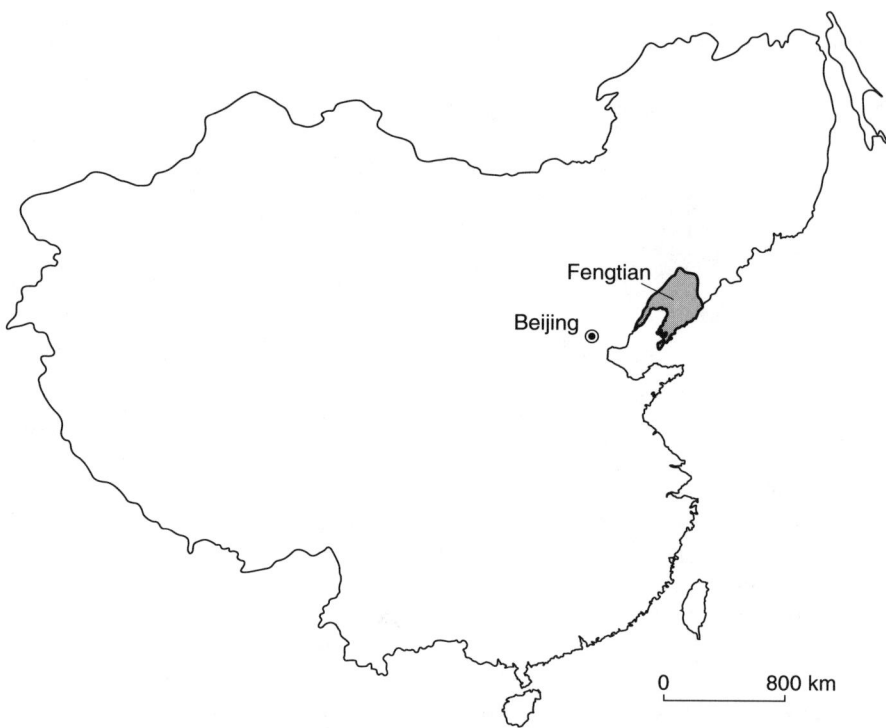

Map 7.1. Liaoning (Shengjing) Province ca. 1800
SOURCE: Derived from Tan Qixiang 1975 8.3–4.

All twelve thousand peasants were Han Chinese.[1] They lived in four villages in Shenyang county, which surrounds the provincial capital of what used to be called Fengtian and is now called Liaoning Province (see Maps 7.1 and 7.2). We derive their life histories from ninety thousand individual records preserved in twenty-five triennial population registers, dated 1774, 1780, 1786, 1792, 1795, 1798, 1801, 1804, 1810, 1813, 1816, 1819, 1822, 1828, 1831, 1837, 1840, 1843, 1846, 1855, 1858, 1861, 1864, 1867, and 1873.[2] For each person these registers record his or her name, age, occupation, family relationships, household relationships, lineage relationships, birth date, physical health (males only), police records (males only), recent demographic events, and village of residence.[3] The registers survive today in the Liaoning Provincial Archives of the People's Republic of China and are available on microfilm at the California Institute of Technology.[4]

The registers are a product of the Eight Banner system, which we have described in detail elsewhere (Fu 1983; Lee and Eng 1984; Lee and Fu n.d.). Unlike ordinary *baojia* registers, these records were heavily relied upon by

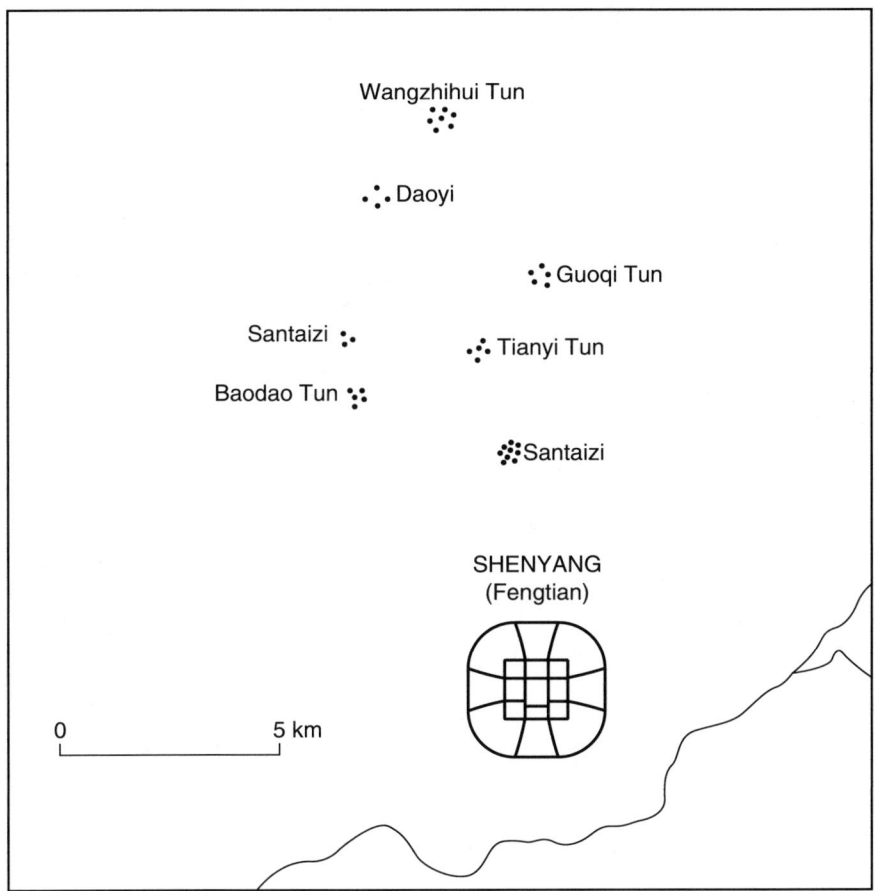

Map 7.2. Daoyi and Surroundings ca. 1800
SOURCE: Derived from Army map series 1.542, sheet NK 51–8, and *Shenyang XZ* (1917 ed.), 1.806–81a.

the Qing for civilian and military administration. They accordingly devised a remarkable system of internal checks for consistency and accuracy. Every person in the Banner population was assigned to a residential household (*linghu*) and had to be registered on a household certificate (*menpai*). These households in turn were organized into clans (*zu*), which had to compile annually updated genealogies (*zupu*).[5] Every three years local authorities compared these genealogies with the household certificates to compile the population registers. Thanks to such efforts, the Banner registers provide far more comprehensive and accurate data than population registration elsewhere in China (Skinner 1987). To the best of our knowledge, no other material records a Chinese peasant population before 1900 with similar detail, accuracy, and completeness.

Nevertheless the registers are far from perfect. Table 7.1 provides a crude demographic profile of all twenty-five registers in our possession. We identify four problems with these data. First, the data are incomplete, especially for females and for the very early age groups. As we can see from Table 7.2, almost no one is registered at one *sui*.[6] Indeed, the mean age at "birth" summarized for all twenty-five registers in Table 7.3 was approximately five *sui*. As mortality was concentrated among these early age groups, we are missing a significant proportion of all deaths.

Second, ages at entrance and exit are often unreported or reported incorrectly. The exact ages at marriage, migration, or death, therefore, elude us. We only know the three-year period during which the event occurred. We accordingly cannot calculate precise age-specific demographic rates. We can only calculate approximate rates.

Third, while exits are distinguished in the registers themselves, entrances are not annotated. We must infer births, in-marriages, and immigration by comparison with preceding registers. We cannot, therefore, identify many of the people who entered and exited during the interval. Our records of entrances accordingly are far less complete than those of exits. Moreover, our dependence on context makes us extremely vulnerable to missing registers.

Finally, fully one-quarter (nine) of the registers from the century under consideration are damaged or lost.[7] Consequently, our record of demographic events for twenty-seven years is highly incomplete. Moreover, whenever a register is missing, not only does the number of entrances and unannotated disappearances rise but the distinctions between disappearances due to emigration, out-marriage, and death and those between the entrances due to immigration and birth are lost. Because out-marriage occurs only for women, we confine our calculations of female mortality to the sixteen intercensal periods for which we have successive registers (1792–1795–1798–1801–1804, 1810–1813–1816–1819–1822, 1828–1831, 1837–1840–1843–1846, 1855–1858–1861–1864–1867). Our calculations of female life expectancy therefore cover only fifty-four years of the century under observation. Our calculations of male life expectancy by contrast include thirty intercensal periods (1774–1777–1780–1783–1786–1789–1792–1795–1798–1801–1804–1807–1810–1813–1816–1819–1822–1825–1828–1831–1834–1837–1840–1843–1846, 1855–1858–1861–1864–1867–1870–1873) and cover virtually the entire century.

Given our incomplete demographic records, an appropriate technique to calculate mortality would be by the intercensal death rates of age cohorts (Shryock et al. 1971). In a closed population the sole influences on the size of any age group at a census will be the size of the cohort comprising the age group at the last census and the level of fertility and mortality during the period between censuses. From the age structure of the population at two successive censuses, the probabilities of dying at any age before the next census can be calculated, and from these in turn the full range of life-table data can be calculated.

The method of mortality estimation is simple and straightforward. But it requires a population closed to migration, as well as accurate age reporting. In practice the application of this method has very often proved disappointing. Migration can distort survival as much as death. Age misreporting, especially selective under- and overenumeration, can cause insuperable problems. Finally, changes in enumeration completeness can completely swamp the effects of mortality and give rise to extremely misleading results.

In our study, however, we can directly meet these requirements by individual record linkage and subsequent data manipulation. We did this in three steps. Our first step was to trace each individual through every register. We discovered during the process of machine transcription that most individuals could easily be linked by hand by a combination of name, age, birthday, and the context of family relationships. In Table 7.1 we list the individuals we could not trace from the preceding register or otherwise account for as entrances through migration. The number is quite small.

Our second step was to close our population to migration. We excluded all immigrants and emigrants from the population at risk. Although people did occasionally disappear between consecutive registers, we identified these missing persons by machine. Table 7.1 also summarizes the number of these disappearances in each register. There are only three hundred sixty-four people missing from the sixteen intercensal registers used for most of our calculations. On average twenty-two people per register disappear. The vast majority of these people are either very old or very young. We believe that they disappeared by an unannotated death and, therefore, include them in the population at risk.[8]

Our third step was to correct any errors in age reporting. To do this we traced the age of each individual through every available register. We then calculated the most consistently reported age (the mode) and corrected all inconsistent ages. Table 7.4 identifies the common errors for the registers now in our possession. Table 7.5 contrasts the net error between the recorded age and the "corrected" age by five-year age groups. According to these figures, in any given register between one-tenth and one-fifth of the population reported an inconsistent age. Two-thirds of these errors are differences of plus or minus three years or less. One-third are differences of plus or minus just one year. These one-year errors may be due to variations in the date of reporting; that is, they may not be mistakes. The remaining errors are as likely to be the result of poor transcription (theirs

TABLE 7.1. A Summary Profile of the Population Registers

Register	Population			Entrances[a]			Exits[b]			Unannotated Disappearances		
	Total	Male	Female	Birth	Marriage	Migration	Death	Marriage	Migration	Total	Male	Female
1774	2373	1317	1056	—	—	—	137	31	15	—	—	—
1777	—	—	—	—	—	—	—	—	—	—	—	—
1780	2720	1546	1174	364	115	260	122	40	4	245	109	136
1783	—	—	—	—	—	—	—	—	—	—	—	—
1786	3021	1711	1310	474	175	220	190	48	34	423	219	204
1789	—	—	—	—	—	—	—	—	—	—	—	—
1792	3112	1732	1380	354	201	43	258	62	9	291	139	52
1795	3179	1767	1412	263	113	21	176	50	17	19	6	13
1798	3248	1805	1443	220	99	15	223	46	4	63	25	38
1801	3261	1809	1452	198	73	13	173	38	14	19	10	9
1804	3513	1947	1566	316	120	22	222	73	11	2	1	1
1807	—	—	—	—	—	—	—	—	—	—	—	—
1810	3525	1986	1539	354	176	37	253	56	15	257	95	162
1813	3524	1979	1545	184	97	27	211	55	7	7	4	3
1816	3471	1947	1524	131	88	4	220	50	3	13	8	5
1819	3416	1929	1487	124	63	5	144	40	10	6	4	2
1822	3618	2027	1591	236	148	24	287	107	2	22	12	10
1825	—	—	—	—	—	—	—	—	—	—	—	—
1828	3603	2061	1542	528	213	36	196	60	14	391	184	207
1831	3649	2088	1561	197	86	4	251	52	—	10	5	5

1834	—	—	—	—	—	—	—	—	—	—	—	—
1837	3633	2107	1526	400	183	16	205	65	4	312	131	181
1840	3587	2109	1478	154	83	1	237	65	1	18	7	11
1843	3424	2066	1358	113	53	2	196	36	1	29	7	22
1846	3374	2034	1340	118	94	—	174	39	3	30	12	18
1849	—	—	—	—	—	—	—	—	—	—	—	—
1852	—	—	—	—	—	—	—	—	—	—	—	—
1855	3460	2110	1350	390	275	15	191	30	6	371	171	200
1858	3435	2115	1321	126	94	8	176	36	2	33	13	20
1861	3479	2164	1315	157	99	6	183	30	1	16	10	6
1864	3533	2223	1310	173	95	25	339	14	1	30	17	13
1867	3466	2198	1268	187	112	17	244	22	4	47	26	21
1870	—	—	—	—	—	—	—	—	—	—	—	—
1873	3565	2253	1313	331	230	28	243	10	2	218	114	104
Total	12,466	6326	6140	6092	3085	849	5251	1155	184	2872	1329	1543

NOTES: Registers were compiled every three years. Most numbers, therefore, represent the cumulated events over a three-year intercensal period. Due to missing registers some numbers, however, represent the cumulated events over six years, and in one case, over nine years. The numbers reflecting six years are italicized.

[a] With the exception of adoptions, we infer all entrances by comparison with preceding registers.

[b] All exits are recorded in the registers. Marriages include remarriages. Emigrants are listed as AWOL (*taoding*).

TABLE 7.2. Ages at First Appearance ("Birth") 1774–1864

	Females	Males	Totals
1	52	108	160
2	170	436	606
3	244	664	908
4	241	598	839
5	222	627	849
6	180	512	692
7	123	293	416
8	91	217	308
9	60	159	219
10	44	111	155
11	31	87	118
12	27	75	102
13	19	46	65
14	17	44	61
15	12	25	37
16	14	17	31
17	2	13	15
18	2	6	8
19	5	4	9
20	1	6	7
21	0	2	2
Total	1573	4066	5639

NOTE: All ages in *sui*.

and ours) as incorrect reporting. Correct ages are usually consistent with the first age at appearance. Nevertheless, not all these "corrected" ages are necessarily correct.

We can distinguish three patterns in age misreporting in the registers under consideration. First, men were more prone to misreport their age than women. Approximately one-third more men did misreport. Second, men were far more prone to overreport their age than women. Approximately one-half more men did overreport. Third, old people were more likely to misreport their age than young people. In all registers the pattern is monotonic, with an abrupt increase in the proportion misreporting from at most one-twelfth to as much as one-eighth sometime during middle age. The causes for such selective misreporting are open to surmise. We suspect they were often deliberate.

From Table 7.5, however, we see that net error in age reporting was slight. Indeed once we organized the population into five-year age groups most

TABLE 7.3. Frequency and Mean Ages at First Registration

	Females	Mean Age	Males	Mean Age
1774	—	—	—	—
1780†	114	4.8	231	5.1
1786†	151	4.6	283	4.8
1792†	114	4.3	215	4.2
1795	59	4.3	120	4.3
1798	86	5.6	129	4.5
1801	68	4.6	126	5.3
1804	115	5.9	199	5.8
1810†	114	6.7	211	6.2
1813	64	5.2	118	5.3
1816	36	5.2	93	5.0
1819	37	6.0	86	7.5
1822	66	4.5	165	4.8
1828†	140	6.4	351	5.9
1831	65	5.3	130	4.1
1837†	96	6.0	274	5.7
1840	39	4.4	114	4.3
1843	20	4.4	93	4.0
1846	27	3.5	91	3.8
1855†	42	7.6	331	7.4
1858	9	3.0	114	4.0
1861	14	4.1	142	4.6
1864	10	3.9	162	5.2
1867	12	7.3	175	5.7
1873†	27	6.59	288	6.16

NOTE: Registers were compiled every three years. Most numbers, therefore, represent the cumulated events over a three-year intercensal period. Due to missing registers some numbers, however, represent the cumulated events over six years, and in one case, over nine years. Such numbers are indicated by the † symbol. All ages in *sui*.

errors canceled each other out. In almost all age groups, the mean absolute discrepancy was below three years. The worst discrepancies occurred among the older age groups (above fifty *sui*), where discrepancies of between three and five years became more common. These results compare favorably with population registration elsewhere, even in modern times. Indeed our data are apparently almost as accurate as the 1960 U.S. census for nonwhites (Ewbank 1981). Even uncorrected ages may, therefore, be sufficiently precise for most demographic analysis. Our registers, if they are representative of all Banner population registers, place the Chinese demographic records among the most accurate of world historical data.

Finally, having closed the population and corrected the age structure, we trace each live person in the first register forward to the next register by

TABLE 7.4. Common Discrepancies between Reported Age and Corrected Age

Errors	1774	1780	1786	1792	1795	1798	1801	1804	1810	1813	1816	1819	1822	1828	1831	1837	1840	1843	1846	1855	1858	1861	1864	1867
+4 or more	1.2	1.3	1.6	0.6	0.6	0.8	1.2	1.7	1.2	1.4	1.0	1.7	1.6	1.1	1.6	1.2	0.9	0.8	0.8	0.7	0.3	0.8	1.5	2.0
+3	0.8	0.8	0.5	0.3	0.2	0.2	0.3	0.5	0.5	0.5	0.5	0.6	0.6	0.6	0.6	0.5	0.5	0.6	0.5	0.4	0.3	0.3	0.3	0.5
+2	0.4	0.6	1.2	0.5	0.6	0.5	0.7	0.9	0.7	0.7	0.7	0.8	0.8	1.0	0.7	0.5	0.6	0.7	0.7	0.6	0.4	0.4	0.3	0.4
+1	1.4	1.7	1.5	1.0	0.9	1.1	1.1	1.2	1.3	1.2	1.2	1.4	1.7	1.6	1.8	1.3	1.1	0.9	1.2	1.3	1.1	1.3	1.6	2.1
None	87.1	85.5	88.4	91.6	93.2	92.5	91.6	89.6	92.1	92.9	91.4	89.2	88.3	87.5	89.7	91.8	92.7	92.7	92.4	92.1	94.0	93.6	91.6	88.4
-1	2.4	3.1	2.6	1.5	1.5	1.3	1.9	2.0	1.3	0.8	1.3	1.6	2.1	2.5	1.6	1.5	1.1	1.2	1.2	1.0	1.0	0.9	1.0	1.8
-2	1.7	2.0	1.9	1.7	1.0	0.8	1.1	1.5	0.6	0.7	0.7	0.9	1.1	1.3	0.7	0.5	0.4	0.4	0.5	0.3	0.2	0.4	0.3	0.5
-3	1.1	1.0	0.4	0.6	0.6	0.6	0.6	1.0	0.9	0.8	1.4	1.3	1.2	1.5	1.4	0.9	1.0	1.1	1.0	1.0	0.9	0.9	1.6	0.9
-4 or more	3.4	3.6	1.8	1.7	1.2	1.8	1.4	1.4	1.4	1.0	1.6	2.4	2.6	2.9	1.9	1.5	1.7	1.5	1.5	2.4	1.4	1.3	2.1	2.8

NOTE: Age differences in *sui*.

TABLE 7.5. Discrepancies in Age Reporting by Age Group (%)

Age Group	−5.00	−4.00	−3.00	−2.00	−1.00	0.0	1.00	2.00	3.00	4.00	5.00	Total
1–5	.5	.1	.6	.5	1.6	94.3	1.8	.4	.2	–	–	3512
5–10	.6	.1	.4	.4	1.1	92.7	2.0	1.0	.8	.4	.5	5589
10–15	1.0	.2	.3	.6	.9	91.3	2.0	1.2	.9	.5	1.2	5954
15–20	1.3	.2	.4	.7	1.3	91.2	1.4	1.0	.8	.3	1.5	6268
20–25	1.4	.2	.4	.5	1.1	91.9	1.5	.8	.7	.4	1.0	6925
25–30	1.4	.2	.3	.5	1.0	92.1	1.2	.8	.7	.4	1.5	6777
30–35	.9	.1	.3	.5	1.1	92.3	1.3	.7	.7	.3	1.8	6425
35–40	1.1	.1	.4	.5	1.0	92.5	.8	.6	.7	.2	2.0	6185
40–45	.9	.2	.5	.6	1.4	91.5	1.5	.6	.8	.1	1.8	5643
45–50	1.2	.2	.6	.8	1.6	91.2	1.2	.6	.8	.2	1.5	4940
50–55	1.2	.2	.8	.8	1.4	90.6	1.3	.5	.7	.5	2.1	4259
55–60	1.1	.3	.6	1.0	1.9	89.3	1.6	.5	1.1	.5	2.1	3709
60–65	1.4	.5	.9	1.1	2.1	88.1	2.0	.4	1.5	.4	1.7	3074
65–70	1.3	.4	.9	.8	2.3	88.1	1.5	.6	1.9	.3	1.8	2292
70–75	1.2	.4	.9	.7	2.2	85.5	2.2	.6	3.0	.5	2.7	1383
75 and up	5.8	.5	.6	1.3	1.6	75.5	2.6	1.7	4.2	.8	5.3	1650

NOTE: All ages in *sui*.

five-year age cohort. We divide the number of deaths in the second register by the person-years at risk from the first register to calculate the central death rates over three years.[9] We adjust these rates for five years and then calculate the possibility at age x of dying before age x + 5 according to a conventional method known as the Reed-Merrill technique (Shryock et al. 1971:443).[10] From these probabilities, called $_5q_x$, we then derive the full range of life-table functions, including life expectancy and the standard deviation of life expectancy (Chiang 1968: 209–11).[11] The result is a life table by five-year age cohorts based on the distribution of deaths during specific three-year periods.

According to these calculations, mortality during the century under observation was relatively moderate. Tables 7.6 and 7.7 summarize our results for males only and females only for the intercensal periods for which we now have data. On average men at six months of age, that is, two *sui*, could expect to live to thirty-five. Women at six months of age could expect to live past twenty-eight. Life expectancy at birth was, therefore, probably in the high twenties for women and in the low thirties for men.[12] Of course, given the missing deaths in our early age groups, mortality may in fact have been higher. Nevertheless, these conclusions suggest that mortality during the late eighteenth and early nineteenth centuries was lower than during the early twentieth century, when life expectancy at birth for both sexes was in the middle to low twenties (Barclay et al. 1976). Indeed

TABLE 7.6. Female Life Table, 1792–1867

Age Group	$_5N_x$	$_5N_{x+3}$	$_5M_x$	$_5q_x$	Life Expectancy	Standard Deviation of Life Expectancy
1–5	572	464	.06396	.2766	28.0	0.5
5–10	994	940	.01909	.0913	35.8	0.4
10–15	954	903	.01987	.0949	35.0	0.4
15–20	515	463	.02600	.1225	33.2	0.4
20–25	1145	1093	.01729	.0931	33.2	0.3
25–30	1737	1652	.0169	.0813	31.1	0.2
30–35	1761	1672	.0180	.0865	28.6	0.2
35–40	1688	1586	.0206	.0984	25.9	0.2
40–45	1557	1464	.0215	.1025	23.4	0.2
45–50	1384	1305	.0206	.0983	20.7	0.2
50–55	1187	1094	.0259	.1222	17.5	0.2
55–60	1088	991	.0303	.1416	14.6	0.1
60–65	921	797	.0442	.2000	11.5	0.1
65–70	733	582	.0692	.2957	8.6	0.1
70–75	435	318	.111	.4333	6.2	0.1
75 and up	475	289	.1388	.5100	3.7	0.1

NOTE: 1792–1795–1798–1801–1804, 1810–1813–1816–1819–1822, 1828–1831, 1837–1840–1843–1846, 1855–1858–1861–1864–1867. All ages in *sui*.

life expectancy in China at the turn of the nineteenth century appears to have been approximately as high as life expectancy in France at that time.[13]

In China, however, the pattern of mortality by sex and age differed greatly from the common experience of other historical populations. Not only did men generally live longer than women but mortality for both sexes was lower between the twenties and fifties than before or after. We believe that this pattern of mortality was probably the product of the unequal distribution of resources within the Chinese household. The incidence of death, in other words, reflects a social hierarchy that placed males before females and healthy adults above the young and the old.

In Table 7.8, we contrast male and female life expectancy by five-year age group and compare the implied mortality level of each age group with Model West populations from the Coale and Demeny (1966) regional model life tables.[14] On the basis of this comparison, we can elaborate on the Chinese pattern of mortality by sex and age. First, mortality was generally higher among females than among males. Young men could expect to live seven or more years longer than young women. Women did not begin to

TABLE 7.7. Male Life Table, 1792–1867

Age Group	$_5N_x$	$_5N_{x+3}$	$_5M_x$	$_5q_x$	Life Expectancy	Standard Deviation of Life Expectancy
1–5	1721	1455	.05461	.24123	35.2	0.3
5–10	2650	2527	.01985	.09485	43.3	0.3
10–15	2767	2697	.00853	.04182	42.9	0.2
15–20	2595	2531	.00995	.04863	39.7	0.2
20–25	2458	2399	.00802	.03939	36.4	0.2
25–30	2367	2312	.00819	.04023	32.7	0.2
30–35	2205	2138	.01058	.05162	28.9	0.2
35–40	2212	2123	.01322	.06414	25.2	0.2
40–45	1933	1838	.01612	.07169	21.8	0.2
45–50	1645	1520	.02737	.12856	18.3	0.2
50–55	1376	1245	.03145	.14638	15.4	0.1
55–60	1203	1019	.04832	.21647	12.6	0.1
60–65	980	822	.06097	.26549	10.4	0.1
65–70	668	517	.07456	.31500	8.1	0.1
70–75	349	234	.13233	.49297	5.7	0.1
75 and up	382	202	.17109	.58717	3.5	0.1

NOTE: 1792–1795–1798–1801–1804, 1810–1813–1816–1819–1822, 1828–1831, 1837–1840–1843–1846, 1855–1858–1861–1864. All ages in *sui*.

live longer than men until around age thirty. Moreover, the level of male mortality suggested by comparison with Model West populations remained significantly higher than the level of female mortality until age forty. Below age forty, in other words, men experienced fewer deaths than was common in populations with similar levels of female mortality elsewhere in the world. Above that age, however, the pattern was reversed. Not only did women live longer than men in an absolute sense, but their life expectancy was greater than that of women of similar ages in populations with equivalent levels of male mortality.

Second, men and women in their prime experienced fewer deaths than would be predicted by the mortality of the very young or the very old. Thus for men the mortality level upon adulthood first shifts upward from a Model West mortality level of six to a mortality level of seven or more (the equivalent of a life expectancy at birth in the upper thirties) and then declines in the older age groups to a mortality level of two or less (the equivalent of a life expectancy at birth in the upper teens or low twenties). Similarly, for women the mortality level shifts upward from West level one to West level six, then declines to below one. The distribution of deaths over age in our

TABLE 7.8. Differences in Male and Female Life Expectancy (F–M)

Age Group	Male Life Expectancy	West Mortality Level[a]	Female Life Expectancy	West Mortality Level[a]	Differences in Life Expectancy	Standard Deviation of the Differences in Life Expectancy
1–5	35.2	6	28.0	1	−7.2	.8
5–10	43.3	6	35.8	1	−7.5	.7
10–15	42.9	6	35.0	1	−7.9	.6
15–20	39.7	6	33.2	2	−6.5	.6
20–25	36.4	6	33.2	4	−3.2	.5
25–30	32.7	6	31.1	5	−1.6	.4
30–35	28.9	8	28.6	5	−.3	.4
35–40	25.2	7	25.9	5	.7	.4
40–45	21.8	7	23.4	6	1.6	.4
45–50	18.3	6	20.7	6	2.4	.4
50–55	15.4	6	17.5	6	2.1	.3
55–60	12.6	5	14.6	6	2.0	.2
60–65	10.4	5	11.5	6	1.1	.2
65–70	8.1	5	8.6	4	.5	.2
70–75	5.7	2	6.2	2	.5	.2
75 and up	3.5	< 1	3.7	< 1	.2	.2

SOURCE: Tables 7.5 and 7.6.
[a] To perform this approximation we assumed that ages in *sui* are one year rather than one and a half years less than Western ages. Actual mortality levels should be slightly higher, especially in the early age groups.

population, in other words, was quite different from the distribution of most other historical populations.

Mortality, of course, was far from constant. Figure 7.1 summarizes the annual crude death rates for sixteen three-year periods between 1772 and 1840. Figure 7.2 summarizes average life expectancy by age for both sexes combined for eight intercensal periods between 1798 and 1840. The differences are considerable. Life expectancy varied by as much as fifteen years, from an e_5 in the low fifties during the period from 1817 to 1819 to an e_5 in the middle thirties during the period immediately following, from 1820 to 1822. None of these years appears to have been a year of major famine.[15] Nevertheless, the contrast in mortality by age and sex between good and bad periods can tell us much about the differential access to resources in Daoyi.

Although the distribution of deaths by age remained relatively constant between good and bad periods, the distribution of deaths by sex differed considerably in our population. Male life expectancy apparently fluctuated

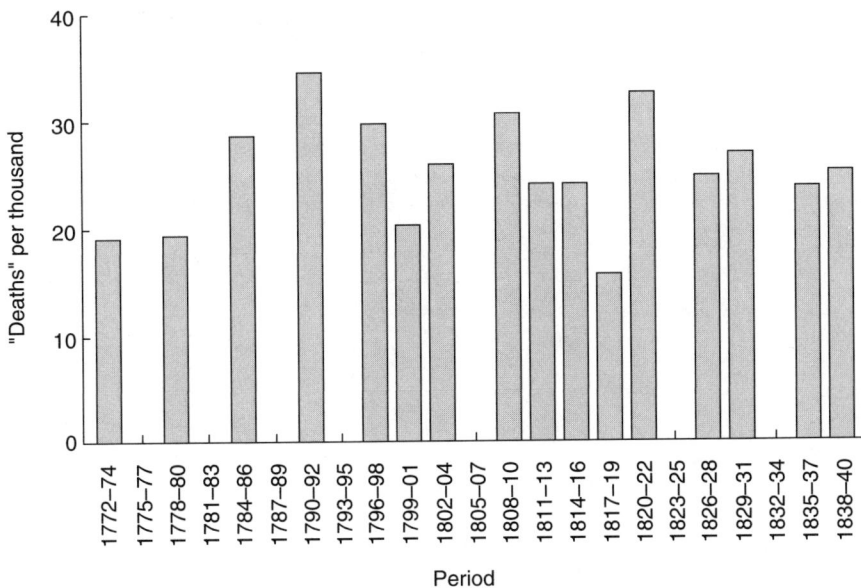

Figure 7.1. Annual Crude "Death" Rates
NOTE: Registered deaths only.

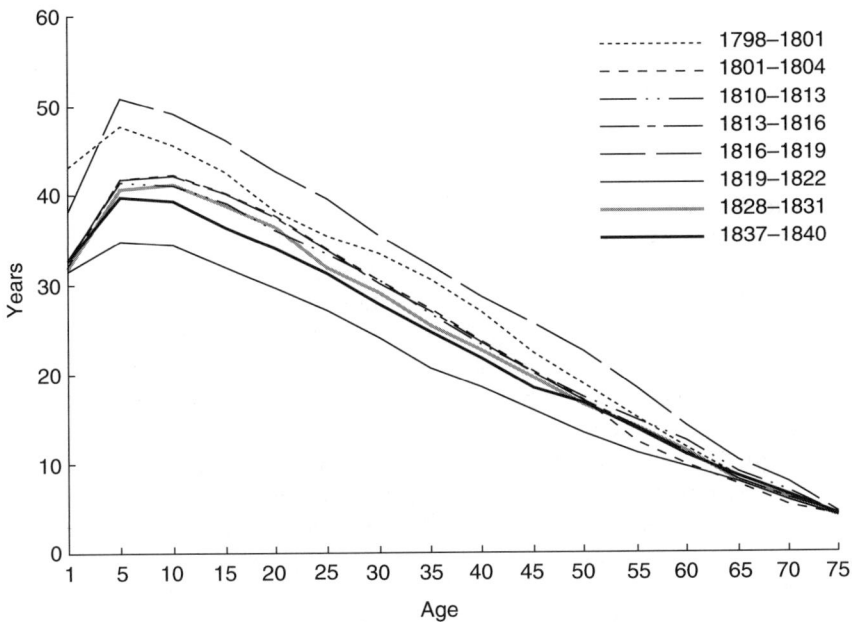

Figure 7.2. Intercensal Life Expectancy, Both Sexes

TABLE 7.9. Female Life Expectancies during Good Periods versus Bad Periods

Age Group	Life Expectancy in Good Periods	West Mortality Level[a]	Life Expectancy in Bad Periods	West Mortality Level[a]	Differences in Life Expectancy	Standard Deviation of Differences in Life Expectancy
1–5	37.119	4.043	26.767	<1	10.351	5.100
5–10	43.082	4.833	34.832	<1	8.249	5.127
10–15	41.964	5.964	32.984	<1	8.980	5.042
15–20	40.099	7.169	31.360	1.131	8.738	4.999
20–25	36.128	6.692	32.929	4.245	3.198	3.435
25–30	33.738	7.261	30.564	4.575	3.173	2.583
30–35	32.024	8.575	26.644	3.511	5.379	2.405
35–40	29.515	9.319	24.613	4.036	4.902	2.216
40–45	26.672	9.879	21.411	3.392	5.261	2.041
45–50	23.066	9.564	19.191	4.031	3.875	1.905
50–55	19.912	10.016	16.511	4.426	3.400	1.678
55–60	16.026	8.787	12.351	1.993	3.675	1.549
60–65	12.322	7.192	9.026	<1	3.295	1.339
65–70	9.381	5.836	7.352	<1	2.029	1.235
70–75	7.271	5.943	4.345	<1	2.925	1.087
75 and up	4.068	<1	3.658	<1	.409	.706

SOURCE: Table 7.6: (1799–1801) + (1817–1819) − (1838–1840).

[a] To perform this approximation we assumed that ages in *sui* are one year rather than one and a half years less than Western ages. Actual mortality levels should be slightly higher, especially in the early age groups.

far more than female life expectancy. In Tables 7.9 and 7.10 we contrast life expectancy by sex during two low-mortality periods (1799–1801 and 1817–1819) with that during two high-mortality periods for each sex (1838–1840 for females and 1820–1822 for males). In spite of the high standard deviations, the differences in male life expectancy are striking. By comparison the differences in female life expectancy seem almost insignificant. Male life expectancy at birth differed by fifteen years, with a standard deviation of 3.8. Female life expectancy at birth differed by only ten years, with a standard deviation of 5.10. The implication is a consumption pattern where females consumed fewer resources than males and where female consumption remained relatively constant. Males may not only have consumed a greater share of resources but also have appropriated much of the surplus to themselves in good years.

These behavioral results, of course, do not explain why our population behaved the way it did. Were the differences in life expectancy by sex in the younger ages largely a result of neglect of younger women or were they the

TABLE 7.10. Male Life Expectancies during Good Periods versus Bad Periods

Age Group	Life Expectancy in Good Periods	West Mortality Level[a]	Life Expectancy in Bad Periods	West Mortality Level[a]	Differences in Life Expectancy	Standard Deviation of Differences in Life Expectancy
1–5	44.790	8.386	30.141	1.157	14.648	3.766
5–10	53.545	12.903	35.115	< 1	18.430	2.912
10–15	51.546	14.472	35.113	2.292	16.432	2.520
15–20	47.916	15.146	31.931	2.545	15.984	2.355
20–25	43.790	15.214	29.015	2.783	14.774	2.246
25–30	40.731	16.145	26.166	2.684	14.564	2.106
30–35	36.500	15.976	22.698	1.971	13.802	2.013
35–40	32.947	16.593	19.164	< 1	13.783	1.869
40–45	28.748	16.362	16.402	< 1	12.345	1.767
45–50	24.705	16.102	13.804	< 1	10.900	1.655
50–55	21.239	16.618	11.483	< 1	9.755	1.555
55–60	17.268	15.467	9.394	< 1	7.874	1.444
60–65	13.279	12.750	8.370	< 1	4.909	1.346
65–70	9.544	8.885	6.734	< 1	2.810	1.252
70–75	6.956	6.673	4.656	< 1	2.300	1.086
75 and up	4.118	< 1	3.658	< 1	.459	.772

SOURCE: Table 7.7: (1799–1801) + (1817–1819) − (1820–1822).

[a] To perform this approximation we assumed that ages in *sui* are one year rather than one and a half years less than Western ages. Actual mortality levels should be slightly higher, especially in the early age groups.

result of conscious discrimination? Similarly, were the increases in female life expectancy during their thirties and forties a reflection of the higher status of age or were they simply a consequence of a fall in maternal mortality? Direct evidence on such questions must come from other sources if it is to come from anywhere.

Our findings do, however, give us some insight into the rise in Chinese population during the eighteenth and nineteenth centuries. Until recently virtually the only precise demographic study of a "traditional" rural Chinese population was the Barclay, Coale, Stoto, and Trussell reexamination of the population data collected by Buck in his 1929–1931 survey of Chinese agriculture (1976). Relying very heavily on a body of indirect techniques of demographic estimation, they concluded that life expectancy at birth in rural China was in the low to middle twenties. Moreover, according to these authors, such high mortality was probably characteristic of the demography of late imperial China. The problem that then confronted historians was how to explain the sustained rise in Chinese population in the face of such high mortality. The present study using techniques of direct analysis on eighteenth- and nineteenth-century materials suggests that life expectancy in late imperial China on the contrary was considerably higher than had been previously thought. As our analysis progresses we look forward to a more complete understanding of Qing population dynamics.

NOTES

This work was supported by grants from the California Institute of Technology, the National Academy of Science, the National Endowment of the Humanities, and the Wang Institute of Graduate Studies. We would like to thank them for their assistance.

1. According to the 1864 title page, these are the "Daoyi Village population registers from the Han army of the Plain Yellow Standard" (*Zheng huangqi Daoyi tun Hanjun rending hukou ce*). The population is not Manchu. In 1983 of the 17,100 people who live in Daoyi Xiang, of which our four villages are part, 400 were Korean, 700 were Manchu, and 16,000 were Han Chinese. Zhou Yuanlian (1981, 1982) describes the establishment of the Liaoning Han banners in some detail.

2. All twenty-five registers have been transcribed into machine-readable form. The process has been very labor intensive. James Lee transcribed the registers for 1774 and 1792. Robert Eng transcribed the registers for 1780 and 1786. Julie Sun transcribed the registers for 1798 and 1819. Liu Guiping transcribed the register for 1855. Wang Yuanqing transcribed the register for 1861. He Ti transcribed the register for 1864. Anna Chi transcribed the registers for 1795, 1843, 1846, 1858, and 1873. Alice Suen transcribed the remaining registers: 1801, 1804, 1810, 1813, 1816, 1822, 1828, 1831, 1837, and 1840. Lawrence Anthony, Cameron Campbell, and Martin Hunt wrote machine programs to identify transcription errors. Anna Chi and James Lee "cleaned" the entire data set. The total process has taken several thousand hours stretching over the last five years.

3. All ages are in *sui*. Birth dates are by lunar calendar. The registers only record disappearances by death, marriage, and migration. We infer all appearances by birth, marriage, and immigration from context by comparison of consecutive registers.

4. Altogether there are over three thousand such population registers in the Liaoning Provincial Archives. I would like to thank the archival authorities for making the thirty-six Daoyi registers available to me. Ju Deyuan introduced me to their existence in 1981. Wu Fusheng and Liu Kuizhi collected and copied the registers in 1982 and 1985. I am deeply grateful to them and their colleagues for their assistance. I could not have proceeded without their help.

5. According to my survey of Daoyi in October 1986 and July 1987, although most of these genealogies were destroyed during the cultural revolution, several still survive. See Lee and Campbell forthcoming for an anlysis of these data.

6. Apparently the Chinese did not consider children during the first year of life to be fully "human." The *Collection of Important Documents of the Tang* records an imperial edict in 623: "People when they are first born are just young animals

[*huang*]. At four *sui* they become minors [*xiao*]. At sixteen *sui* they become youths [*zhong*]. At twenty-one *sui* they become adults [*ding*]. At sixty *sui* they become old [*lao*]" (*Tang huiyao* 1991). According to a famous passage from the *Rites of Zhou*, a compendium of statements on early political institutions and policies probably completed in the second century B.C., "people should be registered after they have grown their teeth." In a well-known commentary on this passage Qiu Jun, a fifteenth-century statesman, explained: "The human body is not fully developed until teeth are grown. Boys grow their first set of teeth in the eighth month and their second set in their eighth year. Girls grow their first set of teeth in their seventh month and their second set in their seventh year. They should then all be recorded in the population register" (Qui Jun 15th century).

7. These nine registers are dated 1777, 1783, 1789, 1807, 1825, 1834, 1849, 1852, and 1870. Until recently I had assumed that these missing registers were lost. It was not until a trip to Liaoning in October 1986 that I discovered that several (how many is still not clear) of these registers actually survive, but in damaged form. The Liaoning Provincial Archives has agreed to make the damaged registers eventually available to me.

8. We have done our calculations both with and without including these unannotated disappearances as deaths. The results are very similar. They are slightly smoother in the oldest age groups with this procedure.

9. To perform this calculation, we assign each person alive in the second register three person-years according to his age in the first register. As we do not know the exact year of death, we assign one-third of a death to each of the three years in the period. We then distribute the one and a half person-years lived by all people who died during the intercensal period to each of the three years in the period by 4/6, 3/6, and 2/6 per year of age. We would like to thank Tom Pullum for suggesting this method of calculation.

10. We would like to thank Richard Barrett for suggesting the Reed-Merrill method to us. In Anthony, Lee, and Suen 1985 we have estimated life expectancy by the rates of survival according to the methods suggested in Hill and Trussell 1983. The results are approximately the same.

11. We would also like to thank Ronald Lee for introducing us to Chiang's 1968 analysis on how to calculate the standard deviation of life expectancy.

12. We make these estimates by comparison with the regional model life tables calculated by Coale and Demeny. These life tables unfortunately do not distinguish the first year of life by month.

13. In France, according to Blayo 1975, life expectancy from 1770 to 1779 was 28.2 for males and 29.6 for females at birth, 38.6 for males and 38.5 for females at age one, and 46.0 for males and 45.6 for females at age five. Life expectancy from 1780 to 1789 was 27.5 for males and 28.1 for females at birth, 37.6 for males and 37.1 for females at age one, and 45.5 for males and 44.3 for females at age five. By contrast, in England, according to Wrigley and Schofield 1981, life expectancy at birth for both sexes was 36.3 from 1750 to 1775, 37 from 1775 to 1800, and 41.5 from 1800 to 1825.

14. The Coale and Demeny model populations and life tables were constructed to facilitate extrapolations from incomplete or partial demographic data. They found that the range of human mortality can be divided into four distinct age

patterns of death that they labeled west, north, east, and south. Each of these four sets of regional model life tables was based on historical data from different regions of the world, and contains twenty-four "mortality levels" ranging from a life expectancy at birth of eighteen to seventy-five. These mortality levels are defined so that the higher the life expectancy, the greater the mortality level.

15. The year 1802 was apparently the only bad harvest year during the period under consideration. According to the local gazetteer, "in 1802 there was inadequate spring rain. Moreover, violent winds during the fourth and fifth months devastated the fields. The harvests were extremely poor—approximately half the normal yield" (*Fengtian tongzhi*, 36.723). The result was a considerable decline in life expectancy at six months of age to thirty for females (with a standard deviation of 2.8) and thirty-two for males (with a standard deviation of 1.9).

EIGHT

Migration in Two Minnan Lineages in the Ming and Qing Periods

Wang Lianmao

Translated by Stevan Harrell

Minnan (present-day Quanzhou, Zhangzhou, and Xiamen) has historically been a typical immigrant society. Today, many lineages can trace the history of their gradual southward migration from North China in the Jin (260–311), Tang (618–908), Five Dynasties (908–960), Song (960–1280), and other periods. And the area's ancient language, drama, music, and social customs all can be traced to the influence of the remains of the medieval culture of the North China area brought there by immigrants.

Minnan is also a society with an unbroken history of out-migration; because of this it has become famous as a homeland of overseas Chinese and as the most important ancestral home of the inhabitants of Taiwan. The beginning of the out-migration of Minnan people can be traced to the period of large-scale maritime foreign trade from the port of Quanzhou in the Tang, Song, and Yuan periods. But the most important trend during those periods was the in-migration of large numbers of Arab merchants, missionaries, and others.

Beginning in the middle years of the Ming, following upon the decline of official trade at Quanzhou, the gradual rise, under difficult circumstances, of private free trade, the uneven development of the feudal economy, the growing seriousness of the land problem, and the social unrest brought about by armies fighting locally, the outward migration of people from all areas of Minnan increased steadily and eventually became a large-scale population movement, which continued in various forms until the 1940s.

This population movement, aside from a period of sale of coolie labor, generally consisted of free migration and, from the beginning, had a strong basis in kin and locality connections, with its most basic form being migration of agnatic groups as units. For this reason, genealogies are an ideal source for investigation of this population movement.

In the last few years I have carried out various investigations of lineages in the cities, towns, and villages of Minnan and have looked at over 100 genealogies of various surnames. I have chosen the *Genealogy of Dongxiating Branch of the Yan Lineage, Anping* (a printed genealogy in sixteen volumes, revised in 1942, and called "the Yan genealogy" below) and *The Genealogy with Records of the Generations of the Lin Lineage of Pushan, Longhai, Zhangzhou* (a written genealogy in five volumes, revised in 1774, and called "the Lin genealogy" below) for detailed research. I use various kinds of tabulations, analyses, and comparisons from these two lineages to explore the different natures and characteristics of migration in lineages living in two different kinds of economic environments during the Ming and Qing.

THE YAN AND LIN LINEAGES

The Yan Lineage of Anping, a Coastal Commercial Town

Anping, also called Anhai, formerly belonged to the eighth *du* of Jinjiang County, Quanzhou Prefecture. It is located on Weitou Bay at the south end of that county and in former times was one of the most important foreign trade centers in Quanzhou. In the Song period, the port of Anhai was already a place where "the ships reached around the world, and foreigners and natives traded together" (Anhai ca. 1600). In the Shaoxing period of the southern Song (1131–62), two large stone bridges were built over the bay—the Anping Bridge, five *li* in length, and the Tongyang Bridge, three *li* in length. These bridges helped to concentrate trade and contributed to the strength of the economy. Even though official trade at the ports of Quanzhou diminished during the Ming, the flourishing town at Anping did not decline but actually developed further.

He Jiaoyuan, a famous historian of the late sixteenth and early seventeenth centuries, makes frequent reference to the situation in Anping at that time. He says:

> The town of Anping is to the southeast of the city, on the edge of the ocean, with over 100,000 inhabitants; there are literary gentry equivalent to those of a large county. Its people plow and weave, and many of them conduct trade with the two capitals [Nanjing and Beijing], Shandong, Henan, Jiangsu, Zhejiang and Lingnan; in addition they sail the seas to trade with many foreign places, increasing their financial strength.

He also commented on the social customs of Anping:

> It is much like Huizhou, in that there are a lot of people in a small area, so that seven of ten households depend for their living upon [trade with] the outside. (He Qiaoyuan ca. 1600)

Another famous author, He's contemporary Li Guangjin, also mentions Anping in his writings:

> Anping belongs to traders, and has gradually become dominant. They don't rely on their local market either, but husbands and sons put on their hats as soon as they are born, and in pursuit of riches travel and trade all over the country. They go north to Hebei, south to Jiangsu, east to Guangdong, west to Sichuan. Or braving the winds and bucking the waves, they wrest profit from barbarian villages on oceanic islands. Those close to home return once a year; those far away return only after several years. They pass through the county and don't go home, but make their abode in other cities. Affairs of the household are managed by women. This is a general summary of their customs. (Li Guangjin ca. 1600)

This kind of lively internal and external commercial activity not only brought about the emergence in Anping of a commercial stratum containing a large number of households (many of them wealthy merchants) but also took the residents forward a step in establishing their economic position in the country. According to the *Gazetteer of Anhai* from the Ming period:

> There is no direction in the straight streets or narrow alleys that does not have commercial shops; there are over a thousand of them, and those from all over who go after profits must hurry there; they will be able to do business all around. (Anhai ca. 1600)

As Professor Fu Yiling of Xiamen University has pointed out, Anping has a special place in Ming economic history. Fu goes so far as to say:

> The foreign trade of the Ming period, in the first place, was created by Fujian merchants (including Anping merchants definitely playing an important part) and Huizhou merchants together; with merchants from Guangdong and other places also participating. (Fu Yiling 1983)

I am very much in agreement with this view. Anping was a nuclear area of Minnan trade in the middle and late Ming, and flourished during this period. But, unfortunately, in the Shunzhi period of the Qing, in 1656 and again in 1661, the town was subjected to damage by Qing troops and to the coastal deportation order. But after 1684, when the order was rescinded and coastal people were allowed to return, the refugees rebuilt their homes; from then until the Qianlong period, Anping gradually recovered its prosperity and did not lose its place as the commercial center of southern Jinjiang County.

The Yan lineage of Anping lived on the edge of this outward-oriented, commercially flourishing town. This point is important when we look at the reasons for and nature of migration of the people of that lineage. Members of the Yan lineage today are still concentrated in two places: in Xingco, to the north of town, and in Xi'an, to the west. The town itself was very small in the Ming period, and these settlements at that time were right up against the town walls; today they are continuous with the town. In addition, many of the residents today have given up the traditional style of architecture and have built many new multistoried buildings, giving the place an even less rural appearance. The surrounding farmland is scarce and poor, with the primary crops being sugarcane and squashes. There are now over three thousand Yans, most of them engaged in nonagricultural labor. As a result of several centuries of out-migration, there are now over a thousand descendants of this lineage living overseas, in such places as the Philippines, Indonesia, Malaysia, Singapore, Vietnam, Burma, Thailand, Hawaii, and Taiwan (Yan 1978).

As to when the Yans settled Anping, there is still no evidence. The current branch is descended from Zhang Jun'an of Nan'an County, who was married uxorilocally to the daughter of Yan Balang. The Yan genealogy says:

> The founding male ancestor's ... personal name was Deliang, and his *zi* was Jun'an. The founding female ancestor, Yitai, was posthumously named Guizhang. He was the second son of Zhang Fushi of Zhongcun village, Panlu township, Nan'an county. He was married uxorilocally to the daughter of Balang. Their descendants occupied Shuilu township in the 8th *du*, which today is Shangxian township, and Qinchang divided off to reside in Zhugui ward, which is today's Xi'an township. Their descendants are the Yans of Anping.

Zhang Jun'an and Yan Yitai had two sons, the elder of whom was Shiyuan, born in 1305. From this we know that Zhang Jun'an and Yan Yitai married before 1305, at the beginning of the Dade period of the Yuan. Their descendants all took their mother's surname, but after they died the son's ancestral tablets were still inscribed "So-and-so, Zhang surname ancestor," in order to express the continuation of worship in the patriline. The Heyuan Zhang and Yan Combined Surname Association, active today in the Philippines, was organized according to this principle. The Yans of Anping recognize that they are a branch of the Fujian Yans but at the same time have not forgotten that they are also a branch of the Zhangs; and until recently they always took part in the lineage ancestral worship activities of the Zhangs of Jinjiang. These ties to two surname groups were very useful in increasing the power of the lineage.

This Zhang-Yan lineage of Anping did not arrive in the area any earlier than other lineages. But by the latter part of the Ming, they had clearly become one of the best known lineages in this area. We can see this from the biography of a Yan wife of Ke Rifan of Anping, written by Li Guangjin in the Wanli period: "The Kes and the Yans are the prominent lineages of this township [*li*]" (Li Guangjin ca. 1600). Even earlier than this, in Jiajing 36 (1557), the fact that Yan Qinfu, known as a village bully, dared to beat to death the famous gentryman Ke Shixiang, a retired former prefect who was in charge of the building of the Dongyang Bridge (Anhai ca. 1600), also testifies to the power of the Yan lineage at that time. From the genealogy we can also learn that after the middle of the fifteenth century there were a group of men in the Yan lineage who began to gain personal status and enter the official world through the examination system. Between the Chenghua and Chongzhen periods of the Ming (1465–1644), there were twenty-eight men in the lineage who held degrees of *shengyuan* or above, including one *jinshi*, four civil *juren*, and six military *juren*. The highest office attained was supervising secretary of the Office for Scrutiny of Rites. Of course, this record looks pale compared to those of some of the other Anping lineages, such as the Huang, Wang, and Chen, but it demonstrates that the social and political position of this lineage was on the increase.

We know that there was a particularly close connection in Ming times between the power of lineages in coastal communities and the private trading activity along the coast. For example the large Chen, Ke, Huang, and Yang lineages of Anping all acquired their reputations from trading. The Yans were not unusual:

> [Yan Jubian] came home from Jinling . . . after this, he traveled overseas, having contact with foreign kings, and trading in Jiangsu with Zhu and Tao. He was scholarly, filial, and friendly, and his liberality of mind brought him great success, so that he controlled great capital and developed a large business. (Yan 1942)

> Yan Lixue was a merchant in Guangdong. He was of sympathetic disposition and placed great store on generosity, and gained the respect of all merchants through his goodness of character. When he went to deal in overseas trade on an official commission, someone swindled him, and another merchant, Hu Tingshen, protected him, so that he could return without injury. He was thrifty in nature, and extremely economical in food and clothing. If someone he respected became poor, he was never tight; if they were in his debt, he would burn their promises and not ask for repayment. (Quanzhou 1736–96)

> Yan You, as soon as he was grown and married, was poor and so he traveled north as far as Hebei and south as far as Guangdong, using his profits to support his mother and brothers. There was someone from Zhangzhou who owed three hundred dollars to You; it had already been returned, but the note still existed. The man's son did not know; when his father died You went to see him; he thought You had come to collect his money, but You simply told him the reason and gave him back his note. (Quanzhou 1736–96)

> Chushi [Chen Douyan], when he had just become an adult, fled chaos to come to Anping. Yan Jundao, considering his character and morals, greatly respected him, and allowed him to marry his daughter. He staked a lot of money and capital on them, which Chushi used to ship goods, which he and his Yan wife together handled very frugally; what surplus they earned, they did not

treat as profit, but used it to compensate his father-in-law, who thus regarded them as trustworthy, and continued to stake money on them without asking about their accounts. At first Chushi struggled to learn his trade, but in the end struggled for enough time; his money flowed in and out like water; when he went on an expedition he was like fierce beasts or birds of prey, so that no one who dealt with him could match him in the end—whether people sold to him at a loss or owed him interest, in the end they all paid money to him. Chushi's business took him north to Hebei and Jiangsu, south to Guangdong. When the overseas trade was opened with Luzon, he earned money in Luzon. He became widely respected for his ability to earn money, so he was made [local] wine-libationer. In the end, when he had gained maximum wealth, it was attributable to his affines [the Yan family], and his affines also became wealthy. (Li Guangjin ca. 1600)

That Yan Daomou could "stake a lot of money and capital," that afterwards he staked money "without asking about their accounts," and that Chen Keyue, having gone through a struggle for knowledge and competition for time, in the end became extremely wealthy from his dealings in the market and his success was due to his affines, make it clear that Yan Daomou himself was a man of considerable wealth.

Thus by the middle of the Ming, the Yan lineage had already become one of the best known lineages in that area, and its power in the local area already allowed it to confront other lineages on equal terms. Some members of the lineage had already become members of the intelligentsia or joined the lower and middle ranks of the bureaucracy, and even more of them, owing to the hardships caused by the scarcity of land, had become merchants and traveled to the four quarters, increasing their property and wealth. In sum, the Anping Yan lineage of this period was a periurban, primarily commercial lineage.

The Lin Lineage of Pushan, a Farming Community

Pushan of Longhai County is the old Pushan village of Baishi Township in the twenty-ninth *du* of Longxi County and is now Baishi village, Jiaomei Township, Longhai County. It is about seven kilometers from Jiaomei town, about twenty-five kilometers from Longhai county town, and about thirty *li* from Haizheng town, which was Yuegang, the famous port for private trade, during the Ming dynasty. Pushan is a pure agricultural village of the kind often seen in the Minnan flatlands. The village is surrounded by a large expanse of rice and cane fields and banana orchards. To the south, the village abuts on the lower course of the Jiulong River, forming a small plain; there are a few little hills to the north. In the entire village there are 2060 people, 95% of whom are members of the Lin lineage. The labor force constitutes 29% of the population and farms for a living. The average amount of land per person is not more than one *mu*;

in addition to wet rice and sugarcane, the residents cultivate bananas and mushrooms on a large scale. The income of agricultural households has become more or less respectable in the past few years, as newly built houses demonstrate; but the houses still retain the traditional domestic architecture of the area.

According to the preface to the Lin genealogy, the founding ancestor of the lineage, Lin Yin'an, was originally from Qinbei village, Changtai County, Zhangzhou, and in the Dade period of the Yuan dynasty (1297–1307) came to Baishi *bao* and married uxorilocally into a Chen family, whereupon he settled down in the Pushan area. Because the Lins of Qinbei village of Changtai are a division of the Lins of Puyang, Lin Yin'an wrote the two characters "Pushan" on his house in order to record his place of origin. His descendants have used "Pushan" as a lineage emblem through the generations.

From the genealogy we can see that, although the members of this lineage living in the village exerted much effort and struggled to try to gain fame and glory for their lineage, the results didn't amount to much. The most glorious thing was that they produced a *jinshi*, Lin Tigui, who became a senior secretary of the board of revenue and vice governor of Guangdong and was given the honorific rank of *zhongfeng daifu*. After he retired and returned home, in 1533 he led the people of the village in reconstructing the waterworks of the official harbor, which "reached upstream as far as Liuying, downstream as far as Shimei harbor, was over twenty *li* in length, and irrigated over two hundred *qing* of land" (Lin genealogy). The waterworks made a large contribution to the agricultural production of the area. From the Hongzhi period of the Ming through Qianlong 39 of the Qing (1488–1774), lineage members who achieved the degree of *jiansheng* or above or held official posts, including honorary ones, numbered nineteen. Other than Lin Tigui, they produced a military *juren* in the Wanli period, who rose to the rank of lieutenant general, and in the Qianlong period they produced a *juren* and *zhou* magistrate. The other officials were either county or prefectural *shengyuan* or *jiansheng*. These numbers demonstrate that this lineage, after time of Lin Tigui, was not very prominent in politics.

In the economic sphere, there were a few lineage members who traveled by land to a few places in Guangdong and Jiangsu to make a living, but their number was far short of that of the Yan lineage of Anping. Those such as Lin Meihou of the twelfth generation, who "pursued his living at the edge of Southern Guangdong, and came back with a full coffer," and Lin Guzan of the fourteenth generation, who "made profits in Guangdong," were not many. We can thus infer that the real economic power of that lineage also must have been very limited. To sum up, the Lin is a typical traditional Minnan village lineage, making its living from agriculture. Because of the growth of population and the limited amount of land, it was difficult to meet the basic needs of survival. When we investigate the reasons for out-migration of the population of this lineage, this is one of the important factors.

MIGRATION OF THE YAN LINEAGE OF ANPING
The Numbers and Destinations of Migration

There were 404 men recorded in the Yan genealogy who died and were buried somewhere else. This number is quite respectable for a lineage that was not founded particularly early. In addition, the number does not include those who were lost track of, migrants of the Republican period, or people who migrated to do business but then returned. I believe the latter were quite numerous: Yan Chaibian, Yan Sha'ou, and Yan Lixue, mentioned above, are all examples of those who migrated and returned.

The wide distribution of destinations in this lineage is rarely seen in other lineages of Minnan. Outside the country, there are Shunta (Jakarta), Semarang, and Jiugang in Indonesia; Luzon and Lulai in the Philippines; Shili (Singapore), Perak, Kuala Lumpur, and Penang on the Malay Peninsula; Annam (Vietnam); also Thailand; and Japan. Inside the country there were Guangzhou, Chaozhou, Xiangshan Ao, Biqing, Luoding, Hainan, Leizhou, Nanxiong, Gaozhou, Xuwen, Dongguan, and Nan'ao in Guangdong; Nanning, Lianzhou, Wuzhou, and Yulinzhou in Guangxi; Hangzhou, Wenzhou, Ningbo, and Taizhou in Zhejiang; Chengdu in Sichuan; and Fuzhou and Xiamen in Fujian—altogether over twenty cities, as well as many places in Taiwan.

The destinations of migrants are given in Table 8.1, in which we can see clearly that the migrants to Guangdong were particularly numerous, 182 people (45% of the total number of migrants). Of these, the largest concentrations were at Guangzhou, with 103 migrants; Chaozhou, 23; Hainan, 12; Xiangshan Ao, 10; Leizhou, 8; and Gaozhou, 8. The next largest number were in the Southeast Asian countries and Japan, with 120 people (29.7%); of these places, Jakarta had the most (43) and was followed by Luzon (18) and Thailand and Semarang (8 each). The third largest number of migrants went to Taiwan, which had 75 people (18.5% of the total).

The Time and Direction of Migration

The time of migration is the most frustrating question because of the 404 migrants, the genealogy records an exact date of migration for only three: Yan Xianyou of the eighth generation, who migrated to Guiyu in Chaoyang with his wife and his sons Tiansi and Tianyu, in 1519; Yan Tingwei of the eleventh generation, born in 1574, who migrated with his son Kecong to Qiongshan County, Hainan, in 1617; and Yan Shifang of the fifteenth

TABLE 8.1. Destinations of Yan Lineage Migrants

	Male Migrants	Female Migrants	Total Migrants
Jakarta	38	5	43
Semarang	7	1	8
Jiugang	1	0	1
Borneo	1	0	1
Luzon	18	0	18
Lulai	1	0	1
Singapore	3	0	3
Perak	2	0	2
Penang	1	0	1
Kuala Lumpur	1	0	1
Thailand	8	0	8
Annam	4	0	4
Champa	1	0	1
Japan	1	0	1
Other Unspecified Southeast Asian Countries	27	0	27
Taiwan	63	12	75
Guangzhou	80	23	103
Chaozhou	21	2	23
Xiangshan Ao	10	0	10
Manzhou	1	0	1
Biqing	1	0	1
Fanyu	1	0	1
Anzhou	1	0	1
Huizhou	1	0	1
Luoding	1	1	2
Leizhou	6	2	8
Nanxiong	1	0	1
Gaozhou	8	0	8
Qiongzhou (Hainan)	8	4	12
Xuwen	2	0	2
Dongguan	5	0	5
Yulinzhou	2	0	2
Nan'ao	1	0	1
Nanning	1	0	1
Lianzhou	3	0	3
Wuzhou	1	0	1
Wenzhou	2	0	2
Hangzhou	2	0	2
Ningbo	1	0	1
Taizhou	3	0	3
Fuzhou	6	0	6
Xiamen	6	1	7
Chengdu	1	0	1

generation, born in 1722, who went to Jarkarta in 1745 and died and was buried there in 1756.

This practice of not recording the dates of out-migration is very common in the genealogies of Minnan; all the unrevised genealogies from the Ming dynasty on lack out-migration dates. Some scholars have used the birth date as the date of migration. This is clearly incorrect; in cases of whole families moving together, it is possible that migrants took infants or children with them, but most of the migrants must have been adults.

In order to solve this question, I have counted migration dates as twenty years after the birth date of the migrant (Zhuang and Wang 1984). Of course this method is not exact either. Of the three examples cited above, two include birth dates: Yan Tingwei, when he moved with his son to live in Qiongshan County, Hainan, in 1617, was already a forty-three-year-old man, and when Yan Shifang went to Jakarta in 1745, he was just twenty-three. These examples show that the ages of migrants at the time they migrated follow no particular pattern. But in a situation with very incomplete data, we can still use the method of adding twenty years to the birth date, because in that era, twenty-year-old males had generally already married and needed to make a living for themselves. This age also fits with "going to the four directions and running into the waves," which was the way things seem to have been in Anping. "When a lad reaches the age of twenty, he should always trade for riches, and go on merchant expeditions around the country" (Li Guangjin ca. 1600). "There are partings of newlyweds, together for a few days and then gone" (He Jiaoyuan ca. 1600). Of course, one must pay attention to those migrants who died before the age of twenty; we can only use their date of death in our tabulations. Figure 8.1 was prepared by this method.

OUT-MIGRATION IN THE YAN LINEAGE DURING THE MING AND QING

Figure 8.1 demonstrates that out-migration in the Yan lineage had already begun by the 1480s, and from the 1520s to the 1750s, there were 287 migrants (not including those who had no birth date recorded). On the average, they migrated at a rate above 1.25 persons per year. This was the high-tide period of migration in that lineage. From the 1760s on, the rate of migration slowed.

If we take the date of the first migration to the above-mentioned locations as an indication, then migration destinations were adopted in the following order:

Thailand	Yan Sixiang	1487
Hainan	Yan Qianhua	1504

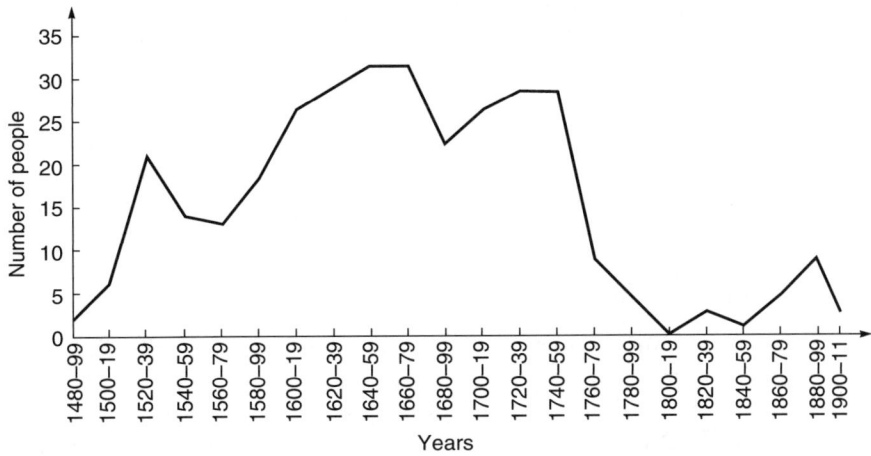

Figure 8.1. Out-Migration from the Yan Lineage during the Ming and Qing

Chaozhou	Yan Xuan	1513
Leizhou	Yan Sheng	1514
SE Asia (unspecified)	Yan Hui	1516
Guangzhou	Yan Fuze	1525
Ningbo	Yan Senhao	1529
Nanning	Yan Kun	1530
Xuwen	Yan Zhengqin	1531
Taizhou	Yan Fu	1534
Annam (Vietnam)	Yan Xi	1535
Nan'ao	Yan Xuangu	1536
Lianzhou	Yan Senpin	1537
Huizhou (Guangdong)	Yan Xuanzhi	1542
Shunta (Jakarta)	Yan Yihun	1551
Xiangshan Ao	Yan Yishen	1551
Chengdu	Yan Futing	1551
Taiwan	Yan Longyuan	1554
Hangzhou	Yan Xihua	1557
Wenzhou	Yan Shijie	1571
Luzon	Yan Jiase	1583
Gaozhou	Yan Tingzhuan	1609
Jiugang	Yan Jiamian	1610
Nanxiong	Yan Kerui	1618
Yulinzhou	Yan Huacai	1624
Wuzhou	Yan Kesi	1638
Fuzhou	Yan Bingchun	1639

Fanyu	Yan Tingzhao	1647
Xiamen	Yan Kehua	1650
Luoding	Yan Chongdao	1671
Biqing	Yan Shimin	1702
Semarang	Yan Shixian	1713
Annam	Yan Zhongzhen	1716
Japan	Yan Dunzheng	1771
Perak	Yan Jiyu	1869
Singapore	Yan Yuyang	1876
Kuala Lumpur	Yan Qicao	1891

Frankly speaking, from this kind of comparison, it is still difficult to determine any general pattern of migration, but if we analyze the data according to the situation in a few of the most important destinations, we can discover that the migration of the Yans to various areas was concentrated in different time periods.

Guangdong	from Hongzhi 17 to Chongzhen (1504–1644)	89 people
	from Shunzhi to Qianlong (1644–1795)	73 people
Thailand	from Chenghua 23 to Jiajing (1487–1566)	5 people
	from Kangxi to Yongzheng (1662–1735)	3 people
Indonesia	from Jiajing 30 to Wanli (1551–1620)	7 people
	from Shunzhi to Qianlong (1644–1795)	29 people
	Guangxu (1875–1908)	1 person
Luzon	from Wanli 11 through Tianqi (1583–1627)	13 people
	Kangxi (1662–1722)	1 person
Malaya	from Tongzhi 8 to Guangxu (1869–1908)	6 people
Taiwan	from Jiajing 33 to Chongzhen (1555–1644)	3 people
	from Shunzhi to Xianfeng (1644–1861)	58 people

An Account of Migration in the Yan Lineage

In about the 1480s, lineage member Yan Sixiang was the first to emigrate to Thailand. The Yan genealogy says:

> Sixiang of the 4th generation . . . was the eldest son of Puzhi. He was born in the *Dinghai* year of Chenghua (1467), and died in Thailand on the 26th of the seventh month in the *Xinsi* year of Chengde (1521).

According to the materials that I now possess, he is not only the first of the Yan lineage but the person with the earliest birth date in any of the lineages of Anping to go abroad. According to their records, four other lineage members—Yan Xiangliang, Yan Senqi, Yan Senli, and Yan Liu—all went to Thailand in the sixteenth century. At that time, Thailand was an important destination for Fujian merchants, and by the Jiajing period there was already a Chinatown there. Fujian merchants exported porcelain and brought back primarily black pepper and Sapan wood. In the Chongzhen period, Quanzhou merchants in Thailand competed with Japanese and Dutch merchants for the trade in deerskins (Fu Yiling 1956). Yan Sixiang and the others were most probably engaged in this kind of trade.

The period from the 1520s to the mid-1600s was a time of considerable out-migration for the Yan lineage. Over one hundred lineage members migrated to various coastal cities in Guangdong, including Guangzhou, Chaozhou, Hainan, Xiangshan Ao, and Leizhou.

> We know that Guangdong in the Ming dynasty was a playground for adventurers; merchants in search of profits all followed each other to eastern Guangdong; they were called "Going to Guangdongers [*zouguang*]." At the same time, Haojing [in the southern part of Xiangshan county] was a center for international trade, so many Fujianese went there to trade; of them, Zhangzhou and Quanzhou people were the most numerous. (Fu Yiling 1956)

The large number of Anping Yans "going to Guangdong" at this time were like a flock of ducks going after the same food; that they were mostly concentrated along a trade route in eastern Guangdong shows that they were merchants hoping for great profits.

Overseas migration started as a gradual process and became a high tide; besides the migrants who went to Thailand, Jakarta, Jiugang, and Annam, there were even more people who concentrated at Luzon. Trade at Luzon in those days occupied a primary place in the trade of the Orient. After the Spanish occupied the Philippines but did not achieve their goal of establishing trade in China, Chinese merchants went in great numbers to establish Luzon as a place for trade. "In Anping, those who are enamored of trading, who ply the Luzon route, bobbing on the great sea in search of profits, constitute nine families out of ten" (Li Guangjin ca. 1600). The Yans did not fall behind; from Wanli 11 to the Tianqi period (1583–1627), we know of thirteen who lived in Luzon, and all of them were merchants.

In the Qing, the century from Shunzhi, in the middle of the seventeenth century, to Qianlong, in the middle of the eighteenth, was another stage in the migration of the Yan lineage. That very few people still went to old destinations such as Thailand and Luzon certainly has something to do with the 1603 massacre of large numbers of overseas Chinese by the Spanish colonial authorities in Luzon, in which several members of the Yan lineage died. Of the new destinations, the ones most worthy of attention are Taiwan and Jakarta. In addition, there continued to be a large number of people going to various places in Guangdong; the practice of "going to Guangdong" continued until late Qianlong times, when it began to diminish. The decline of this practice was probably the reason for the general decline of Anping commerce.

Large numbers of Yans began moving to Taiwan in the Jiajing period, in the middle of the sixteenth century. According to the Yan genealogy:

> Longyuan of the tenth generation had the *zi* Riban. He was the eldest son of Zhengbi. He was born in the *jiawu* year of Jiajing [1534], and [the date of] his death is lost. He is buried in Taiwan. His wife was surnamed Zheng, and they had one son.

Yan Longyuan is one of the earliest among nearly seven thousand Fujianese migrants to Taiwan that we have so far found in over 100 genealogies (Zhuang and Wang 1985). But after the mid-1500s, there are no migrants to Taiwan from the Yan lineage for about a hundred years, until the beginning of the first high tide of migrants to Taiwan in the Chongzhen period, when Yan Kaiyu went with his family to Tainan. Yan Kaiyu's wife Cai Jieqin is one of the earliest female migrants to Taiwan that we have been able to find (Zhuang and Wang 1985). As with that of many other coastal Fujian lineages, the migration of the Yans to Taiwan is apparently part of the third great wave of migration, which occurred in the Kangxi, Yongzheng, and Qianlong periods of the early Qing. After this, there were very few people who migrated to Taiwan.

The migration of Yan lineage members to Jakarta began in the last half of the sixteenth century. The first migrants were Yan Yihun, Yan Hongkui, and Yan Yilan of the ninth generation and Yan Jiazhen, Yan Jiahui, and Yan Jiaxu of the tenth generation; their time of migration was concentrated from the late Jiajing (1522–66) period through the beginning of the Wanli (1573–1619) period, and they appear to also have been commercial migrants. From this period until after the middle of the seventeenth century, about thirty lineage members migrated to Jakarta. This wave of migration is closely connected with changes in Jakarta under Dutch colonial rule. I believe that this group of Anping Yan migrants, like other migrants at this time, were people who pursued ordinary laboring occupations. "From the 1780s to the end of the century, the number of Chinese migrants to Jakarta gradually diminished" (Wen et al. 1985). The situation as portrayed in the Yan genealogy also fits nicely with this: aside from one person who migrated in the Guangxu period, this kind of migration had basically stopped by this time.

From the nineteenth century until the destruction of the Qing, even though there were a few individuals in the Yan lineage who migrated to Annam, Penang, Kuala Lumpur, Singapore, and Semarang, and to Xiamen and other places within Fujian, relatively large-scale out-migration did not occur again.

MIGRATION OF THE LIN LINEAGE OF PUSHAN

We can use the same methods outlined above to describe and tabulate the migration of the Lin lineage of Pushan.

Numbers and Destinations of Migrants

There were 336 members of the Lin lineage listed clearly in the genealogy as having died and been buried in other places. Of these, 201 died in foreign countries, 38 died in other parts of China, and 97 died in Taiwan.

These figures are clearly not complete, since they only include those who died and were buried in foreign countries before the date of the compilation of the Lin genealogy in Qianlong 39 (1774). I have discovered from other sources that people of that lineage continued to migrate out after that time; for example, the famous Lin Pinghou, a landlord of northern Taiwan, emigrated after that date. In addition, as with the Yans of Anping, there were some members of the lineage who emigrated to make a living but afterwards returned home, and there is no way to discover them simply from using the recorded place of burial. But sometimes their migration history can be discovered from their marriage situation. Consider the following example.

> Lin Hedai of the 20th generation, the son of Zijing, whose posthumous name was Dunda, was born in the tenth year of Kangxi (1671) and died in the seventh year of Qianlong (1742). He married a wife named Wei, and married another wife overseas, named Jiang. He is buried at Wangjun Shan. He had three sons. (Lin genealogy)

This quote shows that Lin Hedai lived for a while overseas and also married a wife whom he brought back.

> Lin Keda of the ninth generation was the second son of Ziyong. He was born in the 17th year of Jiajing (1538) and died in the 43rd year of Wanli (1615). His wife was surnamed Chen and his concubine, from Deqing county in Hangzhou, was surnamed Zhu. He had three sons. (Lin genealogy)

This quote shows that Lin Keda had been to Hangzhou. Also, since he had a concubine, he may have been a merchant. But his mercantile success should not get in the way of our general understanding of migration from this lineage from the middle of the Ming through the first part of the Qing.

There are a couple of differences between the Lins and the Yans in terms of the destinations of migration. The first is that there were far fewer Lin commercial migrants to coastal cities in China. The localities include only

TABLE 8.2. Destinations of Lin Lineage Migrants

	Male Migrants	Female Migrants	Total Migrants
Jakarta	58	2	60
Semarang	31	1	32
Banjarmasin	12	0	12
Cheribon	1	0	1
Yalaohan	2	0	2
Demak	1	0	1
Amboina	5	1	6
Luzon	32	0	32
Maomian	1	0	1
Iloilo	1	0	1
Lulai	1	0	1
Cambodia	22	0	22
Thailand	3	0	3
Liukun	1	0	1
Annam	1	0	1
Japan	1	0	1
Foreign countries (unspecified)	24	0	24
Guangdong	9	1	10
Chaozhou	2	0	2
Haifeng	3	0	3
Nanjing	4	0	4
Kunshan County, Suzhou	5	4	9
Taicang	4	1	5
Zhangzhou	2	0	2
Other provinces	3	0	3
Taiwan	92	5	97

Guangdong (which I judge to mean Guangzhou), Chaozhou, Haifeng, Nanjing, Suzhou, Taicang, and Zhangzhou. Another difference is that overseas and Taiwan migrants are more numerous among the Lins than among the Yans. Overseas migrants from the Lin lineage in this period were distributed in Jakarta, Semarang, Banjarmasin, Cheribon, Yalaohan, Demak, Amboina, Makassar, Pekalongkan, Luzon, Maomian, Iloilo, Lulai, Cambodia, Thailand, Liukun, Annam, and Japan.

From Table 8.2 we can tell that the greatest number of migrants from the Lin lineage went to Indonesia (114, 33.9% of the total number of migrants). After Indonesia come Taiwan (97, 28.8%), the Philippines (35, 10.4%), and Cambodia (22, 6.5%). The total number of migrants to foreign countries, 201, comprises 59.8% of the total number of emigrants. Migrants to other parts of the Chinese mainland total thirty-eight people, or only 11.3%. Thus in the two and a half centuries from the Jiajing period to Qianlong

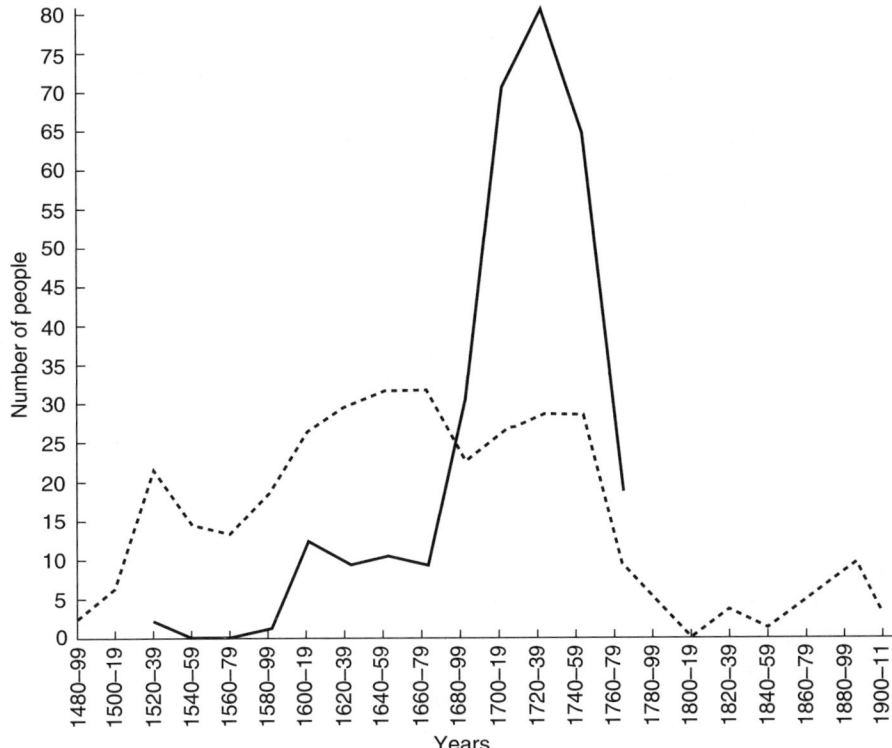

Figure 8.2. Out-Migration from the Lin Lineage during the Ming and Qing

NOTE: Does not include those whose birth dates are not known or second-generation residents in the emigrant communities.

39, Southeast Asia and Taiwan were the primary destinations of the out-migrants from the Lin lineage.

Times and Routes of Migration

The greatest majority of Lin lineage migrants were people born in the early Qing. Of the 336 migrants, excluding 33 whose birth dates are unclear, 267 people were born in the time from Shunzhi to Qianlong 39. Of these, those born in the Kangxi period were particularly numerous, 190 people. From these figures we can see that the migration from that lineage was concentrated in the period from Kangxi to the compilation of the genealogy in Qianlong.

Figure 8.2 shows clearly that emigration from the Pushan Lin lineage did not start in earnest until the seventeenth century (even though there were a few isolated individuals who emigrated before this), a full century later than emigration from the Yan lineage, and the numbers are small by comparison. After the 1680s emigration in the Lin lineage experienced a dramatic increase leading to a kind of high tide not seen in the Yan lineage. The sudden increase in the emigration rate from 0.26 persons per year from 1520 to 1679 to 3 persons per year from 1680 to 1759 cannot help but attract our attention.

Let us look again at the order of emigration in this lineage:

Chaozhou	Lin Xiayu Lin Xiayang	1536
Guangdong	Lin Jiexiang	1590
Eastern Sea	Lin Kelu	1602
Taiwan	Lin Zongchao	1605
Haifeng	Lin Binquan	1608
Nanjing	Lin Diesheng	1611
Cambodia	Lin Zhongyan	1612
Western Ocean	Lin Puzhao	1614
Jakarta	Lin Puguan	1618
Luzon	Lin Pumeng	1628
Semarang	Lin Hezhen	1659
Amboina	Lin Deren	1662
Banjarmasin	Lin Hechao	1684
Kunshan County, Suzhou	Lin Heyun	1684
Taicang	Lin Weilin	1688
Thailand	Lin Weiyang	1696
Demak	Lin Weizhuang	1708
Yalaohan	Lin Weifa	1714
Maomian	Lin Weidao	1719
Annam	Lin Guixia	1721
Japan	Lin Guijiang	1722
Liukun	Lin Wengan	1728
Chaozhou	Lin Wenqi	1728
Cheribon	Lin Guiquan	1739
Lulai	Lin Wendan	1745
Iloilo	Lin Wenzhen	1752

Examination of this order of migration demonstrates that the destinations of migration in the Lin lineage were also overlapping. The data for the Yan lineage of Anping and the migration data for many other Minnan lineages whose genealogies I have examined follow the same basic pattern.

This kind of overlapping migration in different directions does not negate the fact that migration from a particular lineage to a particular place is usually concentrated in time. The Yan lineage of Anping and the Lin lineage of Pushan are both like this. We can attempt to demonstrate this from a few places where emigrants from this lineage were relatively many:

Indonesia	Wanli (1573–1620)	1 person
	Shunzhi (1644–1661)	3 people
	Kangxi to Qianlong (1662–1774)	105 people
Philippines	Chongzhen (1628–1644)	1 person
	Kangxi to Qianlong (1662–1774)	32 people
Cambodia	Wanli (1573–1620)	1 person
	Kangxi to Qianlong (1662–1774)	21 people
Taiwan	Wanli to Chongzhen (1573–1644)	9 people
	Shunzhi (1644–1661)	3 people
	Kangxi to Qianlong (1662–1774)	72 people

A General Discussion of Emigration from the Lin Lineage

The general outline of the migration history of the Lin lineage of Pushan is clear: in the golden age of private trading in the middle and late Ming period, the Lin lineage, though living only thirty kilometers from Yuegang harbor, did not jump into the waves. Even though there were some (Lin Kelu, Lin Fuzhao, Lin Fuguan, and Lin Fuming) who sailed the eastern and western oceans, some (Lin Jiexiang and the brothers Lin Xiayu and Lin Xiayang) who "went to Guangdong" in search of profits, and some (Lin Meihou) who "returned with full coffers," in the end the number of Lin migrants was quite small in comparison with that of the Yans of Anping. It is difficult to find explanations for this kind of situation, which does not fit together with their surrounding environment, other than the preservation of the natural economy and the closed nature of this village.

In the beginning of the Qing, this lineage suddenly was transformed, and there was a flood as if a dam had broken. People flowed to other places to seek a living. Just in the period from Kangxi to Qianlong 39 (1662–1775) there were two or three hundred emigrants. One direction of migration was to the south, concentrated in Jakarta, Semarang, Banjarmasin, Luzon in the Philippines, and Cambodia; another was eastward toward Taiwan.

From the middle of the fifteenth to the beginning of the seventeenth century was the period of great prosperity for Yuegang harbor: "Those who settle among barbarians are seven of ten families" (Zhang Xie ca. 1600). "Farmers and merchants are in equal numbers; going overseas is like going to market" (Zhang Xie ca. 1600). Yet this rural lineage retained a conservative nature. In the end, what was it that caused the Lins to move to large-scale emigration in the early Qing? I have examined the genealogy and have only found this kind of a record: "When the current dynasty was established, Zheng (Chenggong) controlled Xiamen. Since our whole lineage was situated between mountain and sea, we had been moved around by war for several decades." The upheaval caused by war could be one reason. At the beginning of the Qing, the government instituted the maritime prohibition and also enforced the deportation of the coastal population inland, in order to oppose the anti-Qing forces of Zheng Chenggong. At the same time, from Jiangdong to the area east of the Jiulong River was a deserted area, and the best thing for inhabitants was to move out; there are many examples. Baishi village, where the Lins live, is close by the lower reaches of the Jiulong River and was no exception. This perhaps explains why many Lins turned their backs on the village, left the well, and went to the outside to seek a living.

The second reason was the occurrence of seventy-four relatively large-scale natural disasters in this area from Jiajing through Qianlong (Haicheng 1736–96). This situation must have promoted large-scale emigration to a certain degree.

The third reason was that the defeat of the Zheng forces in Taiwan in 1683 and the resulting political unification brought new connections between the two sides of the strait and brought about the opening of Taiwan. At this time, migration from the mainland to Taiwan started its third and largest high tide. This wave of migration lasted until the Qianlong and Jiaqing periods; the numbers of migrants to Taiwan from many Minnan lineages were highest at this time (Zhuang and Wang 1985). The large-scale movement of the Lins of Pushan to Taiwan at this time reflects this development.

The fourth reason was the announcement by the Qing government in 1684, the year after they brought Taiwan under their control, that they were repealing the maritime prohibition order. In the same year the Dutch colonialists forced the Bantan kingdom of Java to sign a treaty making Bantan a protectorate of the Dutch East India Company. The Netherlands not only controlled the coastal areas of Java but also forcibly pacified a popular opposition in Jakarta, consolidating its colonial control. This consolidation coupled with the development of the sugar production meant that the colonialists needed a large amount of Chinese labor. Because of this, Chinese immigrants came incessantly to Jakarta. According to Dutch documents, eleven Chinese merchant ships came to Jakarta from Fujian in 1686; of these, eight came from Xiamen and three from other ports. In addition to bringing Chinese trade commodities, they brought eight hundred laborers. After their arrival, the numbers of these sorts of Chinese commodities and "new guests" (*Nieuweling* in Dutch, *Orang Baru* in Malay) grew year by year (Wen et al. 1985).

I believe that these are the most important reasons for the large-scale emigration of Pushan Lin migrants to Jakarta during these years. They were clearly laborers who filled the needs of this labor market (of course there may be a few exceptions), not the kind of mercantile migrants characteristic of the private trading period of the middle and late Ming.

OTHER QUESTIONS ABOUT THE NATURE OF MIGRATION

Other questions about migration from the Lin and Yan lineages in the Ming and Qing periods that are deserving of research and analysis are, for example, the ordinary forms of migration of households within a lineage, the differences in migration patterns from areas with different kinds of economies, the sibling order of migrants and their domestic organization and relations, emigrant polygamy and the question of ancestral succession, and a comparison of the longevity of migrants in different destinations.

The Ordinary Forms of Household Population Migration

Individual Migration. Migration from households in the two lineages was basically that of individuals, as was migration in other Minnan lineages. (Of course there were some exceptional cases of mass migration and "abolition of villages" in order to escape war, epidemics, or lineage feuding.) These individuals either left their families at home or had not yet formed families, and they migrated individually to seek a living. Even though their original intention was to return home after earning a respectable amount of money from trading or labor, many of them ended up dying and being buried in other countries, though of course some of them actually did return home. These temporary migrants show some differences from permanent migrants. For example, of the 180 members of the Yan lineage who died and were buried in coastal commercial cities, the genealogy records only 50 as *qiaozhu* ("settled as emigrants") or *shiju* ("lived there for generations"). The others simply have their burial places recorded, showing that there were more sojourning or temporary migrants than permanent settlers.

The best corroboration for this judgment of the nature of migration lies in the marital situation of the emigrants. In general, any migrant who is married but emigrates alone is, regardless of the end result, a temporary migrant hoping to return home. Of the 114 male Yans who went overseas to seek a living, 72 were already married. Of these, only 1 took his family with him, 4 married or remarried in the foreign country, and all the rest left all their family members at home. Of the 197 Lin males who went overseas to seek a living, 141 were already married. Of these, only 4 took their families with them, 6 married or remarried overseas, and the rest of them left their families at home.

This sort of single, temporary migrant is also very salient during the early period of migration to Taiwan, but starting in the Kangxi and Qianlong periods, with the continuous growth in the numbers of emigrants, the number of these individual migrants diminished greatly (Zhuang and Wang 1985). The situation in Southeast Asia was different; even after the development of an overseas Chinese society in the latter period of the Qing, individual migration was still extremely widespread. The example of the Chen lineage of Xiato, Shishan, Nan'an County, is quite representative. Of the emigrants to Southeast Asia from that lineage (the majority of whom emigrated during the period from the nineteenth century to the 1940s), there were 446 who were already married. Of these, only 86 took their families with them or married overseas; the rest all left their families at home.

The basic reason for the prevalence of individual migration was the traditional love of the soil found in the lineages of the Minnan area (the respect for "roots"), along with the strong desire to pursue riches abroad in order to enrich the family and bring glory to the lineage.

Successive Migration by Household Members. Some individual migrants established businesses with property overseas. When they reached a certain age, they retired and returned to their original home, passing on their businesses and property to their sons. This practice resulted in multigenerational successive migration. This kind of migration was also very common among the people of other Minnan lineages. For example, take Zhuang Kehui of the nineteenth generation of the Zhuang lineage of Qingyang in Jinjiang County (1833–1908).

> From childhood his family fortunes were thin and his ambition was boundless, so he resolutely went to the Philippines in the South Seas to seek a living. Overcoming difficulties and danger, he determined that he would operate a business, and began to prevail in the trade in Philippine timber. Shepherding his capital, he returned home, where he built a house. After this he made the southern trip again, by sunlight or starlight, not daunted by toil and hardship ... [His wife] had saved something at home and established a landed estate, and the family fortunes prospered because of this, and afterward they built a palatial home to leave to their sons and grandsons. (Xuchuan Zhuang genealogy)

Zhuang Kehui's second son, Zhuang Wangrong (born 1870), followed the same path.

> When I reached the age of sixteen, I went to the Philippines to trade. At this time our father was forty-nine, and recovering at home. My elder brother thus did not take care of our primary affairs, and I was the only one taking care of the business in the Philippines. I succeeded to the endeavors of my father and grandfather, managing the business, and thus our family fortunes were calmed somewhat. When I turned 18, I returned home to take a wife named Su ... and then crossed the ocean again to resume business ... Then I also

took my two sons with me to the Philippines. Then we encountered a period when business was not good, so we changed our line and organization of business, and my two sons began working for other people's profit, but they still inherited my hardworking ambition, as well as my thrift and frankness. Afterwards, they left that store and went into business for themselves, pursuing it with single-mindedness, with thrift and with diligence, and their business achieved daily growth. Saving capital that was left over, I returned home and built a palatial home there; with a total of ten rooms around a courtyard, in order to leave it to my sons and grandsons. (Xuchuan Zhuang genealogy)

Zhuang Wangrong's eldest son, Zhuang Caishi (born 1892), tells the following story:

From my childhood I followed my father doing business in the Philippines in the South Seas . . . From thence pursuing business single-mindedly, with diligence and thrift, the business achieved daily growth. My younger brother then followed me in crossing to the Philippines to trade; supporting each other we managed to have a yearly surplus. At this time my father's age reached five decades, so he shepherded his resources and returned home to build a palatial house to shelter his sons and grandsons. Because my brother was thrifty and diligent in all affairs, and overcame the burdens of his business responsibilities, I also followed my father and returned home to help with the plans; only after two years did we celebrate its completion. Then I followed my father's order to rest at home, and not cross over to the Philippines again. Because my brother and I could take over the business, he could shed his burden of responsibilities, and could stay happily at home, with a joyful fate and amusing his eyes, enjoying the years of Heaven. Even though I am his son and have taken on the burdens of his labor, I was not able to take care of my parents as well as he was. My grandfather was forty-nine when he was able to return home to rest; my father could not achieve his leisure until he was fifty-five. But still, how could I not also be content? (Xuchuan Zhuang genealogy)

Family Members Migrating to the Same Place. In the two lineages, instances of members of the same household—fathers and sons, brothers, or a whole family—moving together to the same place are quite numerous. For example, in the ninth generation of the Anping Yans, "Guomei (Rongchun), Guozhou (Rongduan), and Guoyong (Rongzhuang), all sons of Kuangyan, together with their nephew Ximu established an outside residence at Shengli in Dingyin, Dongguan County, Guangdong" (Yan genealogy). In the tenth generation, the four sons of Yan Zonghan—Tingyu, Tingfan, Tingbao, and Tingqi—all moved to Guangdong. Yan Qianyou of the eighth generation went in Zhengde 14 (1519) together with his wife, surnamed Gao, and his sons Tiansi and Tianming to live in Guiyu, Chaoyang, Guangdong. Other examples come from the twelfth generation of the Pushan Lins; Hezheng, Heyu, and Hehui were three brothers who all went to Jakarta to seek a living. Heguo, Hedai, and Heli, also three brothers, went together to seek a living in Semarang and died and were buried there.

I have tabulated statistics on nearly one thousand members of the Huang lineage of Cannei in Anxi County who migrated to Taiwan, and discovered that there were twenty-nine examples of father and son migrating together, seventeen examples of brothers migrating together (the numbers of individuals are not comparable), forty-four examples of husbands and wives migrating together, and thirty examples of entire families migrating together (Anxi Cannei Huang genealogy). In the migration of Minnan lineage members, this kind of situation is extremely common, and difficult to present case-by-case.

Family Members Migrating to Different Destinations. The situation of members of the same household migrating to different destinations is even more common. Take the entry for Yan Menghua in the Yan genealogy:

> Yan Menghua of the seventh generation: Eldest son, Sentong, *zi* Shiguan, *hao* Maosung, died and is buried at Mahe in Chaoyang. Second son, Senqi, *zi* Shiyong, *hao* Yijiang, born at the *wu* hour on the twenty-ninth day of the tenth month of the *tingsi* year of Hongzhi, died in Thailand on the seventh day of the sixth month of the *bingxu* year of Jiajing. Third son Senpin, *zi* Shizhi, *hao* Nuanyi, born at an auspicious time on the twenty-first day of the first month of the *dingchou* year of Zhengde; died and buried at Lianzhou.

The genealogy entry for Lin Bolian of the Pushan Lin lineage provides another example.

> Lin Bolian of the tenth generation: Eldest son, Zhongpin, born in the eighth year of Kangxi, died in the twelfth year of Yongzheng. [At home] married a wife named Guo, and had four sons. Second son, Zhongzhong, born in the twelfth year of Kangxi, died in the forty-eighth year of Kangxi, buried at Machen in a foreign country. Married a wife named Chen [at home], and had one son. Third son, Zhongpan [at home]. Fourth son, Zhongxiang, born in the twenty-second year of Kangxi, died in the ninth year of Qianlong, buried at Semarang. Married a wife of unknown surname [at home] and had one son. Fifth son, Zhongxin, born in the twenty-fourth year of Kangxi, died in Kangxi, buried at Semarang. Sixth son, Zhongzhu, born in the twenty-fifth year of Kangxi, died in the forty-fifth year of Kangxi, buried at Semarang. Seventh son, Zhongda, born in the twenty-seventh year of Kangxi, died in the twelfth year of Qianlong, buried at Semarang. Married a wife named Shi [at home], and had three sons.

The entry for Lin Heyuan of the thirteenth generation states:

> First son, Weimo, born in the forty-seventh year of Kangxi, died in the thirtieth year of Qianlong, buried in the right side of the bamboo grove at Linjia, Beixinzhuang, Danshui, Taiwan. Married a woman named Zhuang, and took

a second wife named Wang [both at home]. Second son, Weiting, born in the fifty-fourth year of Kangxi, died in the sixth year of Qianlong, buried at Luzon. Third son, Weimao, born in the fifty-sixth year of Kangxi, died in the eighth year of Qianlong, buried at Zhuangshan, Madou, Taiwan. Fourth son, Weituo, born in the sixty-first year of Kangxi, died in the ninth year of Qianlong, buried at Madoushan in Taiwan. Fifth son, Weiqiu [at home].

Differences in Migration Patterns by Area

The Zhang-Quan region is an economic area with common historical traditions and customs, and the patterns and basic tendencies of migration in each of its lineages are similar. Nevertheless, because of differences in the political and economic position and the nature of values in the lineages, their population migration also displays differing individual nature and characteristics. For example, the Anping Yan lineage shows the character of mercantile migration; the Lin lineage of Pushan even more strongly exhibits characteristics of migration by farmers and by ordinary people going out to sell their labor.

We have paid attention to the fact that during the flourishing era of private trade in the middle and late Ming, commercial migrants were concentrated in lineages living near the coastal ports convenient for oceanic transport. The situation of the port of Anping is very typical. From the opening of the market at Luzon in the middle of the sixteenth century, the merchants of Anping who traded silk, hempen thread, porcelain, and tea leaves in the long distance trade to Luzon practically constituted nine families out of ten and existed in every lineage. Those who went returned only once a year, or even stayed long-term without returning. One can find examples of large-scale commercial migration similar to that of the Yans in the genealogies of the Huang, Ke, Chen, Gao, Zheng, and Wu lineages of Anping. Thus the migration of the Yan lineage is not an unusual phenomenon of a single lineage but a common practice characteristic of all living under particular historical conditions in a certain economic area.

In addition, the phenomenon is not peculiar to the single area of Anping; lineages living near other harbors at that time also display similar phenomena. For example, the Gong lineage, living in Huian's largest port, Chongwu Zhen, had quite a few lineage members who engaged in outside mercantile activity, and the lineage thus displayed commercial migration of the same sort as the Anping Yans. Records of the Gongs can be found in Guangdong, Huguang, Beijing, Jining, Linqing, Jiangsu and Zhejiang, Shandong, Taiwan, and overseas in Thailand.

The nature of migration displayed by the Lin lineage of Pushan is also a phenomenon not of that lineage alone but of a large number of rural lineages, particularly the poor and backward lineages of mountain areas. For example, several lineages of Yongchun County are very typical. The Li lineage of Guanlin, the Huang lineage of Penglai, and the Kang lineage of Fengshan all had large numbers of migrants going to Taiwan in the mid-Qing, and in the "indentured labor" period after the Opium War, they migrated overseas to Southeast Asia in great numbers. And the migration from the Kang and Li lineages to other domestic locations in large numbers in the early Qing is concentrated in the mountainous areas of northern and western Fujian and in a few areas in the border regions of Fujian, Zhejiang, and Jiangxi.

The Sibling Position of Migrants and Its Relation to Domestic Organization

In the families within the lineages of Minnan, were the migrants the eldest sons, the second sons, or other sons? Because many genealogies are not sufficiently clear about initial migrants or about the descendants of migrants born in the destination areas, we can only select a few typical lineages from differing economic zones to undertake this kind of statistical comparison. The results are displayed in Table 8.3.

Of the 2,095 migrants from the seven lineages tabulated in Table 8.3, the greatest number were eldest sons, the next greatest, second sons, and after that, third sons and below. If we add only sons to first sons, then the percentages become even larger: 43% for the Yans, 44% for the Lins, 41% for the Chens of Xiazhai, 48% for the Chens of Linbing, 45% for the Kangs, 37% for the Huangs, and 36% for the Lis.

The reasons for this numerical predominance of eldest sons in emigration are not unrelated to the partible inheritance system practiced in Minnan lineages. At the same time, if we look at the household, the responsibilities of the eldest son are the most numerous; he is the first to assume the responsibility of helping the elder generation with the family's production, and he also has to plan for the younger brothers' forming families and establishing their household economies. Because of these duties, he has to struggle on behalf of the family's position, and the elder generation will always support the eldest son's going out to struggle, which will add to the family's economic income earlier and lighten the responsibilities of the remaining members. The above statistics also show that if the eldest son has to stay behind to assist in the management of the household, it is the second son who emigrates to seek a living; the number of second sons emigrating is hardly less than the number of first sons. All these things influenced the relationships and organization in Minnan families in a particular direction.

Remarriage of Emigrants and the Continuity of Ancestral Worship

I have already touched on the fact that the majority of male emigrants were already married. We can also discover from the genealogies that among the married male migrants, those who married again or took concubines at the

TABLE 8.3. Birth Orders of Migrants from Selected Minnan Lineages

Lineage	Lineage Type	Migration Destination	Number of Migrants	Eldest Sons	Second Sons	Third and Later Sons	Only Sons	Adopted Sons	Continuation Sons
Anping Yan	Coastal commercial	Coast cities, Overseas, Taiwan	306	91 (30%)	85 (28%)	77 (25%)	41 (13%)	12 (4%)	0
Pushan Lin	Flatland agricultural	Overseas, Taiwan, coast cities	308	105 (34%)	97 (31%)	74 (24%)	30 (10%)	2 (1%)	0
Nan'an Xiazhai Chen	Mountain	Overseas	819	229 (28%)	222 (27%)	181 (22%)	106 (13%)	32 (4%)	49 (6%)
Nan'an Linbing Chen	Mountain	Overseas, Taiwan	183	60 (33%)	50 (27%)	43 (23%)	27 (15%)	3 (2%)	0
Yongchun Fengshan Kang	Mountain	Overseas	281	81 (29%)	49 (17%)	38 (14%)	45 (16%)	9 (3%)	59 (21%)
Yongchun Penglai Huang	Mountain	Overseas	122	32 (26%)	29 (24%)	33 (27%)	13 (11%)	8 (7%)	7 (6%)
Yongchun Guanlin Li	Mountain	Overseas	76	21 (28%)	14 (18%)	21 (28%)	6 (8%)	10 (13%)	4 (5%)
Total			2095	619 (30%)	546 (25%)	467 (22%)	268 (13%)	76 (4%)	119 (6%)

destination were not at all rare. Polygyny was more common among the Yans than among the Lins. I believe that this is directly connected to the individual economic situations of the migrants.

The number of Yans who took concubines was forty-two. Of these, twelve were overseas migrants, twenty-three were internal migrants, and seven were Taiwan migrants. The number of Lins who took concubines was ten. Of these, four were overseas migrants, three were internal migrants, and four were Taiwan migrants. When unmarried individual migrants died away from home, in order to assure the continuity of their "incense fire" (descendants), often one son (or sometimes two, three, or more sons) of the migrant's brother or other lineage relative of the same generation was chosen as the "continuation son" of the deceased. Also, "received the continuation of the branch" was conventionally written below the name of the deceased in the genealogy in order to avoid the "collapse of the branch" (the lack of descendants to succeed). This kind of phenomenon is not limited to the Yans and Lins and is extremely common in other Minnan lineages as a highly respected way to express the traditional attitudes of continuation of blood relations.

Longevity of Migrants

The figures in Table 8.4 demonstrate the differences in longevity of the overseas, Taiwan, and mainland migrants from the two lineages from the mid-Ming to the early Qing. The average age at death of the overseas migrants is the lowest, between thirty-eight and thirty-nine years; Taiwan migrants come next, and the emigrants with the highest average age at death are the migrants to the coastal commercial cities and towns. In the Yan lineage of Anping, the mainland migrants' average age at death exceeds that of the overseas migrants by more than ten years. This is explicable in that the human and natural hazards to which migrants in coastal commercial cities and towns were exposed were relatively few; their lives were generally relatively safe, and their economic conditions were relatively more prosperous than those of the former two categories.

Emigrants from the two lineages who moved to Taiwan were basically all concentrated in the third high tide of migration, during the Kangxi, Yongzheng, and Qianlong periods. The environment they entered had already rid itself of the difficulties and dangers of an earlier period, so we can understand that they had longer lifespans.

The shortness of the lifespans of the overseas migrants to a certain extent reflected the hardships of their life overseas and the miseries they encountered. We can see from Table 8.4 that there were forty overseas migrants from the Yan lineage who died before forty, constituting 59.7% of the total of sixty-seven migrants; of the Lin lineage overseas migrants there were

TABLE 8.4. Comparison of Longevity in the Yan and Lin Lineages

Age at death	Overseas	Taiwan	Mainland
	Yan Lineage		
Under 20	4	2	2
20–29	16	9	13
30–39	20	6	23
40–49	12	6	27
50–59	10	5	18
60–69	1	6	14
70–79	4	2	15
80+	0	1	5
Total	67	37	117
Youngest death	17	15	18
Oldest death	78	88	96
Average death age	38.82	43.94	48.98
	Lin Lineage		
Under 20	5	4	
20–29	31	14	
30–39	59	10	
40–49	38	10	
50–59	25	13	
60–69	5	3	
70–79	4	3	
80+		1	
Total	167	58	
Youngest death	15	14	
Oldest death	72	86	
Average death age	39.15	41.86	

NOTE: Ages of death for Lin migrants within the mainland not tabulated because there were so few.

ninety-five who did not reach the age of forty, constituting 56.9% of the total.

Neither of the genealogies records the causes of death of the emigrants systematically, so we can only piece together the situation at that time from a few cases in which causes of death are given.

Deaths from Marine Accidents. There were six members of the Yan lineage who died in the Sunda Sea: Yan Hongkui, Yan Yilan, Yan Yihui, Yan Jiahai, Yan Jiayun, and Yan Rugui. Members of the Lin lineage who died in maritime accidents were Lin Fuzha (boat sank in an outside city), Lin Kelu (boat sank in the eastern sea), and Lin Fuzhao (boat sank in the western sea). Because at that time the ocean was navigated in primitive sailboats, I believe that there were probably other migrants who died in maritime accidents.

Massacres by Colonialists. In 1603 (Wanli 31, *guimao*) Spanish colonialists in the Philippines massacred a large number of overseas Chinese; tens of thousands perished (Zhang 1982, chap. 323). There were seven members of the Yan lineage who were killed in this incident. They were Yan Jiasheng, 19; Yan Jiayi, 40; Yan Jiase, 39; Yan Tingcai, 49; Yan Tingbi, 32; Yan Tinggan, 23; and Yan Tingcan, 34. They are all noted in the genealogy.

In 1740 (Qianlong 5), from the fourth to the twelfth day of the tenth month, the Dutch colonialists cruelly massacred nearly ten thousand overseas Chinese. This massacre of Batavia, or the "cruel incident of the river of blood," shocked Java, China, and Europe. Lin Guizhi, 44, of the Pushan Lins, died in this incident, as recorded in the genealogy.

In those times, whether it was in the Philippines under Spanish rule or in Indonesia under Dutch rule, overseas Chinese often experienced cruel treatment. Economically they were restricted, excluded, and plundered; politically they were subjected to discrimination and all kinds of persecution. They had no assurance whatsoever of the safety of body, home, or life. I believe that this was a very common reason why those who did not live to forty constituted the majority of the overseas migrants from the Yan and Lin lineages.

CONCLUSION

In the Ming-Qing emigration of Minnan, the Yan lineage of Anping and the Lin lineage of Pushan are representative of two different kinds of lineages. Because of existing differences in socioeconomic environment, there were differences in the nature of migration. The migrants from the Yan lineage reflect the commercial migrants of the middle and late Ming, while the migrants from the Lin lineage reflect the agricultural and other ordinary migrants of the early Qing.

If we look at the patterns of migration, we see that the migration patterns of the Yan lineage are obviously connected to the rise and fall of trade at Anping. During the period of prosperity of Anping merchants (from the middle of the Ming to the early Qing), the number of Yans who went to do business in the cities of Guangdong or who "sailed the seas to sell to barbarians" was great. When the merchants of Anping declined after the Qianlong period, the population of migrants from the Yan lineage also fell off greatly. The migration of great numbers of the Lin lineage to Indonesia and the Philippines was connected with changes in Dutch and Spanish colonial policy toward overseas Chinese and with the nature of the labor market. The Lin migrations also had a very close connection with the large-scale opening of Taiwan after it was united with the mainland in Kangxi 22 (1683).

I believe that the types of migration found in the lineages described here follow this same pattern. And the marriage styles of the migrants, the adoption of "continuation sons," and regular adoption, as well as the fact that eldest sons (including only sons) constituted the majority of emigrants, reflects from several angles the traditional lineage ideology and the family organization of Minnan. The differences in average lifespan of emigrants are certainly connected with the quality of the environment in the different destinations and constitute a record of the differing fates of the emigrants.

GLOSSARY OF CHINESE TERMS

Bao 堡
Baojia 保甲
Biji 筆記
Dafang 大房
Ding 丁
Du 都
Fang 房
Fusheng 附生
Gongsheng 貢生
Guoxue sheng 國學生
Hang 行
Hao 号
Houxuan 候選
Huang 黃
Jia 家
Jiansheng 監生
Jiantiao 兼祧
Jinshi 進士
Juan 卷
Junxiang 郡庠
Juren 舉人
Lao 老
Li 里
Linghu 另戶
Lingsheng 廩生
Menpai 門牌
Ming 名
Mu 畝
Muzhiming 墓誌銘
Qiaozhu 僑居
Qing 頃
Shengyuan 生員
Shiju 世居
Shixi biao 世系表
Shixi tu 世系圖
Sui 歲
Taixue sheng 太學生
Wu shengyuan 武生員
Wushi tongtang 五世同堂
Wu xiangsheng 武庠生
Xian 縣
Xiao 小
Xiaofang 小房
Xiaoren 小人
Xiangsheng 庠生
Xiucai 秀才
Yao 夭
Yixiang 邑庠
Zengsheng 增生
Zhi 枝
Zhong 中
Zhou 州
Zi 字
Zouguang 走廣
Zh 族
Zupu 族譜

GLOSSARY OF DEMOGRAPHIC TERMS

Age-specific death rate: The number of deaths per thousand person-years among the members of a population in a certain age bracket, e.g., 40–44 years or 55–59 years.

Age-specific fertility rate: The number of births per thousand woman-years among the members of a population in a certain age bracket. In Chinese genealogical demography, an equivalent age-specific male fertility rate, based on man-years instead of woman-years, is used.

Age-specific marital fertility rate: The number of births per thousand married woman-years among those members of a population in a certain age bracket. In Chinese genealogical demography, an equivalent male-based rate may be used.

Age structure: The proportions of a population in various age brackets at a particular time.

Annual rate of population growth: The percentage increase per year in a total population. The population growth rate equals the birth rate plus the in-migration rate minus the death rate and the out-migration rate.

Birth cohort: All the people born in a particular interval, such as 1800–1849.

Birth interval: The time between the birth of one of a woman's children and the birth of the next one.

Completed marital fertility: The total number of children a woman bears by the time her marriage ends. Since there is little divorce in traditional Chinese populations, this usually means the total number of children a woman bears before she dies or becomes a widow.

Complex families: Families that include more members than just the elementary family of a married couple with children.

Conjugal families: Families that include a married couple and their children only; nuclear families.

Consort: As used here, any legal sexual partner of a male lineage member, whether wife or concubine.

Death rates: The number of deaths per thousand population per year.

Demographic regime: The combined fertility, nuptiality, mortality, and migration rates of a particular population.

Developmental cycle: The sequence of structures a family passes through in the course of a generation.

Extended household: A household that contains more than the conjugal family of a married couple and their children.

Fecundability: The ability of a woman to become pregnant.

Fertility: The number of children born. There are various specific measures of fertility, defined elsewhere in this glossary. In demography, fertility does *not* carry its meaning in everyday or medical language, i.e., the ability of a woman to become pregnant. This is referred to in demography as fecundability.

Frèrèche: A family consisting of at least two brothers and their wives and children, without the parents of the brothers. Frèrèches and grand families are forms of the joint family.

Grand family: A family consisting of three or more generations, with at least two brothers and their wives and children in the second generation. The grand and *frèrèche* families are forms of the joint family.

Gross (intergenerational) reproduction rate: The ratio of the number of members born in a particular generation to the number of members born into the previous generation. This is conventionally calculated for females, but in Chinese genealogical demography an equivalent male-based rate can be used.

Infant mortality rate: The number of deaths in the first year of life per thousand births.

Intercensal death rates: The number of deaths per thousand person-years in the interval between two censuses.

Joint families: Families containing at least two brothers, with their wives and children, in the same generation. A joint family that also contains one or both of the brothers' parents is a grand family; a joint family without the brothers' parents is a *frèrèche*.

Life expectancy (e_x): The average number of years a member of a population can expect to live after age x. For example, a life expectancy at age twenty of thirty-five years means the average person who is alive at twenty will live to age fifty-five.

Life table: A table of life expectancies at particular ages (usually five-year intervals) for a particular population.

Major marriage: A marriage in which a woman enters her husband's household as a young adult.

Maternal mortality: The number of maternal deaths per thousand term pregnancies.

Mean length of generation: The mean interval between the date of a man's birth and the average of the birth dates of his sons.

Minor marriage: A marriage, also called a little daughter-in-law marriage, in which a girl is adopted by her future husband's parents and raised in their household.

Model life table: Life table (q.v.) prepared from large sets of reliable data, used for matching to data from incomplete data sets.

Mortality: A rate of deaths in a certain population. Specific measures of mortality include crude death rates, age-specific death rates, mean age at death, etc.

Natural fertility: The fertility of a population that is practicing no sort of birth limitation procedures.

Natural increase: The excess of births over deaths in a population. May not be the same as the population growth rate because it does not account for in- or out-migration.

Net paternal intergenerational reproduction of males: The male-based equivalent of net reproduction rate (q.v.).

Net reproduction rate: The ratio of the number of people born in a particular generation to the number of people born in the previous generation who survive to maturity, minus one. This ratio is zero if the population size is stable. In ordinary demography, the net reproduction rate is calculated as a ratio of daughters to mothers; in Chinese genealogical demography, it can be calculated as a ratio of sons to fathers.

Nuclear family system: A form of the developmental cycle in which married couples regularly establish independent households. In this system, families ordinarily do not grow more complex than the nuclear or conjugal form.

Nuptiality: A measure of marriage, usually the proportion of a population ever married or the proportion of a population married at a certain age.

Parity: Conventionally, the number of children a woman has borne. In Chinese genealogical demography, an equivalent male measure can be calculated.

Parity progression ratio: A series of ratios of the number of parents who have borne a certain number of children to the number who have borne one fewer children. For example, if half the women who bear one child also bear a second child, the parity progression ratio from one to two is .5.

Reproduction rate: The size of one generation compared to the size of the previous generation. See also specific reproduction rates (gross and net).

Sex ratio: The number of males per hundred females in a population.

Stem families: Families with married couples in at least two generations but with no two married couples in any one generation.

Total fertility: The average number of children a woman would bear if she were at risk for childbearing for the whole span of her reproductive years, ages fifteen to forty-five. Differs from the number of children ever born because some women die before completing the normal reproductive span. Total fertility is a summation of age-specific fertility rates.

Total marital fertility rate: The average number of children a woman would bear if she were married during her entire reproductive life span, ages fifteen to forty-five. Total marital fertility rate is a summation of age-specific marital fertility rates.

Vital dates: Date of birth and date of death.

REFERENCES

Ahern, Emily. 1976. Segmentation in Chinese lineages: A view through written genealogies. *American Ethnologist* 3(1):1–16.
Anhai. ca. 1600. *Anhai zhi* (Gazetteer of Anhai [Anping]).
Anthony, Lawrence, James Lee, and Alice Suen. 1985. *Adult mortality in rural Liaoning 1795 to 1820*. California Institute of Technology Humanities Working Paper 115. Pasadena.
Averill, Stephen C. 1983. The Shed People and the opening of the Yangzi highlands. *Modern China* 9:84–126.
Bai Juyi (772–846). 1965. *Bai Xiangshan ji*. Wanyou wenku ed.
Banister, Judith. 1987. *China's changing population*. Stanford: Stanford University Press.
Barclay, George W. 1954. *Colonial development and population in Taiwan*. Princeton: Princeton University Press.
Barclay, George W., Ansley J. Coale, Michael A. Stoto, and T. James Trussell. 1976. A reassessment of the demography of traditional rural China. *Population Index* 42(4):606–35.
Bean, Lee L., and Geraldine Mineau. 1986. The polygyny-fertility hypothesis: A re-evaluation. *Population Studies* 40(1):67–81.
Beattie, Hillary. 1979. *Land and lineage in China: A study of T'ung-ch'eng County, Anhwei, in the Ming and Ch'ing dynasties*. New York: Cambridge University Press.
Bielenstein, Hans. 1987. *Bulletin of the Museum of Far Eastern Antiquities, Stockholm*.
Birge, Bettine. 1985. A study of the marriage age of women in Sung China, 960–1279. Master's essay, Columbia University.
Blayo, Y. 1975. La mortalité en France de 1740 à 1829. *Population* (November–December):138–39.
Bongaarts, J. 1983. *Fertility, biology, and behavior: An analysis of the proximate determinants*. New York: Academic Press.
Brass, William. 1975. *Methods for estimating fertility and mortality from limited and defective data*. Occasional Publication, Carolina Population Center, Laboratories for Population Statistics. Chapel Hill: University of North Carolina.

Buck, John Lossing. 1937. *Land utilization in China*. Nanking: University of Nanking.
Cartier, Michel. 1974. Nouvelles données sur la demographie Chinoise à l'époque des Ming, 1368–1644. *Annales: Économies Sociétés Civilisations* 28:1341–59.
Chaffe, John W. 1985. *The thorny gates of learning in Sung China*. Cambridge: Cambridge University Press.
Chang Chung-li. 1955. *The Chinese gentry*. Seattle: University of Washington Press.
Chang Pide. 1977. *Songren zhuanji ziliao suoyin*. Rev. ed. Taipei: Dingwen shuju.
Chen Ta. 1946. *Population in modern China*. Chicago: University of Chicago Press.
Cheng Ju (1078–1144). 1929. *Beishan xiaoji*. Sibu congkan ed.
Cheng Yi (1033–1107). 1981. *Erh Cheng ji*. Xinhua shuju ed.
Chiang Chin Long. 1968. *Introduction to stochastic processes in biostatistics*. New York: Wiley.
Coale, Ansley J. 1985a. Fertility in rural China: A reconfirmation of the Barclay reassessment. In *Family and population in East Asian history*, ed. Susan B. Hanley and Arthur P. Wolf, 186–95. Stanford: Stanford University Press.
———. 1985b. Reassessment defended. *Population and Development Review* 10(3): 471–80.
Coale, Ansley J., and Paul Demeny. 1966. *Regional model life tables and stable populations*. Princeton: Princeton University Press.
Coale, Ansley J., and James Trussell. 1974. Model fertility schedules: Variations in the structure of childbearing in human populations. *Population Index* 40(2):185–258.
———. 1975. Erratum. *Population Index* 41(4):572.
———. 1978. Technical note: Finding the two parameters that specify a model schedule of marital fertility. *Population Index* 44(2):203–13.
Cohen, Myron. 1968. A case study of Chinese family economy and development. *Journal of Asian and African Studies* 3:161–80.
———. 1970. Developmental process in the Chinese family group. In *Family and kinship in Chinese society*, ed. Maurice Freedman, 21–36. Stanford: Stanford University Press.
———. 1976. *House united, house divided: The Chinese family in Taiwan*. New York: Columbia University Press.
Cole, James H. 1980. The Shaohsing connection: A vertical administrative clique in late Qing China. *Modern China* 6(3):317–326.
Dickeman, Mildred. 1975. Demographic consequences of infanticide in man. *Annual Review of Ecology and Systematics* 6:107–37.
Dunstan, Helen. 1975. The late Ming epidemics—a preliminary survey. *Ch'ing-shih Wen-t'i* 3(3):1–59.
Eberhard, Wolfram. 1962. *Social mobility in traditional China*. Leiden: E. J. Brill.
Ebrey, Patricia. 1981. Women in the kinship system of the Southern Song upper class. *Historical Reflections* 8:113–28.
———. 1983. Types of lineages in Ch'ing China: A reexamination of the Chang lineage of T'ung-ch'eng. *Ch'ing-shih Wen-t'i* 4(9):1–20.
———. 1984a. Conceptions of the family in the Sung dynasty. *Journal of Asian Studies* 43(2):219–45.

———. 1984b. *Family and property in Sung China: Yuan Ts'ai's precepts for social life.* Princeton: Princeton University Press.
———. 1984c. The women in Liu Kezhuang's family. *Modern China* 10:415–40.
———. 1986. The early stages in the development of descent group organization. In *Kinship organization in late imperial China, 1000–1940*, ed. Patricia Ebrey and James L. Watson, 16–61. Berkeley: University of California Press.
———. 1988. Dynamics of elite domination in Sung China. *Harvard Journal of Asiatic Studies* 48(2):493–519.
———. 1991. Shifts in marriage finance, sixth to thirteenth centuries. In *Marriage and inequality in Chinese society*, ed. Rubie S. Watson and Patricia Buckley Ebrey, 97–132. Berkeley and Los Angeles: University of California Press.
———. 1993. *The inner quarters: Marriage and the lives of Chinese women in the Sung period.* Berkeley and Los Angeles: University of California Press.
Ewbank, Douglas. 1981. *Age misreporting and age-selective underenumeration: Sources, patterns, and consequences for demographic analysis.* Washington, D.C.: National Academy Press.
Fei, John, and Liu Ts'ui-jung. 1982. The growth and decline of Chinese family clans. *Journal of Interdisciplinary History* 12(3):375–408.
Fei Hsiao-t'ung (Fei Xiaotong). 1939. *Peasant life in China.* London: Routledge and Kegan Paul.
———. 1946. Peasantry and gentry. *American Journal of Sociology* 52(1):1–17.
Fengtian tongzhi. [1934] 1982. Reprint, Dongbei wenshi congshu bianji weiyuanhui, August.
Feng Zigang. 1935. *Lanyu nongcun diaocha* (Investigation of villages in Lanyu). Hangzhou: Guoli zhejiang daxue.
Fogel, Robert. 1986. Nutrition and the decline in mortality since 1700. In *Long-term factors in American economic growth*, ed. Stanley Engerman and Robert Gallman. Chicago: University of Chicago Press.
Freedman, Maurice. 1958. *Lineage organization in southeastern China.* London: Athlone.
———. 1966. *Chinese lineage and society.* London: Athlone.
Fu Kedong. 1983. Baqi zhidu huji chutan (A preliminary study of the Eight Banner household registration system). *Minzu yanjiu* (Ethnic studies) 6:34–43.
Fu Yiling. 1956. *Ming-Qing shidai shangren ji shangren ziben.* (Merchants and merchant capital in the Ming and Qing periods). Beijing: Zhongguo renmin chubanshe.
———. 1983. *Xinbian Anhai zhi xuyan* (Preface to the newly edited Gazetteer of Anhai).
Gamble, Sidney D. [1954] 1968. *Ting Hsien: A north China rural community.* New York: Institute of Pacific Relations. Reprint, Stanford: Stanford University Press.
Goldman, Noreen. 1980. Far Eastern patterns of mortality. *Population Studies* 34(1):5–22.
Haicheng. 1736–96. *Haicheng xian zhi* (Gazetteer of Haicheng County).
Hajnal, J. 1965. European marriage patterns in perspective. In *Population in history*, ed. D. V. Glass and D. E. C. Eversley, 101–43. Chicago: Aldine.
Hanley, Susan B., and Arthur P. Wolf, eds. 1985. *Family and population in East Asian history.* Stanford: Stanford University Press.

Harrell, Stevan. 1982. *Ploughshare village: Culture and context in Taiwan.* Seattle: University of Washington Press.
———. 1985. The rich get children: Segmentation, stratification, and population in three Chekiang lineages. In *Family and population in East Asian history,* ed. Susan B. Hanley and Arthur P. Wolf, 81–132. Stanford: Stanford University Press.
———. 1987. On the holes in Chinese genealogies. *Late Imperial China* 8(2):53–79.
Harrell, Stevan, Susan Naquin, and Ju Deyuan. 1985. Lineage genealogy: The genealogical records of the Qing Imperial Lineage. *Late Imperial China* 6(2):37–47.
Hartwell, Robert M. 1982. Demographic, political, and social transformations of China, 750–1550. *Harvard Journal of Asiatic Studies* 42:365–442.
Hazelton, Keith. 1990. Crisis mortality in premodern China. Paper presented at the Annual Meeting of the Association for Asian Studies, Chicago, April 1990.
He Qiaoyuan. ca. 1600. *Jingshan quan ji* (Complete collection from the Mirror Mountain).
Henry, Louis. 1961. Some data on natural fertility. *Eugenics Quarterly* 8:81–91.
Henry, Louis. 1967. *Manuel de démographie historique.* Geneva and Paris: Librairie Droz.
Herlihy, David. 1985. *Medieval households.* Cambridge: Harvard University Press.
Hill, Kenneth, and James Trussell. 1983. *Manual X: Indirect techniques for demographic estimation.* United Nations Populations Studies, no. 81. New York: United Nations.
Ho Ping-ti. 1959. *Studies on the population of China, 1368–1953.* Cambridge: Harvard University Press.
———. 1962. *The ladder of success in traditional China: Aspects of social mobility, 1368–1911.* New York: Columbia University Press.
Holmgren, J. 1986. Observations on marriage and inheritance practices in early Mongol and Yuan society, with particular reference to the levirate. *Journal of Asian History* 20:127–92.
Hsu, Francis L. K. 1943. The myth of Chinese family size. *American Journal of Sociology* 48(5):555–62.
Hu Yin (1098–1156). 1983. *Feiran ji.* Siku quanshu chenben ed.
Huang, Philip C. C. 1985. *The peasant economy and social change in North China.* Stanford: Stanford University Press.
Hull, C. Hadlai, Norman Nie, and Dale H. Bent. 1975. *Statistical package for the social sciences.* 2d ed. New York: McGraw-Hill.
Hymes, Robert P. 1986. *Statesmen and gentlemen: The elite of Fu-chou, Chiang-hsi, in Northern and Southern Sung.* Cambridge: Cambridge University Press.
Jannetta, Ann Bowman. 1987. *Epidemics and fertility in early modern Japan.* Princeton: Princeton University Press.
Kirshner, Julius, and Anthony Molho. 1978. The dowry fund and the marriage market in early *Quattrocento* Florence. *Journal of Modern History* 50:403–38.
Lang, Olga. 1946. *Chinese family and society.* New Haven: Yale University Press.
Lavely, William R. 1984. The rural Chinese fertility transition: A report from Shifang Xian, Sichuan. *Population Studies* 38(3):365–84.
Lavely, William R., James Lee, and Wang Feng. 1990. Chinese demography: The state of the field. *Journal of Asian Studies* 49(4):807–34.

Lee, James. 1982. Food supply and population growth in Southwest China, 1250–1850. *Journal of Asian Studies* 41(4):711–46.

———. 1990. Happy families: The developmental cycle in rural Liaoning. Paper presented at the Annual Meeting of the Association for Asian Studies, Chicago, April 1990.

———. N.d. Death during early life among members of China's last Imperial Clan, 1700–1800. Unpublished paper.

Lee, James, Lawrence Anthony, and Alice Suen. 1988. Liaoning sheng chengren siwang lu, 1796–1819 (Adult mortality in Liaoning, 1796–1819). In *Qingzhu diyi lishi dang'an guan liushi zhounian lunwen ji* (Proceedings of the symposium on the occasion of the sixtieth anniversary of the First Historical Archives). Beijing: Zhonghua shuju, 2:885–98.

Lee, James, and Cameron Campbell. Forthcoming. *Fate and fortune in rural China: Population and social structure in Liaoning, 1774–1873*. Cambridge: Cambridge University Press.

Lee, James, and Robert Eng. 1984. Population and family history in eighteenth-century Manchuria: Preliminary results from Daoyi, 1774–1798. *Ch'ing-shih Wen-t'i* 5(1):1–55.

Lee, James, and Jon Gjerde. 1986. Comparative household morphology of stem, joint, and nuclear household systems: Norway, China, and the United States. *Continuity and Change* 1(1):89–112.

Lee, James, and Fu Kedong. N.d. The Eight Banner registration system. Unpublished manuscript.

Legge, James, trans. 1967 [1885]. *Li chi, Book of rites*. Reprint, New York: University Books.

Levy, Marion. 1949. *The family revolution in modern China*. Cambridge: Harvard University Press.

Li Guangjin. ca. 1600. *Jingji ji* (Collection from the scenic stairway).

Li Yuanbi (12th century). 1976. *Zuoyi zizhen*. Sibu congkan xubian ed.

Liang Fanzhong. 1980. *Zhongguo lidai hukou tiandi tianfu tongji* (Statistics of household, population, cultivated land, and land taxation in China throughout the dynasties). Shanghai: Renmin chubanshe.

Liu Ts'ui-jung. 1978. Chinese genealogies as a source for the study of historical demography. In *Studies and essays in commemoration of the golden jubilee of Academia Sinica*, 849–70. Taipei: Academia Sinica.

———. 1981. The demographic dynamics of some clans in Lower Yangtze area, ca. 1400–1900. *Jingji Lunwen* (Academia economic papers) 9(1):115–60.

———. 1983. Ming-Qing renkou zhi zengzhi yu qianyi (Growth and migration of the population in the Ming-Qing period). In *Zhongguo shehui jingji shi yantao hui lunwenji* (Papers from the seminar on Chinese social and economic history), ed. Hsu Cho-yun, Mao Han-kuang, and Liu Ts'ui-jung, 283–316. Taipei: Center for Chinese Studies.

———. 1985. The demography of two Chinese clans in Hsiao-shan, Chekiang, 1650–1850. In *Family and population in East Asian history*, ed. Susan B. Hanley and Arthur P. Wolf, 13–61. Stanford: Stanford University Press.

———. 1986. Ming Qing shiqi Changjiang xiayou diqu dushihua zhi fazhan yu renkou tezheng (Demographic aspects of urbanization in the Lower Yangtze region in China, in the Ming-Qing period). *Jingji Lunwen* (Academia economic papers) 14(2):43–86.

———. 1987. Yi Guangdong Xiangshan Xu shi wei li shilun Zhongguo jiazuzhi chengzhang ji qi gongneng zhi fahui (A discourse on growth and function of the Chinese lineage: An example of the Xu lineage of Xiangshan, Guangdong). *Proceedings of the third conference on Asian clan genealogies*, 369–416. Taipei: United Daily News Cultural Foundation.

———. 1989a. Yihuang Beishan Huang shi zhi chengzhang yu shehui jingji huodong (Growth of the Huang lineage in Yihuang and its socio-economic activities). In *The Second International Conference on Sinology, section on Ming, Ching, and modern history*, 243–74. Taipei: Academia Sinica.

———. 1989b. Hebei san jiazu de renkou tezheng (Demographic characteristics of three lineages in Hebei). *Proceedings of the Fourth Conference on Asian Clan Genealogies*, 61–98. Taipei: United Daily News Cultural Foundation.

———. 1992. Ming-Qing jiazu de hunyin xingtai yu shengyulü (Marriage patterns and fertility rates in Ming-Qing lineages). In *Papers on society and culture of early modern China*. Taipei: Institute of History and Philology, Academia Sinica.

Liu Yingli. 1307 [13th century]. *Xinbian shiwen lei ju hanmo daquan*. 1307 ed.

Luo Yuan (1136–1184). 1983. Hun wen. In *Qingchuan baibian*, ed. Tang Shunzi. Siku quanshu ed.

Marme, Michael. 1981. Population and possibility in Ming Suzhou, 1368–1664: A quantified model. *Ming Studies* 12:29–64.

Meskill, Johanna. 1970. The Chinese genealogy as a research source. In *Family and kinship in Chinese society*, ed. Maurice Freedman, 39–61. Stanford: Stanford University Press.

Niida, Noboru. 1937. *Shina mibunhōshi*. Tokyo: Zayūhō kankōkai.

Pasternak, Burton. 1983. *Guests in the dragon: Social demography of a Chinese district, 1895–1946*. New York: Columbia University Press.

Perdue, Peter. 1987. *Exhausting the earth: State and peasant in Hunan, 1500–1850*. Cambridge: Harvard University Press.

Perkins, Dwight H. 1969. *Agricultural development in China, 1368–1968*. Edinburgh: Edinburgh University Press.

Pressat, Roland. 1972. *Demographic analysis*. Chicago: Aldine, Atherton, Inc.

Quanzhou. 1736–96. *Quanzhou fu zhi* (Gazetteer of Quanshou Prefecture).

Qiu Jun. 15th century. *Daxue yanyi bu* (Commentary on the *Rites of Zhou*).

Sa, Sophie. 1985. Marriage among the Taiwanese of pre-1945 Taipei. In *Family and population in East Asian history*, ed. Susan B. Hanley and Arthur P. Wolf, 277–308. Stanford: Stanford University Press.

Schoppa, R. Keith. 1989. *Xiang Lake—Nine centuries of Chinese life*. New Haven and London: Yale University Press.

Schran, Peter. 1978. China's demographic evolution 1850–1953 reconsidered. *The China Quarterly* 75:639–46.

Shao Bowen (1057–1134). 1983. *Shaoshi wenjian lu*. Beijing: Zhonghua shuju ed.

Sharlin, Alan. 1978. Methods for estimating total age distributions and vital rates in family reconstitution studies. *Population Studies* 32(3):511–21.
Shiga Shūzō. 1981. *Chūgoku kazokuhō no genri* (The principle of Chinese lineage laws). Tokyo: Sobunsha.
Shryock, Henry, Jacob Siegel, and associates. 1971. *The methods and materials of demography*. United States Department of Commerce, Bureau of the Census. New York: Academic Press.
Shryock, Henry, Jacob Siegel, and Edward G. Stockwell. 1976. *The methods and materials of demography (Condensed edition)*. New York: Academic Press.
Sima Guang (1019–86). *Simashi shuyi*. Congshu jicheng ed.
Skinner, G. William. 1964. Marketing and social structure in rural China, part I. *Journal of Asian Studies* 24(1):1–43.
———. 1977. Regional urbanization in nineteenth-century China. In *The city in late imperial China*, ed. G. William Skinner. Stanford: Stanford University Press.
———. 1985. Presidential address: The structure of Chinese history. *Journal of Asian Studies* 44(2):271–92.
———. 1987. Sichuan's population in the nineteenth century: Lessons from disaggregated data. *Late Imperial China* 8(1):1–79.
Smith, James E., and Phillip R. Kunz. 1976. Polygyny and fertility in nineteenth-century America. *Population Studies* 30(3):465–80.
Smith, Thomas C. 1977. *Nakahara: Family farming and population in a Japanese village, 1717–1830*. Stanford: Stanford University Press.
Stone, Laurence. 1981. Family history in the 1980s: Past achievements and future trends. *Journal of Interdisciplinary History* 12(1):51–87.
Tang huiyao (Collection of important documents of the Tang). 1991. Shanghai: Shanghai guji chubanshe.
Telford, Ted A. 1985. Marital fertility in the Ming-Qing transition: Tongcheng County, 1520–1661. Paper presented at the Workshop on Qing Population History, California Institute of Technology, August 1985.
———. 1986. A survey of social demographic data in Chinese genealogies. *Late Imperial China* 7:118–48.
———. 1990a. Mortality and social structure in late imperial Tongcheng county. Paper presented at the Annual Meeting of the Association for Asian Studies, Chicago, April 1990.
———. 1990b. Patching the holes in Chinese genealogies. *Late Imperial China* 11(2):116–35.
———. 1992a. Covariates of men's age at first marriage: The historical demography of Chinese lineages. *Population Studies* 46(1):19–35.
———. 1992b. Family and state in Qing China: Age at marriage in the Tongcheng lineages, 1300–1800. Paper presented at the Conference on Political Process and Family Process in Modern Chinese History, Academia Sinica, Nankang, Taiwan, January 1992.
Telford, Ted A., Melvin P. Thatcher, and Basil P. N. Yang. 1983. *Chinese genealogies at the Genealogical Society of Utah: An annotated bibliography*. Taipei: Ch'eng-wen Publishing Co.

Ukaegbu, Alfred O. 1977. Fertility of women in polygynous unions in rural Eastern Nigeria. *Journal of Marriage and the Family* 39(2):397–404.
Vinovskis, M. A. 1972. Mortality rates and trends in Massachusetts before 1860. *Journal of Economic History* 32:184–213.
Waley, Arthur. 1937. *The book of songs.* New York: Grove Press.
Wang Tinggui (1079–1171). 1972. *Luxi wenji.* Siku quanshu zhenben ed.
Watkins, Susan Cotts, and Jane Menken. 1985. Famines in historical perspective: An exchange. *Population and Development Review* 14(1):145–70.
Watson, Rubie S. 1985. *Inequality among brothers: Class and kinship in South China.* Berkeley and Los Angeles: University of California Press.
Watson, Rubie S., and Patricia Buckley Ebrey. 1991. *Marriage and inequality in Chinese society.* Berkeley and Los Angeles: University of California Press.
Wei Shou (506–72). 1974. *Wei shu.* Zhonghua shuju ed.
Wen Guangyi et al. 1985. *Yinduonixiya huaqiao shi* (History of the overseas Chinese in Indonesia). Beijing: Haiyang chubanshe.
Wolf, Arthur P. 1984. Family life and the life cycle in rural China. In *Households,* ed. Robert Mc. Netting, Richard R. Wilk, and Eric J. Arnould, 279–98. Berkeley and Los Angeles: University of California Press.
———. 1985a. Chinese family size: A myth revitalized. In *The Chinese family and its ritual behavior,* ed. Hsieh Jihchang and Chuang Ying-chang, 30–49. Taipei: Academia Sinica.
———. 1985b. Fertility in prerevolutionary rural China. In *Family and population in East Asian history,* ed. Susan B. Hanley and Arthur P. Wolf, 154–85. Stanford: Stanford University Press.
Wolf, Arthur P., and Susan B. Hanley. 1985. Introduction to *Family and population in East Asian history,* ed. Susan B. Hanley and Arthur P. Wolf, 1–12. Stanford: Stanford University Press.
Wolf, Arthur P., and Huang Chieh-shan. 1980. *Marriage and adoption in China, 1845–1945.* Stanford: Stanford University Press.
Wrigley, E. A., ed. 1966. *An Introduction to English historical demography from the sixteenth to the nineteenth century.* London: Weidenfeld and Nicolson.
Wrigley, E. A., and R. S. Schofield. 1981. *The population history of England, 1541–1871.* Cambridge: Harvard University Press.
Xiaoshan. 1987. *Xiaoshan xian zhi* (Gazetteer of Xiaoshan County). Hangzhou: Zhejiang renmin chubanshe.
Xu Hong. 1989. Mingdai de hunyin zhidu (The marriage system of the Ming period). *Dalu zazhi* 78(1):26–27; 78(2):68–82.
Xu Jingheng (1072–1128). 1975. *Hengtang ji.* Siku quanshu zhenben ed.
Yan. 1942. *Xinjiapo Yan shi gonghui shi nian jinian tekan* (Special publication commemorating ten years of the Yan Clan Association in Singapore).
Yu Jing (1000–1064). *Wuxi ji.* Guangdong congshu ed.
Yuan I-chin. 1931. Life tables for a southern Chinese family from 1365 to 1849. *Human Biology* 3(2):157–79.
Zhang Tingyu (1672–1755). 1982. *Ming shi* (History of the Ming). Taipei: Tingwen.
Zhang Xie. ca. 1600. *Dong Xi Yang kao* (Information on the Eastern and Western Oceans).

Zhou Bida (1126–1204). 1971. *Zhou Wenzhong gong ji*. Siku quanshu zhenben ed.
Zhou Yuanlian. 1981. *Qingchao kaiguo shi yanjiu* (Research on the founding of the Qing state). Shenyang: Renmin.
———. 1982. Guanyu baqi zhidu di jige wenti (Some problems on the banner system). *Qingshi Luncong* 3:140–54.
Zhu Xi (1130–1200). 1929. *Zhu Wengong wen ji*. Sibu congkan ed.
Zhuang Weiji and Wang Lianmao. 1984. Cong zupu ziliao kan Min-Tai guanxi (Looking at Fujian-Taiwan relations through genealogical data). *Zhongguo shi yanjiu* no. 1.
———. 1985. *Min-Tai guanxi zupu ziliao xuanbian* (Selected genealogical materials on Fujian-Taiwan relations). Fuzhou: Fujian renmin chubanshe.

CONTRIBUTORS

Lawrence Anthony did his undergraduate and graduate work at the California Institute of Technology, receiving the M.S. and Ph.D. degrees in materials science in 1993. The research leading to the present paper was carried out while he was an undergraduate. He is currently a postdoctoral fellow at Caltech, where he studies the thermodynamics and kinetics of order-disorder transformations. He is the author of over fifteen technical articles.

Cameron Campbell is a Ph.D. candidate in the Department of Sociology at the University of Pennsylvania. His primary interest is demography, in particular the historical demography of China and the mortality decline in contemporary China. He is also interested in the simulation modeling of the effects on populations of processes of selection in mortality and fertility. Two of his most recent publications are "Differential Fertility and the Distribution of Traits: The Case of IQ" (with Samuel Preston), and "The Last Emperors: An Introduction to the Demography of the Qing Imperial Lineage" (with James Lee and Wang Feng).

Patricia Buckley Ebrey, professor of East Asian languages and cultures at the University of Illinois, is a specialist in Song social history. Her most recent books are *Confucianism and Family Rituals in Imperial China: A Social History of Writing about Rites* (1991) and *The Inner Quarters: Marriage and the Lives of Chinese Women in the Sung Period* (1993).

Stevan Harrell is professor and chair of the Department of Anthropology at the University of Washington. He has recently edited *Chinese Families in the Post-Mao Era* (1993, with Deborah Davis), *Cultural Change in Postwar Taiwan* (1994, with Huang Chun-chieh), and *Cultural Encounters on China's Ethnic Frontiers* (1994). His current research concerns ethnic relations in the Liangshan area, southern Sichuan.

James Lee is an associate professor of history and social science at the California Institute of Technology. He has written widely on the historical demography of China and is currently working on the contemporary demography of sub-Saharan

Africa. His most recent publication (with Wang Feng and Cameron Campbell) is "Infant and Child Mortality among the Qing Nobility: Implications for Two Types of Positive Checks."

Liu Ts'ui-jung is a research fellow of the Institute of Economics, Academia Sinica, and professor in the Department of History, National Taiwan University. Her research and teaching are mostly related to Chinese economic history and population history. Her work on Chinese lineage population, based on fifty genealogies, was published in 1992 as *Lineage Population and Socio-economic Change in the Ming and Qing Periods.*

Thomas W. Pullum is professor in the Department of Sociology, University of Texas at Austin. His main research interests are fertility and contraceptive use in developing countries and methods to adjust for various kinds of misreporting in demographic surveys. He is currently working on such topics in the modern Chinese context with the World Health Organization.

Ted A. Telford is adjunct professor of sociology at the University of Utah, specializing in Chinese demographic and social history. He is currently working on a Chinese bibliographic project supported by the National Endowment for the Humanities and continues to extend his historical demographic study of Tongcheng County into the early twentieth century.

Wang Lianmao is director of the Fujian Provincial Museum of Maritime History in Quanzhou, Fujian. He is the author of numerous books and articles on the local history of Quanzhou, the history of overseas commerce centered in Fujian, and the migration connections between Fujian and Taiwan.

INDEX

Adoption, 126, 140n4
Age at marriage: age at birth of first son as proxy for, 80–81; calculations of, and generational span, 145–146; and education, 39–41; and family composition, 150; and family organization, 21; and fertility, 21; fluctuations in, 7; and genealogical records, 11–13, 38; and nuptiality, 13; regional variations in, 21–22, 36–41, 45n18; and social status, 39; and social stratification, 14, 22; in Song dynasty, 23–29; temporal variations in, 13, 22; variations of, for Song men, 37–41
Anhai. See Anping
Anhui Province: genealogies from, 94, 100; mortality, 109–117; population growth, 48
Anping: historical significance and description of, 184–186; migration of Yan lineage from, 190–197; prosperity of lineages from, 186–188

Banner Populations, 91n18, 164, 165
Bielenstein, Hans, 1
Birge, Bettine, 43–44n3, 45n17
Buck, John Lossing, 22

Church of Jesus Christ of Latter-Day Saints, 4, 19n4
Concubines. See Polygyny
Confucius, 26, 28, 59

Daoyi: differential access to resources and mortality, 176; ethnicity of population, 180n1; family structure in, 142
Dingxian, 22
Dowry, 40, 41–43
Dynastic cycle: and mortality rates, 8–10; and population growth, 7; regional manifestations of, 6

Economic conditions: and family organization, 2–3; and marriage, 7; and mortality, 7; and population growth, 120; and regional variation, 2–3
Epitaphs, 6; and age of death, 30; and age differences between husbands and wives, 28–29, 44n4; and age at marriage, 23, 39–41; biases of, 24; components of, 24–25; as evidence of marriage strategies, 41; and family structure, 33–35; Ming, 41, 46n23; and number of children, 32–34; regional variation of, 37
Europe, western: life expectancy, 181n13; marriage system and fertility, 88; mortality and social classes, 90n6

Family, grand, 141, 155. See also Family, joint
Family, joint, 2, 3, 16, 17; definition, 122, 161n1; frequency of, 141, 142; and generational overlap, 144–145; possibility of belonging to, 130–139, 143, 155–161

233

Family, stem, 3, 16, 17; definition of, 122, 161n1; frequency of, 141, 142; and generational overlap, 144–145; potential for belonging to, 150–155, 161
Family developmental cycle, 2; and family organization, 16–17; and methodological considerations, 142–143
Family organization and structure: and age at marriage, 21, 145–146; and concubinage, 130; definitions of terms, 19n3; and the development cycle, 16–17; and fertility, 127–135; *frèrèches*, 17, 155; and mortality, 16, 127, 135–138, 146–150; and parental authority, 35; potential of living in complex family, 130–139, 141; reconstruction of, and methodological considerations, 95, 121–127, 142–143, 160; and remarriage, 130; and sibling position of migrants, 208; and social status, 155–156; among the Song, 34–36. See also Family, joint; Family, stem
Family size: distribution of, 107–108; and fertility, 128; in North Taiwan, 141–142
Fei Xiaotong, 3
Fertility: and age difference between spouses, 30; and age at marriage, 21; age specific marital, 6, 7, 15, 49, 57, 90n3; calculation of marital, 49, 56, 90n3, 95; as component of natural increase, 57, 89n2; estimation of, based on records of male sons, 100–108; and family composition, 127–135, 150, 156–157; and lineage size, 56; marital, 2, 15, 19n2, 96–98; measures of total completed, 67, 98–100; natural, 15, 50, 56; and polygyny, 64, 100; regional variation, 2, 105; and social stratification, 56; and wife's status, 64–65. See also Population growth; Reproductive rates

Genealogical Society of Utah, 4, 19n4
Genealogies: biases of, 5, 13–15, 46n20, 148–150; and calculation of age at marriage, 145–146; criteria for selection of, 121; effects of poor recording, 66; as evidence of marriage strategies, 41; and fertility estimates, 50–51, 94, 95–108; and migration, 183, 192; and mortality estimates, 95, 108–120; omissions in, 5, 38, 49, 66–67, 79, 95; representativeness of, 14–15, 17, 20n9, 38; rules on composition of, 4; as sources for demographic research, 3–6
Great Proletarian Cultural Revolution, 4
Guangdong, 66, 94, 109

Hajnal, J., 2, 21
Hanley, Susan, 2
Hartwell, Robert, 37
Hebei, 22
Ho Ping-ti, 2
Household records, 6
Hsu, Francis, 3
Hubei: family structure, 121; fertility, 99; mortality, 109–117; records of, 94
Hunan, 94; family structure, 121; fertility, 100; mortality, 109; population density, 105
Hymes, Robert, 37

Illegitimate births, 57
Imperial family, 37, 45n1, 46–47n18
Infanticide, 7, 15, 32, 57

Jakarta, 202
Japan, 2, 21
Jiangdu, 105, 106
Jiangnan, 48
Jiangsu, 22, 100, 105; family structure, 121; mortality, 109–117
Jiangxi, 109, 121

Lee, James, 142
Liaoning: bad harvest year, 182n15; content of population registers, 164–166, 180nn1–4, 181nn7,9; life expectancy, 174–175, 177–179; mortality rates, 173–174; problems with population registers, 166–167
Life expectancy: in Liaoning, 174–175, 177–179; and Ming-Qing transition, 8; of Song elite, 30; variation and environment, 117–120; and Western Europe, 181n13; in Yunnan, 45n10
Life tables: construction of, 109–117, 174–175; model, 15, 120n1, 148, 162n6, 181n12, 181–182n14

Marriage: and age differences between spouses, 28–29, 30, 36, 67–68; delay, 26; and economic conditions, 7; length of, 29–32; minor, 67; proxy for dura-

tion of, 81–82; and social status, 61–63, 79, 87–88; strategies, 36–43; timing of, 2; variables and population growth, 56–57. *See also* Age at marriage
Marriage market: lineage dominance of, 14; and sex ratios, 59; skewing of, 7; and social status, 20n9
Migrants: as commercial traders, 186–188; longevity of Minnan, 210–212; and massacres by colonialists, 212; Minnan, and ancestral worship, 211; from rural lineages, 197–203; sibling position of, 208–209
Migration: calculations of times of, 192; differences in patterns of, 207–208; and differences in socioeconomic environment, 212–213; and domestic organization, 208–209; of family members, 205–207; and family process variation, 18–19; and genealogies, 183; individual, 203–205; of the Lin lineage of Pushan, 197–203; and population growth rates, 79; regional variation 2, 17–19; and social status, 80; studies of, 139n2; successive, by household members, 204–205; temporal trends in, 201–203; of Yan lineage of Anping, 190–197
Ming-Qing transition: and fertility, 120; and migration, 18; and mortality, 7–10, 72–73, 120; and nuptiality, 11; and reproductive growth rate, 68
Minnan: individual migration, 203–204; longevity of migrants, 210–212; migrants and sibling position, 208–209; migration by family members, 204–207; migration and rural lineages, 188–190, 197–203; migration of successful commercial traders, 184–188; migration patterns by area, 207–208; trends in migration, 183
Mortality: and crisis periods, 1, 70; differentials between males and females, 174–175; differentials and unequal access to resources, 174, 176, 178; and economic conditions, 7; estimates from genealogical records, 108–120, 146–150; European, and social class, 9on6; and family organization, 16, 127, 135–138, 146–150, 156–157; Far-Eastern pattern of, 117; and generational overlap, 146–

147; infant, 15, 19n2, 49, 63, 108; and length of marriage, 30–31; methods of estimation based on population registers, 167–176; and Ming-Qing transition, 7–10; and model life tables, 181–182n14; as primary factor in demographic regime, 6, 15–16, 48, 56–57, 88; and social status, 14, 61, 63; of southern lineage populations, 109–120; temporal trends in, 9, 163, 176–179; trends in, and cohort analysis, 117–120

Nuptiality, 7, 10–11, 78–79; and age at marriage, 13; and economic success, 11; and Ming-Qing transition, 11; and representativeness of genealogies, 20n9; and social stratification, 14
Nutrition, 61, 63

Polygyny: and fertility, 64, 82, 100, 106–107; frequency of, and family structure, 130; and Minnan migrants, 210–211; and net reproductive rates, 63, 64; and number of children, 32, 33
Population density, 105
Population growth: and degree of formal lineage organization, 65–67; and economic conditions, 120; and elites, 89; formula used to calculate annual rate of, 58; and geographic variations in, 70–75, 82; and in-migration, 91n17; and intergenerational reproduction of males, 57–58, 63; and life expectancy, 179–180; and marriage variables, 56–57, 61–63; and mortality, 48, 61, 63, 87, 88; multiple regression analysis of, 82–88; one-sex models of, 57–58; rapid, and Jiangnan, 48; reduction in, and technological innovation, 89; spatial-ecological factors influencing, 59; statistical models of, 59–60, 82–88, 90–91nn7,8, 91n12. *See also* Fertility; Reproductive rates
Property, 78
Public health, 16, 90n6
Pushan: description of population, 188–190; migration of Lin lineage from, 197–203

Quanzhou, 183. *See also* Minnan

Reproductive rates: and age at birth of first son, 80–81; and age at birth of last son, 81–82; and age differences of spouses, 67–68; and concubines, 63, 64; and dynastic cycle, 8; and husband's birth order, 78–82; intergenerational, of males, 57–58, 82–88; and lineage membership, 75–79; and marriages with no sons, 79; and mortality factor, 15–16; and number, status and order of wives, 63–65, 82; and out-migration, 79–80; and periods of crisis, 68–70; and population density, 59; and proportion of sons unmarried, 78–79; reasons for downturns in, 10–11; and residence, 70–75, 82, 83; and social class, 59; and social status, 60–63, 83, 85, 87–88; temporal analysis of, 68–70; and total surviving sons ever born per wife, 67. *See also* Fertility; Population growth
Ritual segments (of lineages), 75, 78, 82

Sa, Sophie, 22
Sex ratio: at birth, 49; at marriage, 57
Shaoyang, 105, 106
Shenyang, 164
Sichuan, 1
Sima Guang, 25–26
Skinner, G. William, 1, 2, 14
Social status: definitions of, 90n5; and family organization, 155–156; and infant mortality, 63; and marriage differentials, 61–63, 79, 87–88; and migration, 80; and mortality differentials, 61; and population growth rate, 59, 61–63
Song elite: age differences between husbands and wives, 28–29; age at marriage, 24–28; family structure, 33–36; length of marriages, 29–31; marriage strategies, 26–43; number of children, 32–33
Successor wife, 23, 43–44n3
Sui: defined, 19n7

Taipei city dwellers, 22
Taiping rebellion, 9
Taiwan: age at marriage, 22; complex families in, 141, 155; family size in, 141–142; migration to, 19–20, 202
Tongcheng lineages: fertility, 49–57; geographic variations in growth rates, 70–75; and one-sex models of population growth, 57–70; reproductive rates in, 8

Uxorilocal marriage, 57

Watson, Rubie, 17
Widowers, remarriage of, 34
Widows: age of, 45n11; and fertility rates, 30, 31; as matriarchs, 17; and mortality rates, 14; and remarriage, 7, 45n12, 56, 64
Wolf, Arthur, 2, 3, 141, 161

Xiamen, 183. *See also* Minnan
Xiaoshan, 143–144, 155
Xu Hong, 22

Yangzhou, 105
Yangzi, 19n8, 39, 48, 105
Yunnan, 22, 45n10

Zhangzhou, 183. *See also* Minnan
Zhejiang, 22, 109, 143–144

Compositor: Braun-Brumfield, Inc.;
glossary by Asco Trade Typesetting, Inc.
Text: 10/12 Baskerville
Display: Baskerville
Printer: Braun-Brumfield, Inc.
Binder: Braun-Brumfield, Inc.